The End of All Things Is at Hand

The End of All Things Is at Hand

A Christian Eschatology in Conversation
with Science and Islam

VELI-MATTI KÄRKKÄINEN

CASCADE *Books* · Eugene, Oregon

THE END OF ALL THINGS IS AT HAND
A Christian Eschatology in Conversation with Science and Islam

Cascade Books
An Imprint of Wipf and Stock Publishers
199 W. 8th Ave., Suite 3
Eugene, OR 97401

www.wipfandstock.com

PAPERBACK ISBN: 978-1-6667-3054-8
HARDCOVER ISBN: 978-1-6667-2220-8
EBOOK ISBN: 978-1-6667-2221-5

Cataloguing-in-Publication data:

Names: Kärkkäinen, Veli-Matti [author]

Title: The end of all things is at hand : a Christian eschatology in conversation with science and Islam / Veli-Matti Kärkkäinen.

Description: Eugene, OR: Cascade Books, 2022 | Includes bibliographical references.

Identifiers: ISBN 978-1-6667-3054-8 (paperback) | ISBN 978-1-6667-2220-8 (hardcover) | ISBN 978-1-6667-2221-5 (ebook)

Subjects: LCSH: Eschatology | Hope—Religious aspects—Christianity | Christianity and other religions—Islam | End of the world (Astronomy) | Religion and science

Classification: BT821.3 K37 2022 (print) | BT821.3 (ebook)

Contents

Acknowledgments

I WISH TO THANK Ms. Ulrike Guthrie for her careful and insightful editing of the manuscript. She helped "translate" my Finnish-English into proper American prose! My doctoral student Jae Yang at Fuller's Center for Advanced Theological Studies completed the meticulous and most accurate work of double-checking all references and citations.

As always, I am grateful to my wife Anne-Päivi with whom I celebrated the fortieth wedding anniversary during the strange and novel coronavirus times when I put the finishing touches on the book. As a fitting reminder of the coming to an end of all life, at the time of delivering the manuscript to the publisher, we had to travel to our native land Finland to take care of our ailing parents following a severe heart-attack experienced by my beloved dad.

Last but not least, I also wish to acknowledge the long-term continuing support and inspiration from Fuller Theological Seminary for my research, writing, and teaching. The world's largest interdenominational theological seminary with three faculties (theology, psychology, and intercultural studies) currently with over 3,500 students from ninety countries and 110 denominations (with 43,000 alumni serving in 130 nations) is a "theological laboratory" without precedent in theological education!

Abbreviations

ANF   *The Ante-Nicene Fathers: Translations of the Writings of the Fathers down to A.D. 325.* Edited by Alexander Roberts and James Donaldson et al., 9 vols. Edinburgh, 1885–97. Public domain; available at www.ccel.org

ER   *Encyclopedia of Religion.* Edited by Lindsay Jones. 15 vols. 2nd ed. Detroit: Macmillan Reference USA/Gale, Cengage Learning, 2005.

EWEG   *The End of the World and the Ends of God: Science and Theology on Eschatology.* Edited by John Polkinghorne and Michael Welker. Harrisburg, PA: Trinity, 2000.

I&E   *Islam and Ecology: A Bestowed Trust.* Edited by Richard C. Foltz, Frederick M. Denny, and Azizan Baharuddin. Cambridge: Harvard University Press, 2003.

ISHCP   *Islam and Science: Historic and Contemporary Perspectives.* Edited by Muzaffar Iqbal. 3 vols. Surrey, UK: Ashgate, 2012.
        ISCHP 1: Studies in the Islam and Science Nexus
        ISCHP 2: Contemporary Issues in Islam and Science
        ISCHP 3: New Perspectives on the History of Islamic Science

JBC   *Jesus beyond Christianity: The Classic Texts.* Edited by Gregory A. Barker and Stephen E. Gregg. Oxford: Oxford University Press, 2010.

OHE   *Oxford Handbook of Eschatology.* Edited by Jerry L. Walls. New York: Oxford University Press, 2009. Online edition.

OHM	*The Oxford Handbook of Millennialism.* Edited by Catherine Wessinger. New York: Oxford University Press, 2011. Online edition.
NPNF[1]	*A Select Library of the Nicene and Post-Nicene Fathers of the Christian Church.* 1st ser. 14 vols. Edited by Philip Schaff. Edinburgh, 1886–90. Public domain; available at www.ccel.org
NPNF[2]	*A Select Library of the Nicene and Post-Nicene Fathers of the Christian Church.* 2nd ser. 14 vols. Edited by Philip Schaff and Henry Wace. Edinburgh, 1886–90. Public domain; available at www.ccel.org
Pannenberg, *ST*	Wolfhart Pannenberg. *Systematic Theology.* Translated by Geoffrey W. Bromiley. 3 vols. Grand Rapids: Eerdmans, 1991, 1994, 1998.
RTSA	*Resurrection: Theological and Scientific Assessments.* Edited by T. Peters, R. J. Russell, and M. Welker. Grand Rapids: Eerdmans, 2002.

Bible references, unless otherwise indicated, are from the Revised Standard Version of the Bible, copyright 1952 [2nd ed., 1971] by the Division of Christian Education of the National Council of the Churches of Christ in the United States of America. Used by permission. All rights reserved.

Unless otherwise indicated, all citations from patristic writers come from the standard series listed above.

The Qur'anic references, unless otherwise indicated, are from *The Holy Qur'ān: A New English translation of Its Meanings* © 2008 Royal Aal al-Bayt Institute for Islamic Thought, Amman, Jordan. This version of the Qur'ān is also available online at http://altafsir.com.

Hadith texts are from the Hadith Collection website: http://www.hadith-collection.com/ (2009-).

CHAPTER 1

Introduction

The why and what of the doctrine of the last things?

Why be concerned about the "End"?

ONLY A VERY SMALL group of people, I assume, lose sleep at night wondering what the End of all things will be like. Perhaps a few more worry about what the last day of their own lives will be like. But when it comes to life at large, let alone our planet—and the immensely vast universe—that worry is left to us theologians, along with the professional guild of futurologists.

Why, then, write a whole book on the topic of eschatology, the doctrine of the last things? Wouldn't it be more profitable to devote time and energy to reflecting on how to best redeem our limited time in this world and how to help life flourish here and now?

Indeed, these two perspectives, one regarding the life-to-come and the other regarding today and its responsibilities, are not necessarily alternatives. What if our lifestyle before physical death, our mundane life in the quotidian, is affected and even guided by what we believe and imagine about what, if anything, happens after this life? What if devotion to today's responsibilities were thwarted or energized by the vision of what will be— or what we hope for—in the "sweet by and by"?

This is what I argue in this essay. I would like you to consider the suggestion that, as important as it is to focus on the task at hand, that alone is not enough. Why? Because there is a surplus to human life, a something more—the hope and anticipation of something beyond this world. In the words of the late twentieth-century Roman Catholic theologian Karl Rahner, the human being is "a being who ex-ists from out of his present 'now' towards his future."[1] That kind of anticipation does not have to be utopian in nature, that is, to take away your focus from what is important at this moment. Hope in the future may instead allow you to invest your best in the challenges, struggles, and potentials of today in anticipation of a completion and fulfillment of your deepest longings. That is what a sound and solid Christian eschatological expectation could be at its best.

Of course, this kind of anticipation and hope may be a product of self-deception. The atheist Karl Marx reminded us of the danger of religion—for our purposes here, of hope inspired by Christian religion—turning out to be an opiate. But it doesn't have to be. Hope can also be reasonable and rational, even though it cannot be argued irrefutably. Hope is risky. It may end up being unstable, like a house built on sand. Nonetheless, I challenge you to consider the idea that hope is a risk worth taking. Complacency toward and oblivion with regard to the future, to what happens to us after the end of this physical life, may well turn out to be tragic as well.

Sure, faith is more than knowledge, more than a *scientific* knowledge. Faith is a mystery. "But mystery," so Rahner reminds us, "is not to be identified with a statement which is senseless and unintelligible for us."[2] Although the meaning and depth of the mystery may not be able to be totally exhausted, it can be reflected on, considered, and assessed with regard to its truthfulness and reliability. So here I go with the confidence of the seventeenth-century French philosopher Blaise Pascal, who spoke of faith in God and God's promises in terms of a "wager." Advises Pascal: "Let us weigh the gain and the loss in wagering that God is. Let us estimate these two chances. If you gain, you gain all; if you lose, you lose nothing. Wager, then, without hesitation that He is."[3] If God is, there is life after this life. If God is not, then who knows!

Although I am writing about the future as a theologian, from the perspective of Christian tradition, this preoccupation with eschatology is not the commodity of religionists alone. It is a theme that interests a much wider range of people.

1. Rahner, *Foundations of Christian Faith*, 431.
2. Rahner, *Foundations of Christian Faith*, 12.
3. Pascal, *Pascal's Pensées*, #233, 57.

INTRODUCTION

Non-religious speculations about the "future"

Although the technical term "eschatology" is typically confined to the fields of religion and theology, speculation into what, if anything, might happen beyond this life is hardly limited to those fields alone. From of old, sages, philosophers, and cultural leaders have been inspired by visions of the after-life. And this desire to know—or at least to imagine—the "distant future" has not evaporated, despite the advent of modernity and modern science.

Just think of the growing concern in our present culture over the impending "end" of our planet or of human life due to pollution, nuclear war, pandemics, or similar threats. Not surprisingly, in contemporary sciences we have lately heard expressions such as "physical eschatology," which investigates the future of the cosmos and life, whether in the near or distant future.

Indeed, it can be claimed that "[e]very culture has an eschatology; it is part of our inescapable human attempt to make sense of the world"[4] and its future—if it has any future. Consider in this respect the Marxist tripartite outline of the world's history: "A primal state of innocence, followed by a period of social tension, which is, in turn, supplanted by a new era of harmony, the communist society of the future."[5] This is an eschatological vision on steroids. And, counterintuitively, it is not so different from the tripartite religious Christian vision of the medieval mystic-theologian Joachim of Fiore, who intuited the course of world history in terms of three eras, that of the Father, Son, and Spirit. Surprisingly, a similar kind of pattern can be found even in aggressive atheist Friedrich Nietzsche's scheme of history in three stages, the premoral, moral, and ultramoral ages.

What about politics, domestic and international? Do we find any traces of "eschatology" in them? Many of us still remember vividly the American political philosopher Francis Fukuyama's widely circulated pamphlet, ominously titled *The End of History and the Last Man?* At the time of the collapse of Soviet Communism at the end of the 1980s, the author envisioned the final victory of free-market capitalism and its version of democracy over other political ideologies; that was the final stage of evolution, leading to peace and prosperity. While only a few neoconservatives still stick with this naïve and utopian dream, it is a telling example of a political eschatology. It looks like "eschatology" dies hard even in the secular realm.

4. Gillman, *Death of Death*, 21.
5. Gillman, *Death of Death*, 21.

3

Going back to the realm of religions, this book will show that it is not only Christians but also adherents of other traditions who embrace a dynamic and robust vision of eschatology. The counterpart to Christianity in this book will be Islam, the youngest Abrahamic faith, known for an unusually vibrant and deep eschatological imagination. While different in content and form, even the great Asiatic faiths, like Hinduism and Buddhism, have their own distinctive visions of the "End."[6]

The ups and downs of eschatology in Christian spirituality

Whereas for the church fathers in the beginning of the Christian tradition, and in keeping with the New Testament church, a fervent and dynamic eschatological anticipation was a defining feature,[7] by the time of Christendom in the fourth century, a more this-worldly focus began to challenge such an orientation to the future. It seemed like the kingdom of God was not only coming through the church but that the church age itself was the manifestation of God's rule. Or so it seemed when the emperor extolled as the religion of the land a previously outlawed sect, one distinct from its parent religion of Judaism.

Eschatology did not have a central place in Christian spirituality or in the theological curriculum of the church throughout the church's history. More often than not, it was associated with marginal and at times even heretical groups, such as the late second-century prophetic-charismatic Montanists or the sixteenth-century challengers to the Protestant Reformation, the Anabaptists. Even if the expectation of the return of Christ to establish the heavenly kingdom was never deleted from church manuals or theological treatises—and even if mainstream reformers such as Luther at the height of their enthusiasm might have anticipated the Lord's imminent return—by and large the church pushed any preoccupation with the future to the margins.

The eclipse of eschatology reached its zenith in the aftermath of the Enlightenment when the critical principle sidelined any reliance on the supernatural nature of Christian revelation. Almost all defining doctrines seemed to be discarded. Relatedly, among nineteenth-century atheists, any reference to eschatology was not only a laughing matter (because of its

---

6. For a discussion of Asiatic faiths' visions of the future and their relation to Christian eschatology, see Kärkkäinen, *Hope and Community*, ch. 3.

7. Daley, *Hope of the Early Church*.

alleged incredibility) but also an indication of mental perversion or incapacity. As is well known, Ludwig Feuerbach understood the human desire for life after death as a form of egotism. And Sigmund Freud's rejection of (religious) imagination of the afterlife merely as a (neurotic, or at least immature) form of illusion attracted many followers.

We find programmatic work on the demise of eschatology in modernity in the little book *What Is Christianity?* (1901) containing the lectures of the (then) leading Protestant historical theologian Adolf von Harnack. The liberal professor argued that there are only three things at the heart of the original message of Jesus, namely the fatherhood of God, the ethical teaching of Jesus, and the infinite value of the soul. Gone are all supernatural manifestations and powers, including eschatology in its traditional sense.

It was no less a theological giant than the "church father" of the twentieth century, Karl Barth, who strongly resisted the domestication of hope and issued this famous call: "If Christianity be not altogether thoroughgoing eschatology, there remains in it no relationship whatever with Christ. Spirit which does not at every moment point from death to the new life is not the Holy Spirit."[8] Domesticated eschatology, complains Barth, ends up being not much more than a "harmless little chapter at the conclusion of Christian Dogmatics."[9] While this Swiss Reformed theologian was not able to work out the details of his profound vision, his call is as urgent today as it was almost a hundred years ago when he first made it.

The 1964 publication of the German Reformed theologian Jürgen Moltmann's *Theology of Hope* launched a new movement appropriately called "theology of hope."[10] For him, eschatology is the "first" chapter of Christian theology. Another German, the Lutheran Wolfhart Pannenberg, talked about the "causal priority of the future"[11] and made the surprising and counterintuitive claim of "the present as an effect of the future, in contrast to the conventional assumption that past and present are the cause of the future."[12] As counterintuitive as Pannenberg's complex and at times obscure terminology might be, its relevance for our discussion is clear: eschatology is alive and well—*the future matters!* Similarly, think of the late leading American Anabaptist theologian Thomas N. Finger. In his general

---

8. Barth, *Epistle to the Romans*, 314.

9. Barth, *Epistle to the Romans*, 500.

10. Kärkkäinen, "Hope, Theology of," 404–5.

11. So named by Russell, *Time in Eternity*, 117–19.

12. Pannenberg, *Theology and the Kingdom*, 54.

presentation of Christian doctrine, ominously titled *Christian Theology: An Eschatological Approach*, the doctrine of the last things is not the last topic to be treated but rather the *first!* And the rest of the unfolding of Christian dogmatics is geared towards the anticipation of the coming of the kingdom.

What then is eschatology? So far we have used the term as if everybody knows its meaning and agrees about its content. Let's take a closer look at the meaning of the central theme of our book and the ways it is conceived in this project.

What then is Christian eschatology?

In light of the number of interlocutors, perspectives, and viewpoints already presented on eschatology, it is only fair to the reader of this little book that I as the author show my cards and give a brief account of the Christian eschatological vision to be presented. I am not claiming that this book is the final word on Christian eschatology. Neither am I trying to paper over the disagreements and divergences among Christians about many details of eschatology.

The disagreements and debates among theologians are understandable, not only in light of the complexity of the issue, but also because of the extreme difficulty of interpreting biblical teaching on the topic. As the late premier Reformed theologian Daniel Migliore succinctly put it: "The language of Christian hope is language stretched to the limits, language rich in symbols and images."[13] No other book—or genre—in the Bible has been subject to as many differing interpretations as the book of Revelation (originally known as the *Apocalypse*). The same can be said of other eschatologically loaded portions of the Bible, such as the book of Daniel in the Old Testament and the so-called apocalyptic sections in the Gospels (Mark 13; Matthew 24–25; Luke 21).

Before I offer any "definitions," let me mention something obvious, yet essential: The basis for any Christian vision for the future is what the Triune God—Father, Son, and Spirit—has done in the "beginning." We are talking about God who created, who sustains and redeems, and who is going to bring about the promised kingdom. This Christian vision of the future is not a human project of progress, like communism or humanism—although they too aim to fulfill the highest needs and aspirations of men and women. It is not about the "League of Nations" bringing about eternal

---

13. Migliore, *Faith Seeking Understanding*, 340. Italics removed.

peace—although the kingdom of God will usher in prosperity, tranquility, and peace. Eschatology is about what the Triune God, the Almighty and Loving Creator, our Father, alone is able to deliver.

That said, eschatology is not only about God and what God is going to do in ushering in the promised new creation. As much as it is about God, it is also about "man insofar as he is a being who is open to the absolute future of God himself."[14] The human being, despite her limited perspective on life and the world, including her partial and fallible knowledge of the universe, is at the same endowed with an "infinite horizon," a capacity to be open to transcendence, that which goes beyond the physical, visible world—and ultimately to the "absolute mystery" of God.[15] While the human person is not able to bring about the promised eschatological consummation, he or she is endowed with the capacity to intuit, imagine, and envision it. This is a distinctive feature of *homo sapiens*.

What is the meaning of the term "End" of which eschatology speaks (and which I have put in quotation marks so far)? It is a notoriously polyvalent term. As any English speaker knows, the "end" can mean either *cessation* (the coming to an end of an action) or *completion* (or fulfillment, that is, actually reaching the desired goal). It is important to note that both meanings are present in the Christian eschatological expectation. When put in the wider context of religions, "[i]n its broadest sense the term 'eschatology' includes all concepts of life beyond death and everything connected with it, such as heaven and hell, paradise and immortality, resurrection and transmigration of the soul, rebirth and reincarnation, and last judgment and doomsday."[16]

While present in all religions, each in their own distinctive ways, what makes Christian eschatology distinctive is its scope and domain: it encompasses *all* of creation, not only humans, nor merely the earth, but rather the whole vast cosmos.

That said, unfortunately this widest horizon of eschatology has been grasped only slowly in theology and spirituality and is still missing in most eschatological presentations. For too long, the Christian eschatological hope has encompassed only a limited scope, mostly the personal hope of bliss in the life to come. As important as that is, in light of the Triune God's role as the Creator—not only of our own planet but also of the virtually

---

14. Rahner, *Foundations of Christian Faith*, 431.

15. Rahner, *Foundations of Christian Faith*, 61.

16. Schwarz, *Eschatology*, 26.

infinite cosmos—something much bigger has to be intuited. The hope for the "new earth and new heaven," about which the biblical authors prophesied, must be conceived by the theology of the third millennium in its widest terms: this hope relates to the human person, the whole of humanity, the earth, *and* the vast cosmos. What an incredibly vast horizon!

In sum: the development of a viable Christian eschatology has to encompass the following spheres:

- Personal and communal hope
- Human and cosmic destiny
- Present and future hope

Now to parse this broad and comprehensive statement!

Personal and communal hope

A foundational problem in Christian eschatology relates to the relationship between personal eschatology (what happens to me as a human person at and after the end of my physical life) and communal hope (what happens to human beings as a collective, as humankind, and, as a part of this, as a church community at the End of all things). Only an eschatology that envisions the relationship between personal and communal hope as mutual and dynamically conditioned can hold together "the perfecting of individual life after death . . . [and] the consummation of humanity and the world in the kingdom of God."[17]

It is instructive to note that in the Bible the eschatological vision emerges slowly and begins to develop only in the final parts of the Old Testament canon (such as at the end of the book of Daniel). What is particularly important to this discussion is that in the Bible communal hope was primary and was expressed much earlier on, and individual hope emerged only later and gradually. Even when this personal hope finally did begin to surface, it was subservient to the community. Personal hope was tightly connected with the hope for all of humanity.

The Christian church, while embracing this view, also faced the challenge of expanding it radically with the need and desire to incorporate gentiles in the same hope of destiny. Whereas in the old covenant only Israel were designated as God's people, with the coming of the new covenant all

17. Pannenberg, *ST* 3:546.

other people were also to be grafted into the community of Israel's God, the Father, Son, and Spirit.

At this point we see a radical departure from the End-time expectations of non-Christian and non-Jewish religions. For example, the pagan philosopher Plato's idea of the immortality of the soul had no connection to the "salvation" of the whole people; his hope was totally individualistic. The same can be said of modern and contemporary secular hopes with regard to the fulfillment of human desires. For example, even at its best, the communist utopia refers only to the group of people living that ideology's dream of peace and prosperity at the time of the consummation—which, of course, never materialized. But had the communist utopia ever taken place, none of the men and women of earlier generations would have been a part of it, nor would they have had any hope that wrongs and injustices of the past would have been righted or reconciliation taken place.

In sum: in the Christian eschatological vision, an integral link between the consummation of personal and communal hopes links the whole of humankind together, all of them having been created in the image of the Triune God, whether or not they acknowledge or even know it.

Human and cosmic destiny

A foundational argument of the present project is that not only can personal hope not be separated from that of the rest of the humanity, neither can personal-communal hope be separated from that of the planet earth, which is our home and mother. Even more: the Christian hope for humanity and the globe likewise cannot finally be "separated from the destiny of the universe"[18] (including this tiny little planet earth in one corner of our galaxy, among at least 10 billion other planets).

This is an amazingly wide and broad expectation and it tests the capacities and boldness of the Christian imagination. It means that the distinctively Christian eschatological consummation includes *the whole of God's creation*. It includes "history" and "nature," as masterfully expressed by the late American Anabaptist theologian Thomas A. Finger: "Since the new creation arrives through God's Spirit, and since it reshapes the physical world, every theological locus is informed by the Spirit's transformation of matter-energy."[19]

18. Tillich, *Systematic Theology*, 3:418.

19. Finger, *Contemporary Anabaptist Theology*, 563.

No wonder we have had a hard time expanding the vision of our theology of the End beyond the hope for human bliss. Even those few theologians (like Moltmann) who have embraced the destiny of nature on our planet into their eschatological purview have almost totally neglected the widest horizon, that is the truly "cosmic" one.[20]

There is one more interrelated layer to the Christian hope for the End, alongside the mutual integrity of the personal and communal as well as the human and cosmic. It has to do with the linking together of present and future hope, that is, hope for today and for the life to come after this physical existence.

Present and future hope

As I mentioned at the very beginning of this introduction, theologians and many of the faithful believe that what really matters in faith is that which relates to and helps facilitate our duties in everyday life. Why fantasize about the distant future of which we know precious little? Some people even conclude that too much hope regarding the future may thwart our efforts to improve life on this earth. Without denying the potential danger of escapism—whether in our own religion or, say, in Islam—this project contends that, rightly understood, our hope for this world and for the world to come belong together. Indeed, they presuppose each other. Only an approach to life that is confident about the consummation in the life to come can best facilitate the struggle for justice, flourishing, and the well-being of both humanity and the environment. By trusting that all that there is will not come to an end at the moment of my death but rather that my life in this body matters beyond my short lifetime and by believing that our deepest longings may be fulfilled in the new creation brought about by the Triune God, by this we are freed and empowered to dedicate our lives to the service of others.

How would we construct the tight link between our present and future hopes theologically? From Pannenberg I have learned that the Holy Spirit is the key, the eschatological Spirit, the Spirit of life. Through the life-giving power and presence of the divine Spirit "the eschatological future is present already in the hearts of believers" and anticipates the consummation.[21] In

---

20. When he refers to cosmic hope, he means our globe. See Moltmann, *Coming of God*.

21. Pannenberg, *ST* 3:552.

the Christian understanding, believers—to whom is granted the pledge of the Spirit in the new birth—already live the life of the world to come. In the terminology of the unknown author of the book of Hebrews, such people have "tasted . . . the powers of the age to come" (6:5) and live anticipating the new creation.

This both-present-and-future orientation is the needed corrective for two kinds of problematic postures. On the one hand, there is the posture of the merely this-worldly "eschatologies" mentioned above. On the other hand, as I will explore shortly, there is also the opposite posture of fundamentalism and other movements that major in otherworldly eschatological speculations that are deeply escapist and dismissive of the work of improving the current world.

This constructive dynamic between "already" and "not yet" will be explored below through the dynamic of "continuity" and "discontinuity."

The road ahead of us

With these caveats and themes in mind, I briefly preview the road ahead of us in this book. Before we get into too many details of directly eschatological topics, I first raise in the following chapter the foundational question about the meaning and meaningfulness of life. Does it make any sense to speak of the meaningfulness of life—that of humans and of nature—if the cosmos at large, as it appears to many, lacks any ultimate meaning? Astonishingly, this question has not garnered much interest at all in theology (although philosophers have paid it more attention). Arguing that indeed the cosmos at large, as the handiwork of the loving and wise Creator, must have meaning, as must life on this particular planet, the chapter also constructs a trinitarian theology of Christian hope. Based on Christ's resurrection by his Father in the power of the Spirit, Christians can hope for the overcoming of death and life everlasting as a gift from the Creator. Both life in this cosmos and the cosmos itself are full of meaning!

Chapter 3 titled "What do the sciences say about the future of life and the cosmos?" delves into many details of scientific conjectures regarding the end of human life and particularly life on this globe and in the cosmos at large. Whatever *theological* Christian eschatology is, it simply cannot be constructed ignoring what men and women have discovered about the origin, workings, and possible end(s) of nature. While it is not surprising that the visions of the End in Christian eschatology and in the natural sciences hardly coincide—indeed, there is a robust conflict between the two, as is detailed below—this does not mean that the one neglects the other. Both theologians and scientists may benefit from a mutual dialogue and exchange of ideas.

In chapter 4 I expand the discussion of Christian eschatology yet further by engaging another religious tradition as a dialogue partner, in this case the youngest Abrahamic tradition, Islam. Since I expect that only a tiny fraction of the potential readers of this work have much (or any) knowledge of Islam as a religious and theological tradition, I preface this fourth chapter with a crash course on Islam's basic doctrines and beliefs, and a reminder of how each religion's eschatological hope is integrated into the wider fabric of that tradition's belief-system. The other half of the chapter gives a concise overview of basic Islamic eschatological beliefs. Into each of the subsequent chapters I invite Islamic doctrines and convictions as dialogue partners when discussing a specific topic, say, resurrection or final destinies.

Chapter 5 considers a theological and spiritual challenge or problem common to both Islam and Christianity. This problem is apocalypticism, an eschatological expectation gone awry. While apocalypticism in its historical form (flourishing between the two testaments of the Christian Bible) is an essential category in the formation of Christian tradition, in its current form apocalyptic movements pose a threat to both theology and the peaceful existence of the followers of the two religions—and by extension the peace of the world. In their extreme forms, some overly fundamentalist apocalyptic movements in both religions have, for example, been linked to terrorism and other violent acts.

Chapters 6 and 7 belong together and could form one entity. They have been separated merely for the practical reason of trying to avoid overly long individual chapters. They focus on the relationship between the hope for today and the life to come by delving into two case-studies, namely justice and the environment. The basic question behind the two chapters is simply this: Would a robust and dynamic eschatological expectation take away from the church's responsibility for social and economic justice or the well-being and flourishing of the environment? The answer is no, such an expectation does not. Instead, rightly conceived, a healthy expectation of the coming of the new creation facilitates and empowers work for the betterment of the conditions of the present world.

The last two chapters (8 and 9) likewise belong together. They will raise the question as to what happens at death—and what death means theologically in the first place—and what to expect in terms of the "future" of humanity and the cosmos as considered from a Christian perspective. In chapter 8 the focus is on the theologies of death, judgment, and the resurrection. While focusing on Christian materials, I also give detailed consideration to Islamic views, similarly to the previous chapter. Chapter 9 continues the conversation about what to expect in the life to come by zooming in on the religious ends of men and women. Carefully considering various options from hell to annihilationism to universalism, traditional options for those to be condemned, and heaven and the new creation for those who are saved, I develop a constructive Christian proposal. The question of the relationship between life on earth and the life to come reappears when delving into the question of the nature of life and life-conditions in the new creation, for the Christian vision entails embodied life rather than merely a "spiritual" one (as if we could separate the two). The center of Christian eschatological hope, as I repeatedly affirm, is the resurrection of the body, an event made possible through Christ's bodily resurrection.

CHAPTER 2

For what can we hope in a meaningless cosmos?

Why does meaningfulness matter to eschatology?

To speak of the "End" as in having reached the goal, not merely as cessation, presupposes that what has reached the goal—either human life or
the life of the cosmos at large—is *meaningful.* Or how else would it make
sense to establish the goal? When running aimlessly in a forest for, say,
three hours and landing randomly in a certain place, it does not make sense
to claim that the activity has reached its goal. The activity itself, in this case,
running, had no meaning, let alone a predetermined end in view.

Similarly, it hardly makes sense to speak of hope regarding something
that appears to be void of meaning. If human life is a random process made
of physical stuff and energy, it would be absurd to speak of hope as a distinctive human capacity. Machines, aimless processes, or random events do
not have a capacity to hope.

Hope for the future consummation of human life can only be had if
human life in itself is meaningful. And human life in itself can be meaningful only if life at large has some meaning. For in no way is human life
an island, something separated from the environment that facilitates its
birth, growth, and flourishing. That being so, the cosmos at large is likewise
meaningful. An aimless, meaningless process is hardly able to sustain a life
full of meaning.

Only against this horizon of the meaningfulness of life can a valid and reliable hope be established. Therefore, meaningfulness matters—and matters very much—for any talk about eschatological hope.

With this in mind, I develop the argument of this chapter in two inter-related phases. The first section enquires into the conditions and possibility of establishing meaning in a cosmos that appears to be meaningless. The second section focuses on the conditions and power of hope in a world full of meaning, including of meaningful human life.

Meaningful life—in a meaningless cosmos?[1]

In search of meaning

One doesn't have to be struck by a global pandemic such as that caused by COVID-19 to try to come to grips with ultimate issues of life and death—namely whether there is any meaning in all that we are going through. Often a personally sized tragedy suffices to raise the question that we typically push to the margins.

For many of us, the question of meaning first emerges in our youth. That's what happened to me as well. A feeling of cosmic loneliness combined with sense of amazement filled me during wintery night walks in the snow under starry skies in my native land of Finland. The significance and meaning of these experiences—which Karl Rahner would have called "transcendental experiences"—was far from clear to me as a youth. Nor have they become totally clear to me even now, many decades later.

Those moments were sacred to me. And they were meaning*ful*, full of meaning. I had the sense that this cold, lifeless cosmos (as it appeared to me then) was there not because of a happenstance, nor for nothing. Instead, in those Rahnerian moments I had a sense of the purpose, intelligence, and order of the world.

In one form or another, over the years I have recaptured the same kind of feeling of meaningfulness—and cosmic loneliness—when staring at the beauty of nature, the wonder of small kids playing, strangers helping each other, or a loving parent caring for their child. And certainly I have felt it often in religious services, not the least when ministering at the altar or in times of quiet prayer and meditation.

---

1. This section was first published as Kärkkäinen, "*Meaningful Life*," 1–4.

This conviction of the meaningfulness of life has never left me. It inspires and intrigues as much as it bothers and concerns me. There has to be some kind of explanation for such a conviction. Or does there?

This question is extremely complicated and complex, as it has to do with far more than simply the sphere of my own life. Simply put: ultimately my own life can have meaning *only* if there is meaning in this bigger game of which I am a part, namely this (almost) infinitely vast cosmos!

That's a good question—or is it?

In the introduction to his textbook on various views on the topic of the "meaning of life," the British literary critic Terry Eagleton wittily observes: "'What is the meaning of life?' looks at first glance like the same kind of question as 'What is the capital of Albania?' or 'What is the colour of ivory?' But is it really? Could it be more like 'What is the taste of geometry?'"[2] Indeed, many people believe that the whole question of the meaning of life is meaningless! On the other end of the spectrum, particularly those with religious convictions tend to regard it as an unnecessary question for the simple reason that to them an affirmative answer is self-evident.[3]

Be that as it may, as the philosopher Thomas Nagel argues, the human being is stuck with the question and unable to avoid searching for meaning. How so? His argument is this: even though each person looks at the world (or in this case, at the meaning of life) from a personal perspective, the human person has *A View from Nowhere*, to cite the title of one of Nagel's most well-known books. That is, we also have the special capacity to view the world and life from an external or detached point of view without letting the personal take over. But how to integrate the internal and external, or whether that can even be done, is the most foundational philosophical challenge and calls for careful reflection.[4]

2. Eagleton, *Meaning of Life*, 1.

3. For a straightforward theistic (Christian) defense of the "self-evidential" nature of meaningfulness of cosmos and life, see Wiker and Witt, *Meaningful World*.

4. Nagel, *View from Nowhere*, 3. In this regard, it is highly interesting that Nagel's recent work titled *Mind and Cosmos: Why the Materialist Neo-Darwinian Conception of Nature Is Almost Certainly False* (2012) unabashedly refutes the self-sufficiency of naturalism—the view that all that there is, is nature, the physical reality, and nothing else. Recall that he himself was, and in many ways still is, a naturalist-materialist philosopher, though now in a chastened way!

Many others, including myself, are not particularly confident that humans can look at the world, particularly ultimate questions such as the meaning of life, from an "objective" point of view. For meaning is entangled with our deepest commitments, convictions, worldview, and not least with religious beliefs.

Immanuel Kant remained skeptical about the human capacity to discern meaning and purpose in life and the world. He begins the second part of his 1790 book *The Critique of Judgement*—which focuses on "teleological judgment," that is, judgment concerning purpose(fulness)—skeptical of our capacity to grasp such meaning and purpose. Sure, Kant grants that some kind of "a subjective purposiveness in nature" may be discerned in natural laws, order, and usefulness for a specific task. But when it comes to the big question of the purpose(fulness) of the whole world, that, he says, is not within our reach.[5]

So it is interesting that there are some neuroscientists who seem to believe that the human person is capable of finding answers to these ultimate questions. The Harvard University neuroscientist Paul Thagard's book *The Brain and the Meaning of Life* argues precisely this point.[6] And consider the fact that he himself advocates a naturalist worldview, that is, that he believes that beyond the physical (or "nature") there is nothing like God or an afterlife. Rather, he believes that the meaning of life can be found within this life itself.

It is not totally clear to me whether Kant categorically denies the existence of lasting meaning or whether the Enlightenment thinker merely sets limits on our capacity to know. But there are also others who are convinced of the lack of meaning and, therefore, of the futility of the whole project. Take, for example, the French existentialist Jean-Paul Sartre. Famously, he considered life and the cosmos meaningless in terms of ultimate meaning. Not only that, he also made the counterintuitive claim that we humans are not only free but we are "condemned to be free," that is, we are free even against our own will. Why? Because we did not choose to be—in the world or who we are—and so we are "thrown" into the world. Being thrown into the world, as a free being, also necessarily brings with it responsibility. But if there is no ultimate meaningfulness, what is the meaning of this kind of human life?

5. Kant, *Kant's Critique of Judgement*.
6. Thagard, *Brain and the Meaning*.

And yet Sartre reminds us that unlike plants and animals, human beings by necessity feel the need to reflect on the meaning of life, whether or not it can be found. If life intrinsically lacks transcendent meaning (that is, meaning based on something or someone beyond this physical world), humans are left only with the hope of being able to create their own meaning(s). Technically put, Sartre argues that existence precedes essence. That is, in one sense we create ourselves, and there is no "I" before me. There is just existence, being.[7]

So far we have talked about the "meaning" of life as if the meaning of the term were self-evident—and even more importantly, as if the criteria by which to make the judgment were universally agreed. Obviously that is not the case.

What is the meaning of the "meaning" of life?

What are the typical criteria by which to assess the meaningfulness of life? Both in popular discourse and scholarly literature, by far the leading criterion has to do with the problem of evil. The mere existence of rampant suffering, particularly innocent suffering, pain, injustice, and oppression seem to make any appeal to a meaningful life absurd. Add to the suffering experienced by human beings the suffering either caused by humans or by nature, the universal suffering in nature unrelated to us, in animate and inanimate creatures, and you get the point. But is this criterion powerful enough to thwart the question? I suggest it is not. Because even though no reasonable person would ignore the weight of this challenge to meaning, the question about the meaningfulness of the entire cosmos cannot depend on what happens to creatures on one tiny planet at one end of a galaxy. Furthermore—and this is the key to my argumentation—a single part (human life) of the whole (the cosmos) cannot have ultimate meaning unless the *whole* has it, regardless of suffering. Let me give you a childlike example: while the steering wheel or the brakes in the car may serve a particular purpose in the car, it does not make sense to speak of their meaningfulness unless *the car itself* is meaningful; without the rest of the car, it doesn't matter if they function properly or not!

---

7. In case you do not have the time or energy to check Sartre's massive *Being and Nothingness* (originally published in French in 1943 and available in various English editions), a reliable orientation to basic concepts and claims can be found in Onof, "Jean Paul Sartre: Existentialism."

The same can be said of mortality as a criterion. Of course the fact that we all face death is a serious challenge to meaningfulness. But its weight is severely lessened when you reflect on this thought-experiment: how would the mere extension of the human or other creatures' life in itself ensure meaningfulness, even if it were a happy life, let alone a life full of suffering? From this follows the bigger question: how would "immortality" in a meaningless cosmos support life's meaningfulness? I fail to see that it would.

Beyond suffering and mortality, another criterion by which to judge the meaningfulness of life has to do with the seeming indifference of the cosmos towards us: "The cosmos does not seem to care for our aspirations at all; in particular, it could not care less for our search for meaning."[8] While it would be nice for the vast cosmos to show some kind of support for our search for meaning, the lack thereof can hardly be taken as proof for the lack of meaning.

Am I assuming what I seek to prove? Not necessarily. Rather, I imagine a mutual conditioning between the meaning of life (of humanity and other creatures, as well as of nature) and the vast cosmos—but in a way that understands the whole (cosmos) as the "foundation." The theological justification of my basic argument goes like this: Because the loving and almighty God has created everything that exists (the cosmos) with meaning and a purpose (whether or not we humans can discern it), everything created in this cosmos bears the marks of purpose, design, and meaning. Even when fallen from the ultimate goal, the world is inherently valuable and full of meaning, awaiting the final consummation at the eschaton. Indeed, in order for Christian theology to be a meaningful intellectual exercise, it must assume that "we live in a world that makes sense not just now, but totally and forever." Then, and only then, can the awaited end be a "fulfilment of the history of the universe and the history of humanity."[9]

What if meaning is what we make it?

That said, there might be a way to get around my argument, in other words to establish meaning in life even if the cosmos at large lacks it. How? Through human construction: "Thus, meaning in life is as much constructed as found; it must be literally made through one's living one's unique life. No external Creator or Designer is required for this process

8. Pihlström, "Meaningful Life," 5.

9. Polkinghorne, *God of Hope*, xvii, xvi–xvii respectively.

of meaning construction to take place."[10] Yes, in that scheme, the human construction of meaning would trump the lack thereof in the cosmos. Or would it? Frankly, it would be successful only for the time being. In other words, it would only help establish an interim meaning, so to speak. Why? Because anything built by finite, mortal creatures, can only be—and support—something finite and temporary. Furthermore, the above-mentioned three objections to discerning meaning (suffering, mortality, and cosmic indifference) might well be sufficiently weighty to crush it. But my main point is: even if these three objections could be overcome, the end-result would still only be temporary and partial.

So I return to my main argument: that *a part of the whole can only bear lasting meaning if the whole itself is meaningful.* In this regard, I could use the opening words of Ludwig Wittgenstein's *Tractatus Logico-Philosophicus* (1921), even though he himself might not have endorsed my conclusion: "The world is everything that is the case."[11] The term "world" here refers to something far bigger than our planet, let alone our life. It denotes *everything.* In short, establishing and finding the meaning of life is "fundamentally a problem about the intelligibility of the world as a whole."[12] And from a theological point of view, it ultimately takes God to ensure the meaningfulness of the cosmos and life; mere human construction can never have enduring significance. As the Finnish philosopher Sami Pihlström puts it:

> even if we do succeed in seeing our lives as subjectively meaningful, insofar as the "meaning in life" is our own pragmatic creation, whether through active (ethical) action or through more passive (religious) contemplation, we must realize that it is in the end "self-supportive", something made by us in and through our action and/or thinking, with no higher authority supporting or grounding or justifying it.[13]

In other words, Pihlström insists that a merely naturalist account of the world is not able to allege or substantiate its ultimate meaning.

---

10. Pihlström, "Meaningful Life," 4.

11. Wittgenstein, *Tractatus Logico-Philosophicus*, 1. (p. 25).

12. Neiman, *Evil in Modern Thought*, 7–8, cited in Pihlström, "Meaningful Life," 6.

13. Pihlström, "Meaningful Life," 13.

A meaningful "new song"

Don't think that in citing Wittgenstein and Pihlström's ideas I am attempting a cheap apology for faith in God as a precondition for establishing lasting meaning. I fear they would be offended by such a tactic! As solid philosophers, they did their work: they were brave enough to draw the conclusion that the quest for ultimate meaning in life seems to require a reference beyond the human mind.

It takes Christian—or any other theistic—faith and theology to establish the connection between God and meaningfulness of life and cosmos. What the above-mentioned philosophical observations do is to make theistic argument reasonable, even if not everybody is willing to take that step. An example of a philosopher who took that step is the seventeenth-century Frenchman Blaise Pascal. He derived ultimate meaning of life and cosmos from belief in God. Although he was taken aback by the vastness of the cosmos and the tininess of the human being, he surmised:

> Man is but a reed, the most feeble thing in nature; but he is a thinking reed. The entire universe need not arm itself to crush him. A vapour, a drop of water suffices to kill him. But, if the universe were to crush him, man would still be more noble than that which killed him, because he knows that he dies and the advantage which the universe has over him; the universe knows nothing of this.[14]

Here, Pascal is standing on the shoulders of a long line of theists who saw in the order and intelligibility of creation, as well as in the value and beauty of life, the key to the meaningfulness of life. Indeed, from the beginning of Christian theology, this has been an important argument against atheist and (particularly of non-theistic) religions' explanations. Few Christian thinkers have put it more beautifully than the second-century Eastern father Clement of Alexandria. In his *Exhortation to the Heathens*, a polemical apologetic treatise, he speaks of the divine Word, the agent and principle of creation, as the "New Song" in comparison to futile and fallible "songs" in pagan mythologies and philosophies concerning the creative power of their deities:

> [The Word] also composed the universe into melodious order, and tuned the discord of the elements to harmonious arrangement, so that the whole world might become harmony. It let loose the fluid ocean, and yet has prevented it from encroaching on the land. The

14. Pascal, *Pascal's Pensées*, #347, 97.

21

earth, again, which had been in a state of commotion, it has established, and fixed the sea as its boundary. The violence of fire it has softened by the atmosphere . . . ; and the harsh cold of the air it has moderated by the embrace of fire, harmoniously arranging these the extreme tones of the universe. And this deathless strain—the support of the whole and the harmony of all—reaching from the centre to the circumference, and from the extremities to the central part, has harmonized this universal frame of things, not according to the Thracian[15] music . . . but according to the paternal counsel of God, which fired the zeal of David.[16]

In this light, how "unnatural" is the claim of the materialist D. C. Dennett that "[a]n impersonal, unreflective, robotic, mindless little scrap of molecular machinery is the ultimate basis of all the agency, and hence meaning, and hence consciousness, in the universe"![17]

If cosmos at large bears the qualities of a harmonious symphony, then in human life and history we may discern beauty, value, and meaning—notwithstanding horrendous suffering and pain. With that, I wish to contest the opinion of the German theologian Karl Löwith who, having just returned from exile in Japan following World War II, declared: "Historical processes as such do not bear the least evidence of a comprehensive and ultimate meaning. History as such has no outcome."[18] My reflection sympathetically and boldly suggests otherwise. You can make your own judgment.

Whether we are capable of discerning it fully or not, the notion that life is meaningful and purposeful gives wings to hope, the distinctive human capacity to transcend the limits of the current moment.

Meaningful hope

Hope, a distinctive human capacity

Indeed, only against the horizon of the meaningfulness of cosmos and life therein can the distinctively human capacity to hope flourish and empower the expectation of the coming consummation. That hope is not based on

15. Thracians were a group of Indo-Europeans with their own language and culture.

16. Clement of Alexandria, *Exhortation to the Heathens*, chap. 1; ANF2, 172; for a highly useful discussion, see Costache, "Meaningful Cosmos," 107–30.

17. Dennett, *Darwin's Dangerous Idea*, 203.

18. Löwith, *Meaning in History*, 191, (partly) cited in Moltmann, *Coming of God*, 43.

human resources to overcome evil and bring about the hoped-for future; nor is it an illusion or an utopia that lacks grounding. Instead, that hope is based on God, the Creator, the Sustainer, and the Consummator.

What Paul Tillich, the great German liberal Lutheran theologian, called the "Ground of Being," namely God, is indeed the source and foundation of the human hope for future. He rightly warned us against the utopian: "Hope is easy for the foolish, but hard for the wise. Everybody can lose himself into foolish hope, but genuine hope is something rare and great."[19] Although he himself probably would not have agreed with the current project's focus on the coming of God's kingdom by the all-loving and all-powerful God of classical Christianity, I dare to apply his incisive phrase for my own purposes.

As the discussion on the meaningfulness of life in the apparently meaningless universe has revealed, the finite human person does not have the resources to establish lasting meaning in life—particularly beyond the physical death. If there is a Creator, the loving Triune God, it is reasonable to expect the meaningfulness of my own life, in the context of the meaningfulness of the cosmos.

What makes *homo sapiens* distinctive among all creatures, as far as we know currently, is the capacity to reach out to the future with the help of the incredible gift of imagination, of hope. Hope reaches beyond what is present to something that is not yet visible (Rom 8:24–25). This is made possible by the unique human capacity for self-transcendence: that we are able to "stand outside" ourselves. While a dog, to use an example, may be able to anticipate an impending danger, even death, as far as we know it is not able to reflect on the fearfulness or the meaning of the anticipation. Its anticipation is instinctual, "automatic," and not a function of focused reflection.

As mentioned, hope became the theme of the new theological movement birthed in the 1960s, called the "theology of hope." Initiated by Moltmann and Pannenberg, it argued that alongside keenly staring at the *past*—i.e., the works of the Triune God in creation, providence, and salvation—theologians should also peek into the *future*, the coming redemption in fulfillment of divine promises of the coming kingdom.[20] Not for nothing Moltmann titled his first world-acclaimed book *The Theology of Hope* (1964). Subsequently, towards the end of his luminous theological career,

19. Tillich, "The Right to Hope," 17, cited in Snyder, "Hypothesis: There is Hope," 4.
20. Kärkkäinen, "Hope, Theology of," 404–5.

the German theologian published his groundbreaking eschatological study under the title *The Coming of God* (1996), which testifies to the advent or coming of the Triune God from God's "future" to meet us, in the consummation of the new heavens and new earth.

Consider these theological developments as a counter-argument to and a promise in the face of the loss of hope in modern and contemporary Western culture. Whereas before modernity belief in God served as the source of hope and confidence, in the post-Enlightenment world self-confidence and trust in human resources replaced that belief and hope in God. That led to naïve optimism about progress and further funded secularization and distance from God. In the midst of twentieth-century catastrophes, such as the two world wars, such confidence has proved itself to be futile.

Perhaps, ironically, the loss of hope in human capacities and resources has helped Christian theology to gain perspective. According to the astute analysis of the German Lutheran theologian Hans Schwarz, Christian eschatology helps the confused world discern two vital truths: First, "[i]t shows that the modern idea of progress alienated itself from its Christian foundation . . . [as it] deprived history of its God-promised goal." In so doing, "we promoted ourselves from God-alienated and God-endowed actors *in history* to deified agents *of history*." As a remedy to this dilemma, Christian eschatology, second, "provides a hope and a promise that we are unable to attain through our own efforts."[21] Indeed, it is good news for humanity to embrace the truth that men and women are unable to deliver the promise of everlasting happiness and tranquility. Only God can.

Apart from theology, philosophers as well as psychologists and psychiatrists have joined the investigation of the influence, necessity, and nature of hope.[22] Joint projects such as *Interdisciplinary Perspectives on Hope* (2005) have recently appeared.[23] Already a classic is the massive three-volume work of the Marxist philosopher Ernst Bloch, *The Principle of Hope* (1954–59). While an atheist manifesto that argues for the necessity of hope constructed by the human mind before the end of this life—not so different from that of the existentialist philosopher Martin Heidegger—it helped awaken Moltmann from his slumbers; to that point he had not paid

21. Schwarz, *Eschatology*, 17–21 (20; emphasis in original).

22. Averill et al., *Rules of Hope*.

23. Eliott, *Interdisciplinary Perspectives on Hope*.

attention to the importance of future. Hence, this work ironically helped to launch the Christian project of the theology of hope.

Christian faith proposes a solid hope based on the faithfulness of the Triune God, who in the power of the Spirit raised from the dead the crucified Son. Rather than based on a human utopia, Christian hope intuits history as meaningful based on God's providence. The Creator God is the one who also directs the course of history, as meaningless and absurd as it may look like.

In the biblical worldview, hope is expressed in terms of promise.[24] Divine promises often contradict human expectation. The promise of Christ's resurrection, the "anchor" of concrete hope, illustrates this best. In the biblical drama, the greatest threat is death—and the greatest promise is deliverance from the power of death.

Trinitarian hope

As argued, it is an axiom in Christian theology that the ground of Christian hope for the future consummation lies in the Trinitarian God. God, the Father, is the anchor and source of faithfulness. No one else has argued this with more elegance and clarity than the greatest medieval Christian thinker Thomas Aquinas. The Angelic Doctor avers: "He who hopes is indeed imperfect in relation to that which he hopes to obtain, but has not as yet; yet he is perfect, in so far as he already attains his proper rule, viz. God, on Whose help he leans." The point here is that it is in God that the ground of the hope can be found.[25] As Thomas states: "the hope of which we speak now, attains God by leaning on His help in order to obtain the hoped for good."[26] In other words: "Whatever else hope expects to obtain, it hopes for it in reference to God as the last end, or as the first efficient cause."[27]

Indeed, the Trinitarian God has shown himself to be faithful in relation to the people of God in the First Testament. Similarly, the Father has shown himself to be reliable by raising from the dead, in the power of the Spirit, the crucified Son (Rom 1:4). The triune God is the God of hope. As the American Reformed theologian Daniel Migliore stated succinctly:

---

24. Chapter 2 of Moltmann, *Theology of Hope*.

25. Aquinas, *The Summa Theologiæ of St. Thomas Aquinas*, II–II, 17,1. [hereafter: *ST*].

26. Aquinas *ST* II–II, 17.2.

27. Aquinas *ST* II–II, 17.5.

Apart from hope in God, every Christian doctrine becomes distorted. A doctrine of revelation would be flawed if it did not acknowledge that we now see in a mirror dimly and not yet face to face (1 Cor. 12:12); a doctrine of the triune God would be deficient if it did not recognize that God is an inexhaustible mystery; that God's grace to us is an unfathomable gift, that we must cling to God's promise and "hope in the Lord" (Ps. 131:3) both now and in all eternity; a doctrine of creation would be incomplete if it failed to emphasize that the creation still groans for its liberation and completion (Rom. 8:22); a doctrine of humanity would be dreary and pretentious if it were stripped of eschatology and lacked the conviction that our life is now hidden with Christ in God (Col. 3:3); a Christology would be seriously truncated if it failed to affirm that the Lord is not only the one "who is and who was" but also the one "who is to come" (Rev. 22:20); our doctrines of the church and its sacraments would be masquerades if they succumbed to ecclesiastical triumphalism, portrayed the church as owner and dispenser of God's gifts, and had little interest in the completion of God's reign of justice, freedom, and peace throughout the creation.[28]

As I will explore in more detail in chapter 8, Christ's resurrection forms the basis for the Christian hope (1 Cor 15:14–15). Had Christ not been raised, so the apostle argues, any hope for life beyond physical death has no basis. Indeed, the apostle goes so far as to claim that had Christ not been raised, Christian faith would be futile and there would be no hope for eternal life (vv. 17–19). Even worse: without Christ's resurrection, we are left with only the possibility of falsification of Christian hope:

Such a falsification would come in two forms, one looking backward and one looking forward. Looking backward, we could imagine evidence put forward to claim that Jesus hung on the cross, died, and remained dead. . . . Looking forward, we could imagine a future without a consummation, without the new creation promised by the Easter resurrection. . . . The resurrection of Christ, according to Christian faith . . . was the advent of the world's transformation. Without the consummation of this transformatory promise, the Christian faith is in vain.[29]

What about the challenge from sciences? How likely is it to assume resurrection as the ground of the Christian hope for the future—rather than

28. Migliore, *Faith Seeking Understanding*, 330–31.
29. Peters, "Introduction: What Is to Come," viii.

merely a temporary resuscitation of a dead person, as with Lazarus? Honestly, we have to acknowledge that "there is perhaps no topic that seems less suited for the dialogue between theology and the so-called exact sciences than the topic of the resurrection."[30] The reason of course lies in the current secular naturalist[31] worldview that reigns among the scientific communities in the Global North, with its aversion to all notions of life after death and to the category of the "supernatural." Along with naturalism, the main challenge from the sciences concerning the resurrection is that it seems to violate the regularity of natural occurrences, the role of laws of nature.

Without going into details about it here,[32] suffice it to say that there are weighty reasons for assuming the raising from the dead of the slain Messiah, particularly the empty tomb and the great number of eye-witnesses being the most important evidence. Indeed, a good case can be made for the fact that rather than going against "nature" (i.e., being unnatural), the resurrection of Christ—who, himself, in biblical testimonies is the very agent of creation (Col 1:15–17)—transcends and lifts up the natural. It points to the eschatological consummation when, according to the biblical promises, creation "will be set free from its bondage to decay" (Rom 8:21), so much so that, as a result, even death will be defeated (1 Cor 15:55).

While a Christological event, the resurrection is of course also a pneumatological, Spirit-driven event, as Christ was raised to new life by the Father through the Holy Spirit (Rom 1:4). The indwelling Spirit in believers constantly reminds them of the certainty of their own resurrection by the same Spirit who raised Christ (Rom 8:11). The Spirit of God of whom the Bible speaks is the eschatological Spirit, the One who brings about the promised future of God. The Spirit poured out at the day of Pentecost was already the "last day" Spirit of God. The eschaton began about 2,000 years ago and will soon be consummated.

The power and surplus of hope

In making a recommendation for a robust meaningful hope based in the Triune God, I wish to contest and reject the statements to the contrary by

30. Welker, "Resurrection and Eternal Life," 279.

31. "Naturalism" means that all that there is is nature. There is nothing "beyond" or "above" it. Even the non-material properties, such as thinking, imagination, and religiosity, derive from and can be reduced back to the material base.

32. See further Kärkkäinen, *Christ and Reconciliation*, 125–33.

atheists, secularists, and others who fear that God-given hope may be a diversion from reality. Among those voices, one of the most vocal is that of the pronounced atheist, the pessimistic existentialist, Albert Camus: "For if there is a sin against life, it consists perhaps not so much in despairing of life as in hoping for another life and in eluding the implacable grandeur of this life."[33] While I of course side with Camus that "eluding the implacable grandeur of this life" is a deplorable response for the Christian—as well as for anyone else—I wish to challenge this atheist's underlying assumption that a religious hope for the future of God necessarily leads to it. Similarly, I denounce the accusation against Christian religion of Ernst Bloch, the great Jewish-born atheist with whom Moltmann struggled in constructing his response to a godless hope. Said Bloch: "hope is preached from every pulpit, but is confined to mere inwardness or to empty promises of the other world."[34] To the contrary, I say that Christian hope embraces *both* this life *and* the life to come; it includes *both* the mundane *and* the "spiritual." And its domain is the whole cosmos!

Hoping tells us that we consider the current life incomplete, as it were. Why would anyone hope for something if all things were perfect? That said, the anticipation of the consummation does not have to divert us from to-day's responsibilities. The hope for the future may rather energize and em-power for loving service and caring for the environment, as will be detailed in chapters 6 and 7. At the same time, Christian hope—the expectation of the divine intervention—tells us that we ourselves are not able to bring about the hoped-for future reality, salvation, consummation. *Only God can.*

Hope is a way to liberation, freedom. How so? Pannenberg responds: "The imparting of hope by faith in Jesus Christ frees us from this impris-onment in self and lifts us above the self."[35] Notwithstanding our circum-stances, hopeful imagination gets us beyond the current limitations of life. While, of course, this kind of reaching out to the hoped future may end up being nothing but an "exit-mentality," a desire to depart from this world and its responsibilities, or a utopian dream, it does not necessarily have to be. Hope, grounded in the work and nature of the Triune God, may also serve as a foundation for service, neighborly love, and care for creation. Life is meaningful. Life is valuable. It is worth preserving and cultivating.

33. Camus, *The Myth of Sisyphus*, 122, cited in Louw, "*Cura Animarum* as Hope Care," 1.

34. Bloch, *The Principle of Hope*, 5.

35. Pannenberg, *ST* 3:179.

CHAPTER 3

What do the Sciences say about the future of life and the cosmos?

Introduction: why should theology be concerned about the sciences?

Doesn't modern science simply defeat religious explanations?

WHY SHOULD A BOOK on Christian and Muslim eschatology be concerned about raising the question of what the sciences say about the future of life and the cosmos—let alone seeking to answer it? Doesn't it suffice for the theologian (of any faith tradition) to stick with the resources and questions of religious traditions? Aren't the sciences and religions such totally different fields and rationalities that they have nothing in common?

The philosophical point of view often called "naturalism" says as much. It is a foundational worldview that refers to "the philosophy that everything that exists is a part of nature and that there is no reality beyond or outside of nature."[1] Simply put: it means that all that there is in the world—not only the material/physical, such as the human body and the earth, but also everything that is non-material (we might call it "mental," such as qualities like emotions, imagination, love, and religiosity)—are ultimately to be reduced to the material basis. If that were true, no reasonable case could be made for religious explanations, which, while not downplaying the importance of the material ("natural") as God's handiwork, argue that "behind"

1. Goetz and Taliaferro, *Naturalism*, 6.

and "beyond" the physical there is something else, the mental, the spiritual. While not all the most recent forms of naturalism are necessarily totally religion-defeating,[2] all naturalisms do seek to explain the world without reference to God, the almighty Creator.

I endorse the critique of naturalism that notes that this philosophical stance is not of course a "scientific" result. It is a choice, a particular world-view. Indeed, naturalism's basic claim—namely, that nature is all that there is—cannot be verified within science's self-placed limitations that rely only on empirical, testable, or otherwise indubitably rational explanations. No scientific study could ever "prove," or show irrefutable evidence for, natu-ralism. Indeed, ultimate questions of the origins of the cosmos are beyond scientific inquiry. To the perennial questions of why there is something rather than nothing and of who produced it, naturalism doesn't have the "scientific tools" to respond unless it goes beyond its own limits.

In contrast to naturalism, Christian theological engagement of science takes up these metaphysical challenges and argues boldly for the possibility and necessity of a religious interpretation of nature as creation. The same applies to Islam (and of course, Judaism as well). No reasonable theologian contends that there is irrefutable evidence to defeat all reasonable argu-ments against faith in God as the Creator. But this does not imply that faith in God is blind. Not at all. While faith in God, similarly to atheism, is nei-ther a necessary scientific result, nor the outcome of irrefutable philosophi-cal reasoning, a seasoned and critical theologian may be confident about religious explanations.

In sum: while a case can be made for limiting theological inquiries to biblical and theological resources, this project does not consider such a limitation to be useful. This stance is based on the theological conviction that, if God is the Creator of the vast universe (as all Abrahamic faiths com-monly confess), then there is nothing in the cosmos that escapes God's care and interest. Nor should it escape the theologian's interest. As Pannenberg put it: when "Christians confess God as the Creator of the world, it is inevi-tably the same world that is the object of scientific descriptions."[3] Further-more, in the contemporary world science is a universal phenomenon and, as such, exerts significant influence on all religions and ideologies.[4]

---

2. Kärkkäinen, *Creation and Humanity*. Ch. 2 offers a fourfold typology of naturalisms.

3. Pannenberg, "Contributions from Systematic Theology," 359.

4. McNamara and Wildman, *Science and the World's Religions*.

To conclude that theology should be interested in the results and insights of science is not yet to establish a unified theological approach to sciences and the significance and meaning of their results. There is more than one Christian theological response to science.

A diversity of theological responses to science

This contemporary conviction about the possibility of a mutual collaboration and dialogue between the two, science and Christian religion, has not always been shared by every believer. Even today not all theological traditions embrace this conviction universally, nor in the same manner. To illustrate the diversity of approaches to how one relates theology and science, the following overly simplified typology of Christian views may be useful (Islam's stance towards science will be discussed at the end of the following chapter):

1. Theology in continuity with science (classical liberalism)

2. Science in continuity with theology (pre-Enlightenment theology)

3. Theology and science as separate realms (Barth's neo-orthodoxy)

4. The mutual interaction of theology and science[5] (the approach recommended here)

Classical liberalism—stemming from the work of Friedrich Schleiermacher of the nineteenth century and his followers, who wanted to lessen the categorical distinction between God and the world by arguing for the principle of continuity as opposed to juxtaposition between the two—is a grand example of the first category. With its categorical separation between "nature" (the domain of facts) and "history" (the domain of human values), liberalism made the former the realm of natural sciences and the latter that of "human sciences." Hence, no conflict arises. The obvious liability of this approach is the timidity with which theology engages natural sciences. Rather than challenging and dialoguing with the scientific conjectures about the beginning and the end of cosmos, theology simply uncritically embraces scientific explanations. In other words, this is a strategy of uncritical accommodation.

"Science in continuity with theology" derives from the pre-Enlightenment worldview in which theology was seen as the queen of sciences. In

5. Clifford, "Creation," 1:225–40.

theology, all explanations about the world, whether secular or religious, are founded on the authority of Scripture. With the rise of modern sciences in the eighteenth century, this "Scripture principle" (an unquestioning acceptance of the Holy Scripture's authority) naturally collided with the scientific approach. For the time being this emerging conflict was not widely felt, as most of the pioneers of the modern science were believing Christians and they could hold onto both religious and scientific convictions. Soon thereafter, the separation became evident and inevitable. As a result, on the contemporary scene, the fundamentalist movement known as creationism, with its advocacy of an antievolutionary scientific paradigm, seeks to restore this lost authority of the religious explanations. It provides an alternative to mainline natural sciences, based on literal interpretation of the biblical message, for example with an appeal to the alleged paleontological "evidence" in support of a young earth theory.[6] The obvious problem with this approach is that it lacks scientific credibility and hence, even at its best, remains a purely religious affair.

The third category comes materially close to the first in our typology. It is represented by the "church father" of the twentieth century, the late Swiss Reformed Karl Barth and the so-called neo-orthodox movement. With its fideistic approach (based on faith alone), it chooses to elevate theology as the judge of all matters of knowledge (somewhat similarly to the fundamentalists, although not rejecting historical-critical study) and basically accepts classical liberalism's categorical separation between nature and history. It therefore insists that there is no need to dialogue with the sciences—as happened in Barth's massive multi-volume *Church Dogmatics*.[7] Its main liability, similar to that of the second category, is the failure of theology to have a public voice and also to make its own contribution to the sciences.

The last category, identified here as the "mutual interaction of theology and science,"[8] is the one I recommend here. Its basic conviction is that if God is the Creator of everything, then "everything"—including what sciences are discovering about the world—is of interest to theology. This principle is acutely described by the Roman Catholic Church's important

6. Morris, *The Beginning of the World*.

7. In his almost 2,000-page discussion of the doctrine of creation in vol. 3 (part volumes 1 and 2) of *Church Dogmatics*, Barth totally omits any engagement with scientific challenges and conditions. Instead, he focuses entirely on theological conversations.

8. Adapted from Russell, *Cosmology: From Alpha to Omega*.

Vatican II (1962–65) document "Pastoral Constitution on the Church in the Modern World," namely that "earthly matters and the concerns of faith derive from the same God" and hence in principle cannot violate each other.[9] Among Protestant theologians, Pannenberg represents the same position. Notwithstanding the differences between the two, science and theology ultimately study and reflect on the same world. Many other leading Protestant theologians agree, including another Lutheran, the American Ted Peters, as well as the Reformed German Jürgen Moltmann and the late Scottish scholar T. F. Torrance (as much as he was Barthian otherwise). Prominent scholars with a double-degree in natural sciences and theology, including Robert J. Russell, Ian Barbour, John Polkinghorne, Alister McGrath, and Arthur Peacocke, following the same template, have significantly advanced the science-theology model of inquiry. In this model, theology should not merely serve as science's religious interpreter, but should also challenge and contribute to science's quest.

Having now cleared the way for the theology-science engagement with regard to the "end" of human life, the life of our planet, and ultimately, even this vast cosmos, we will proceed in the following manner. We will first review briefly what sciences are telling us about the origins, the "beginning" of the universe and life, as everything that the sciences are conjecturing about the future is based on their calculations of its origins. Thereafter, I will detail more broadly some commonly agreed upon projections into the future among the natural sciences. The last section of this chapter takes a hard look at what is at stake with theology in regards to sciences' explanations regarding the End.

What are the sciences saying about the origins?

For orientation: two dramatic scientific developments

All scientific explanations in our age are indebted to, and cannot do their work without, two transformative leaps in the theory and methods of natural sciences, namely the relativity theories of Albert Einstein in the early twentieth century and the rise and continuing development of quantum physics in their aftermath.[10] Whereas before the universe was conceived in

9. Paul VI. *Gaudium et Spes*, #36.

10. Most ironically, the genius Einstein never owned—and, indeed, stayed a critic of—mainstream quantum theories until the end of his life, even though their emergence

static and often "solid" terms—such as in terms of Newton's clockwork cosmos—these new theories helped scientists envision the world as evolving, dynamic, relational, in constant "movement." It was a hugely transformative change of vision in a relatively short period of time.

Einstein's special relativity theory in 1905 linked space and time together in a space-time continuum and in so doing made all points of observation relative rather than absolute. His 1916 general relativity theory added gravity to the picture and this helped radically revise the earlier steady view of the world. Whereas in the old Newtonian theory space and time were understood to be some kind of separate backgrounds or "containers" in which matter moved, for Einstein space-time was instead a four-dimensional manifold (three space and one time dimension) that "can stretch, warp, and vibrate."[11] Even more (to overly simplify a complex matter) gravitation, rather than being merely a "field," was now understood in light of relativity theories as some kind of a distortion of space and time. As the physicist John Wheeler's famous dictum puts it: "Matter tells space how to curve," and "[s]pace tells matter how to move."[12] Think of the surface of a balloon covered with colored spots while it is being blown up: it is not that the spots are moving (even though they are) but that the surface of the balloon is expanding!

Enter quantum theory.[13] Among its many contributions, perhaps one of the most far-reaching is its defeat of all naïve mechanisms and the determinism of the old paradigm. What quantum theory reveals is that not only at the smallest, subatomic level (where it primarily functions), but also at the macrolevel, nature reveals surprises, irregularities, and unpredictability—notwithstanding the amazing regularity of natural processes. This is of course not to say that the laws of nature would not be in place: of course they are, and they are surprisingly accurate (relatively speaking even deterministic)—or else no scientific observations would be possible. What quantum theory (in its main Copenhagen interpretation) is saying is that determinism is not ironclad and that natural processes and events are probabilistic in nature.

---

would not have been possible without his theories of relativity! See McGrath, *A Theory of Everything (That Matters)*.

11. Spitzer, *New Proofs for the Existence of God*, 15.

12. Misner et al., *Gravitation*, 5.

13. Polkinghorne, *Quantum World*.

The indications of indeterminacy are well known, such as the wave/particle duality (that is, light appears both as wave and as particle) and the incapacity to measure both the momentum and position of the particle.[14] Or consider the highly counterintuitive quantum "entanglement" (Bell's theorem), according to which, without any "real" reason, the measurement of two chance events—imagine the measurement of the spin of two electrons when they travel as a result of the decay of an atom—shows definite non-local correlation; that is, while it cannot be said that these two chance events really influence each other, they are to a certain extent inseparable.

Add to these developments the whole new field of chaos theory, which shows that, while causality (rightly understood) is of course not to be set aside, the more developed the processes, the less *mechanistically* causal they are—even if they are basically deterministic! Consider the famous "butterfly effect": the slightest change affecting climate in one part of the world, when amplified, may cause a huge storm on the other side of the globe.

This kind of dynamic and evolving world gives rise to what is named "emergence," the constant evolution of new properties, qualities, and species. We know that "new and unpredictable phenomena are naturally produced by interactions in nature; that these new structures, organisms, and ideas are not reducible to the subsystems on which they depend; and that the newly evolved realities in turn exercise a causal influence on the parts out of which they arose."[15]

Now, we are ready to review well-known scientific principles of how all we call cosmos came into being.

The origins of the universe in light of contemporary cosmology

Notwithstanding a number of continuing debates, in scientific cosmology[16] the big bang theory is the standard, established position with a huge

---

14. Roughly speaking, the famous "superposition" principle says that a particle can be said to be both "here" and "there," not of course simultaneously but probabilistically, that is, we can never know for sure where it is. Consider also other celebrated quantum examples of indeterminism and counter intuitiveness, namely, the "double-slit experiment"; that is, imagine a beam of electrons being shot through a metal plate with two narrow slits; the results clearly imply that these particles behaved more like waves as they appear to have entered both slits!

15. Clayton, *Mind and Emergence*, vi; for the history, see ch. 1.

16. Wilkinson Microwave Anisotropy Probe. "Cosmology."; NASA, "Universe 101."

experimental support.[17] Simply stated: the cosmos came into being about 13.7 billion years ago from a singularity of zero size and infinite density (usually marked as $t = 0$ in which t denotes time), and has since expanded to its current form. Since the Hubble discovery in the 1920s,[18] we have learned that the galaxies are receding from us, and that therefore the cosmos is "expanding." Important evidence for this expansion and the big bang came from the discovery in the 1960s of the microwave background radiation that is believed to be an echo of the original big bang.

Based on relativity and quantum theories, and from observing the galaxies flying apart as indications of constant expansion, the big bang theory simply looks back in time to the point when the expansion started, finally reaching the "beginning point." It is assumed that the distribution of matter in the universe is homogeneous and isotropic when averaged over very large scales (the so-called cosmological principle). Importantly for our discussion, the big bang theory was originally proposed (although not so named) by the Roman Catholic priest-physicist Georges Lemaître in the 1920s.

Thanks to continuing refinements, we now know that immediately after the big bang, during the extremely short period of time (so-called Planck time, 10^{-43} seconds, the shortest measure of time) called the "inflation period," dramatic developments occurred, the details of which are still unknown to the scientific community.[19] Ironically, while current science can explain how the cosmos has evolved after 10^{-43} seconds from the big bang to today, no complete explanation can be found for this fraction-second long period!

Although this standard big bang theory is still the foundation of all scientific cosmologies, revisions and challenges are under way—but there is neither need nor space to go into those here. Suffice it to mention only the most well-known: that proposed by the British genius Stephen Hawking and his American colleague James Hartle. Briefly stated, their theory claims that while there most probably is a "beginning" to the world, there is no beginning in time (meaning no singularity).[20]

17. Consult Boisvert, *Religion and the Physical Sciences*.

18. NASA, "Hubble Space Telescope."

19. Wilkinson Microwave Anisotropy Probe. "What Is the Inflation Theory?"

20. For details, consult what is the most widely circulated scientific book of origins, Hawking, *Brief History of Time*.

What about the mystery of life in a "lifeless" cosmos?

Somewhat counterintuitively, the mystery of life remains *mystery* in the sense that at the moment of this writing even the most recent scientific research has not proven capable of explaining how life as we know it emerged. Even though we know quite accurately what kind of biological and chemical processes, in addition to the metabolism and the capacity to reproduce, are the essential conditions for living beings, we are far from having a conclusive answer regarding its emergence.[21]

Theologically we can state that if God is not only the original Creator but also the one who continuously creates and acts in the world, it means that "the stuff of the world has a continuous, inbuilt creativity."[22] Our planet is also striking for its unbelievably rich diversity, with its more than two million known species of plants and animals and many more to be discovered. Yet all organisms are related by common ancestry.

All this tells us that the apparently cold and lifeless universe[23] seems to be "fine-tuned" to bring about creative processes, particularly life. This fine-tuning relates particularly to the values of the universal constants. The constants control the interrelationships among space, time, and energy in the universe to allow life-facilitating conditions. Indeed, it would appear that of all the vast number of possible combinations of universal constants, only a very few could facilitate conditions hospitable to the emergence of life. If the constants were selected in a purely random way it is incredibly unlikely that life would have ever emerged in the history of the universe.[24]

Fine-tuning is also the condition for the emergence of humanity, the highest known life-form. Recall the physicist Freeman Dyson's oft-cited comment that "the more I examine the universe and study the details of its architecture, the more evidence I find that the universe in some sense must have known that we were coming."[25] This is the famous "anthropic principle,"[26] or, more widely, the "biopic principle."

While the anthropic principle is not a religious or theological statement—it is instead a scientific observation—understandably Christian

21. McGrath, *Fine-Tuned Universe*, ch. 10; NASA, "Origins of Life."
22. Peacocke, "Chance and Law," 139.
23. Haught, *Is Nature Enough?* 57.
24. McGrath, *Fine-Tuned Universe*, 119–21.
25. Dyson, *Disturbing the Universe*, 250.
26. Barrow and Tipler, *Anthropic Cosmological Principle*.

tradition sees in it support for a rational and loving Creator. But it is found not only in Christian but also in Islamic tradition.[27] The Qur'anic passage from 21:16 is often invoked: "Not for (idle) sport did We create the heavens and the earth and all that is between!"[28] That said, for a non-religious person, such as naturalists and atheists, fine-tuning does not bespeak for God but can be rather understood (for example) in terms of various "multiverse" theories that posit the existence of infinitely many parallel universes; ultimately, so the argument goes, it is inevitable that among the infinite possibilities a life-bringing option will arise. Be that as it may, science alone cannot resolve the issue; it is ultimately a theological and metaphysical concern.

Both scientifically and theologically, it is significant to acknowledge the extremely slow evolution of life on our planet. After the advent of the most elementary forms of bacterial life, it would take over two billion years to attain higher forms of life. That is a long, long time. From a theological perspective, it looks like the Creator is in no hurry. The Creator who in the first place established the natural laws that govern the evolution and sustenance of the vast cosmos seems to be utterly patient about letting those regularities, combined with accidents, produce ever-more sophisticated life-forms.

Now we turn our attention away from the origins—without however leaving behind what we have learned—to the questions of the "end."

The "end" of the cosmos and life in natural sciences' conjectures

The rediscovery of the "end" as a scientific interest

Understandably, the questions related to the "end" of the cosmos have not been at the forefront of scientific inquiry. Such inquiry has attended mainly to its origins. Only in recent decades, beginning from around 1970s, have "eschatological" issues been taken up in a more concerted manner. Still, only baby steps have been taken when compared to the wide and deep interest in the questions of beginnings.[29]

27. For an up-to-date discussion, see Guessoum, *Islam's Quantum Question*, ch. 7 (on design) and ch. 8 (on the anthropic principle).

28. Translated by Abdullah Yusuf Ali, at www.altafsir.com.

29. See Davies, *Last Three Minutes*.

In principle, the picture painted of the "future" in sciences is not complicated: it leads to eventual decay and annihilation.[30] That is because "Einstein's theory of general relativity gives equations that tell us how any universe containing matter and radiation will change with time under the influence of gravity."[31] Within this universally agreed upon scientific projection, there is the well-known debate about "logistics." Three basic options present themselves on the basis of Einstein's theory: if it is an open universe, then the process of expanding eventually leads to a "freeze"; if it is "closed," then the expansion of the universe will reach the culmination point and eventually "contract" until it results in what is known as a "fry," the big crunch; and if the universe has a "flat" curvature, then, as in the first scenario, it will expand (forever) and finally reach the "freeze" point.[32] A majority of scientists argues for the open universe, observing that its expansion seems to be accelerating.

If this is in fact so, then what are the implications of this for the future of the universe—and for life on this earth or life elsewhere? It is convenient to divide that question into three interrelated time-frames: the near future (the end of life conditions on earth), the distant future (the end of the earth, sun, and our solar system), and the far-distant future (the "end" of the whole cosmos).[33] Let us work our way backwards from the far-distant end to questions related to the future of humanity on this earth.

Scientific predictions about the "future" of the universe

The most distant future of the cosmos (the far-distant future), according to current scientific predictions, looks something like the following:

- In 5 billion years, the sun will become a red giant, engulfing the orbits of Earth and Mars.

- In 40–50 billion years, star formation in our galaxy will have ended.

- In 10^{12} years, all massive stars will have become neutron stars or black holes.

---

30. Davies, *Last Three Minutes*, ch. 2: "The Dying Universe."

31. Wilkinson, *Christian Eschatology*, 12.

32. Russell, *Time in Eternity*, 56–59.

33. With minor adaptations from Boisvert, *Religion and the Physical Sciences*, 229–34.

- If the universe is closed, then in 10^{12} years, the universe will have reached its maximum size and then will recollapse back to a singularity like the original hot big bang.

- In 10^{31} years, protons and neutrons will decay into positrons, electrons, neutrinos, and photons.

- In 10^{34} years, all carbon-based life-forms will inevitably become extinct.[34]

The end result of all that is that the "proton decay spells ultimate doom for life based on protons and neutrons, like *Homo sapiens* and all forms of life constructed of atoms."[35] In that light, it does not really matter which of the three above-mentioned scientific scenarios is true (open, closed, or flat); they *all* lead to ultimate decay. At the end there is going to be "a barren universe devoid of any trace that life had ever existed."[36] It merely takes an awful lot of time for this to take place!

Regarding the distant future prospects, beyond the conditions of life on this earth and in this solar system, what is particularly well documented is the possibility of Earth or another planet being hit by a comet or asteroid.[37] An often-cited example from Earth's history is the dinosaur extinction due to a comet's hitting the planet about 65 million years ago.

Regardless of whether this kind of cosmic accident takes place or not, what we know now is that in about 4 to 5 billion years, the Earth will be uninhabitable and eventually lifeless. Our sun will come to the end of its available hydrogen fuel and will begin to swell up and eventually run out of energy. Regarding whether there are other forms of "life" or platforms other than carbon-based life, scientists can only speculate, without any evidence.[38] It is yet to be seen.

Coming to the closest time-frame with regard to humanity and other life on Earth, the near-future, we are dealing with a number of factors with which humanity has some or even a significant role to play. These threats include pollution, global warming, and nuclear threat. Detailed documentation of these threats can be found everywhere nowadays in print and

34. Russell, *Time in Eternity*, 60–61.

35. Barrow and Tipler, *Anthropic Cosmological Principle*, 684, cited in Russell, *Time in Eternity*, 61.

36. Russell, *Time in Eternity*, 61.

37. Ch. 2 in Davies, *Last Three Minutes*.

38. Wilkinson, *Christian Eschatology*, 7–10.

online (and chapter 6 below also speaks of the threats to the environment). I can sum these up by saying: "if current trends continue, we will not."[39]

Among the leading scientists, pessimism about the future of our globe is common: "by 2600 the world's population will be standing shoulder to shoulder, and electricity use will make the Earth glow red hot."[40] In contrast to the optimism of the Enlightenment (the harbinger of modernity), with its unchecked belief in endless progress and improvement, doomsday visions of the future seem to be the order of the day at the beginning of the third millennium.

I can sum up this position by saying: according to the scientific predictions, what can be said of the future and "end" is that:

- Human life as we know it will come to an end.
- Our planet and its life as well as this galaxy will come to an end.
- The (almost) infinitely vast cosmos will come to an end.

But what about life continuing through other potential forms or platforms of "life" other than carbon-based ones?

Other forms of life?

Not surprisingly, various alternative proposals concerning the hoped-for continuation of "human" life have been imagined, even if no scientific evidence for them has (yet) been advanced. One of them builds on the possibility of multiverses, which might make possible endless fertility. Even if *this* universe comes to naught, there might be other universes with fertility and conditions for life in one form or another.

> In the cosmological context, a multiverse is defined as a hypothetical set of possible universes, either finite or infinite in number (including our own observable universe), that together constitute the entirety of space-time, matter, and energy, as well as an underlying set of physical laws or equations.[41]

At the moment, the concept of a multiverse is highly speculative and under fierce debate: "The critical question is whether the existence of a

39. Maguire, *Moral Core of Judaism*, 13.
40. Hawking, *Universe in a Nutshell*, 1.
41. Cleaver, "Multiverse," 90.

41

multiverse in one form or another is probable."[42] No empirical evidence for it exists. If the multiverse theory (to be more precise: any of the many multiverse theories) were shown to be true, theologically it would hardly bring any major problem. The same God who has created this (almost) infinitely vast "observed" universe can be thought to be able to bring forth innumerable such universes!

Perhaps the best-known proposal for a "human" life beyond human life as we know it is that of physicist Freeman Dyson. His foundational presupposition, shared by a group of thinkers in that camp, is that the existence of life is a "necessity" in the kind of universe we know. In other words, we do not know a universe void of life! As much as this reasoning may appear to be circular, in other words, to presuppose what it attempts to prove, it merits reflection. After intelligent life has come to an end, we may bring into existence new kinds of transformations that guarantee the continuation of intelligence in some nonpersonal form.[43]

Another widely discussed speculative proposal comes from an American cosmologist, Frank J. Tipler (the coauthor of *The Anthropic Cosmological Principle* in 1972). Materially similar to Dyson, Tipler's vision of "the physics of immortality" intuits the continuance of intelligent life as some kind of computational process—after intelligent life as we know it has vanished. More than that: he imagines that ultimately the infinite expansion of intelligence to everywhere in the universe is possible.[44]

The main critical question to both of these proposals—beyond the lack of any empirical evidence—is simply this: in what sense can we even imagine a computational non-personal intelligence to come close to what we know as holistic human life?

In the most recent scientific and philosophical discussion about the possibilities of transcending, extending, or improving human life (as we now know it), two basic mutually conditioned concepts have emerged, namely "posthumanism" and "transhumanism." Basically, they mean something like the following:

- Posthumanism: the ways in which the technologies and innovations are changing humanity, such as the idea of a cyborg.[45] This is some-

42. Cleaver, "Multiverse," 91.

43. Dyson, "Life in the Universe," 140–57.

44. Tipler, *Physics of Immortality*; for an insightful theological engagement and critique, see Russell, "Cosmology and Eschatology."

45. For the concept of a cyborg, a good introduction is Clark, *Natural-Born Cyborgs*;

thing humanity has always attempted with the help of fire, the first tools for gardening, agriculture, weapons, and so forth. A typical current expression of posthumanism includes the "smart home," in which information to regulate functions (such as to turn something on/off) comes directly from brains rather than humans speaking or themselves turning something on/off.[46]

- Transhumanism: future visions of what it means to be beyond humanity: "An intellectual movement that aims to transform the human condition by encouraging technologies to greatly enhance human intellectual, physical, and psychological capacities, producing transhumans (or H+) whose abilities are beyond those of current humans."[47]

What are we to think theologically of these two latest concepts or visions? Briefly stated, at this moment it can be said that, first, posthumanism hardly poses a major problem in principle as long as the extended or improved forms of life are not made an ideal or necessary for a flourishing life. For such a turn would result in the "gradation" of life: for example, the handicapped life or current "normal" life without any posthuman improvements would be considered less valuable. Suffering, liabilities, and other challenges, which are essential aspects of life in the quotidian, will not go away as long as we live in the kind of cosmos God has created; hence, life in happiness and in sadness should be equally valued and honored. Other than that, improving life conditions and means of achieving morally and theologically valid goals are not problems in principle.

When it comes to transhumanism, I join the growing chorus of Christian theologians who are deeply worried and concerned. The foundational reason for my concern is twofold. Unlike posthumanism, transhumanism does not accept the inevitability of death and decay, and hence is, in principle, antagonistic to religion. As Ted Peters, a theologian well-versed in these conversations, puts it: transhumanism opposes "Not only death, but also those who accept death, who advocate deathism. Who advocates deathism? Religious believers."[48] For this reason, most transhumanists "see

---

see also Nusselder, *Interface Fantasy*.

46. Smart and Smart, *Posthumanism*, 7; see also Hayles, *How We Became Posthuman*.

47. Smart and Smart, *Posthumanism*, 103.

48. Peters, "Theologians Testing Transhumanism," 136; I first found this citation in Smart and Smart, *Posthumanism*, 89.

their movement as a replacement for traditional religion."[49] The central tenet of transhumanism can be summarized as the belief in overcoming human limitations through reason and technology. What more fundamental limitation is there than aging and death? Transhumanist optimism predicts average life expectancy exceeding a millennium. There are even some who predict that we already have the means to "live long enough to live forever."[50] Transhumanists offer two paths to this utopia. The first is radical life-extension through genetics, nanotechnology, and robotics. This path remains biological. The second offers immortality through the uploading of consciousness.

In sum: with regard to this brief detour into the current scientific and philosophical speculations into the possibility of either improving human life or transforming it to the point it may overcome death, the current interim status report is that they are just that, *speculations*. With regard to the bigger foundational question behind this chapter, the question is: what has all of this engagement of sciences' conjectures about the "far future" to do with theology? In other words, what is at stake theologically? This is the million-dollar question and to this we turn finally here.

What is at stake for theology?

The foundational challenge between sciences and theology concerning the future can be put like this: is it possible to reconcile Christian (and, in a modified manner, Muslim) eschatological expectation of the *imminent* return of Christ and the bringing about of the "new heavens and new earth" with the scientific conjectures that envision an ultimate inevitable decay and disappearance but under almost infinitely long horizons? Even more importantly: how would the Christian vision accord with the sciences' total lack of any vision of "renewal"?

One does not have to be either a professional scientist or a theologian to acknowledge the hugely wide gulf, even contradiction, between the two.[51] The mutual tension between the two disciplines is intensified by the fact that Christian eschatology envisions not only bodily resurrection but

---

49. Peters, "Theologians Testing Transhumanism," 133.

50. Kurzweil, *Singularity Is Near*, 371.

51. Pannenberg, "Theological Questions to Scientists," 48.

also a radical transformation of life conditions in new creation, as will be discussed in detail in chapters 8 and 9.[52]

Above, we charted major alternatives regarding theology's relation to science. Some of them would either ease or drop this grave challenge by simply ignoring the scientific challenge or considering it to be irrelevant to theological concerns. I am not willing to take those easy outs. It is incumbent upon theology to face the challenge, to take it by the horns. There is no denying that much is at stake in theology as "the idea of a hope after death and an end that fulfills history as a whole is as intrinsic to the Christian tradition as it is foreign to the project of science."[53] As I argued above, Christian eschatology is not content with only envisioning a "happy end" to *human* life; in keeping with its belief in God as the Creator of all, the eschatological vision encompasses the *entire cosmos*.

This current project recommends that theology be confident enough— although not dogmatic—to face the questioning and resistance among the scientists and even the wider public regarding the religious vision of the future. While carefully listening to scientists and learning about the continuous flow of new information and insights, theologians should also continue challenging scientists. Theology's challenge to scientists is that "an unaided scientific account of the world does not succeed in making complete sense of cosmic history,"[54] and that science has no means of reaching beyond the observed world and empirically verified observations.

With these caveats in mind, let us continue this eschatological inquiry by widening the scope to the domain of our Abrahamic cousin faith, Islam. What might our Muslim sisters and brothers intuit about the "End"?

---

52. Russell, *Time in Eternity*, 67–70.
53. Clayton, "Eschatology as Metaphysics," 134.
54. Polkinghorne, "Eschatology," 38.

CHAPTER 4

What does Islam envision about the "End"?

Introduction: Why and how to investigate Islamic eschatology?

What is comparative theology?

ONE OF THE KEY tasks of this project, namely a desire to discuss eschatology not only within the resources of Christian tradition but also to compare notes with the youngest Abrahamic sister faith, Islam, makes this a comparative theological study in nature. Like its cognate disciplines of comparative religions and Christian theology of religions, comparative theology facilitates interfaith learning and engagement.[1]

First, as the name indicates, comparative religion focuses on a scientific comparison of religions' doctrines, teachings, and practices. Comparative religion seeks to do its work from a neutral, non-committed point of view rather than pursuing the comparative work from the agenda of a particular tradition. Second, as the name indicates, Christian theology of religions is a confessional Christian discipline that seeks to "account theologically for the meaning and value of other religions. Christian theology of religions attempts to think theologically about what it means for Christians to live with people of other faiths and about the relationship of Christianity to other religions."[2]

---

1. For details and documentation, see Kärkkäinen, *Doing the Work of Comparative Theology*, 1–10; Clooney, *Comparative Theology*, 8–16.
2. Kärkkäinen, *Introduction to the Theology of Religions*, 20.

What then is the distinctive feature and task of comparative theology? Said non-technically, comparative theology seeks to conduct detailed, specific comparisons between two or more faith traditions from a distinctively Christian point of view. In that project, it of course needs basic knowledge about religions produced by comparative religions. The main difference is that comparative theology is confessional rather than "neutral" in nature.

With regard to the Christian theology of religions, the difference is more subtle: whereas theology of religions usually operates at a fairly general level, for example by looking at the meaning of "salvation" or "revelation" among religions, comparative theology complements and challenges this more generic approach by making every effort to consider in detail specific, limited topics in religious traditions. This is what we are doing in this project: rather than merely comparing "eschatologies at large" between the two faith traditions, the ensuing discussion delves into detailed comparisons with regard to a number of individual topics, including judgment, heaven and hell, and, say, what happens between my personal death and the final end.

What might be the benefits of comparative theology? We can list the following three as a summary statement:

> First, Christians can and should learn something about non-Christian religious traditions for the sake of the religious other; in fact, both the license and the imperative to do so rest on a biblical foundation. Second, Christians can and should expect to learn something about God in the course of that exploration, and the basis for such a belief can be found in who God has revealed God-self to be and how Christians have traditionally understood that divine self-revelation. Third, Christians can and should expect that their understanding of their own faith tradition will be stretched and challenged, but at the same time deepened and strengthened through such interreligious dialogue.[3]

The significance of eschatology in Islam

As in other Abrahamic faiths, in Islam there is an acknowledgment of purposefulness in human life and events. Therefore, it makes sense to hear that "the Qur'ān posits an understanding of meaning and significance to the

---

3. Largen, *Baby Krishna, Infant Christ*, 9.

flow of time and history."[4] There is a definite divinely set plan that moves history from creation to the consummation. This is why eschatology matters to Islam as well.

The main reason for comparing notes between Christian and Islamic traditions concerning the "End" is that eschatology plays an extraordinary role in Islam. Recall that the Prophet's first and continuing message was about the coming judgment and the need for submission to Allah in order to avoid the hell of judgment. The Qur'an and particularly Hadith texts discuss the afterlife at great length.[5]

As one of the three major doctrinal areas, eschatology is named as the ultimate "return." Based on Q 7:29 ("As He brought you into being, so you will return"), the idea is that all men and women, having been created and "covenanted" by Allah, are destined to return to Allah. Indeed, all of life is a long process of (preparing) for this return.[6]

Generally speaking, contemporary Muslims tend to take the traditional teaching on eschatology much more seriously than most Jews and Christians do. The "eschatological narrative" lays claim on everything in the Muslim's faith and life. Similarly to Judaism and Christianity, a rich tradition of apocalypticism can be found in Islam, including radical millenarian and jihadist movements.[7]

Regarding the task of a *comparative eschatology* between the two traditions, a couple of important caveats are in order. First, generally speaking, there is a scholarly agreement that Islamic eschatology seems to be (much) more focused on the *personal* aspects of the doctrine of the End, death, and judgment, rather than the cosmic aspects. Second, of neither tradition is it justified to claim that eschatology denotes only, and at times, even primarily, the "otherworldly." The anticipation of the End, within the structure of each religion, lays claim on the life lived today.

Before outlining the core aspects of Islamic eschatology, for the sake of the reader with little or no knowledge of the counterpart's doctrines and theology, I offer a short account of Islam's main beliefs. This will prepare the reader for a focused look at eschatology. Thereafter, throughout the rest of

---

4. Smith and Haddad, *Islamic Understanding*, 3.

5. Chittick, "Muslim Eschatology," 132–50.

6. See also 89:27–28: "'O soul at peace! Return to your Lord, pleased, pleasing.'" Hermansen, "Eschatology," 310–11.

7. Cook, "Early Islamic," 267–83; Kenney, "Millennialism," 688–716.

Muslims are a 'people of the Book.'"[11] The Holy Qur'an is the beginning and the end of all Muslim thinking and living religiously. It is important for us to recall that the Qur'an does not do away with earlier revelations—the Jewish First Testament and the Christian Second Testament—but rather considers itself their fulfillment and correction.

Similarly to other main faith traditions, linked to later exposition and expansion of the primary Qur'anic materials, a huge and vast secondary Hadith tradition also exists, which consists of the sayings of the Prophet and other sages. The sayings and actions of Muhammad narrated in the Hadith are believed not to be revealed, although they are inspired. Understandably, Islamic tradition has also created a huge commentary literature.

Although the Prophet Muhammad is not a divine figure in Islam, nor a "savior," his role as the recipient of the Qur'anic revelation is unsurpassable: "God is the speaker of the revelation, the angel Gabriel is the intermediary agent, and Muhammad is the recipient."[12] And in contrast to Judeo-Christian traditions, in Islam Muhammad is claimed to have received revelation more or less directly, without personal, circumstantial, or historical mediation, although it did not happen all at one time.[13] Hence, Islam regards the Qur'an as the direct, authoritative speech of God conveyed through the Prophet, but that only in its original Arabic form, which is a holy language ("And thus have We revealed to you an Arabic Qur'an," 42:7). Indeed, there is an old tradition according to which the Qur'an is but a copy of a "Guarded Tablet" in heaven (85:21–22[14]). No wonder that Muslims believe in the strict infallibility of the Qur'an in its original language.

Like the New Testament, the Qur'an defines its main and ultimate goal as the salvation of humankind (although "salvation" in Islam is different from the Christian view, as I will explain below). The Holy Qur'an often refers to itself as the guide or path to salvation and true knowledge of God (14:1).[15]

Not surprisingly, the Islamic tradition has paid close attention to careful and authoritative exegesis (tafsir) of the Qur'an. Indeed, because the

11. Coward, *Sacred Word*, 81.

12. Coward, *Sacred Word*, 82.

13. "And [it is] a Qur'an that We have divided that you may recite it to mankind at intervals, and We have revealed it by [successive] revelation" (Q 17:106).

14. "It is a glorious Qur'an, in a tablet, preserved."

15. "Alif lām rā'. A Book We have revealed to you that you may bring forth mankind from darkness into light by the leave of their Lord to the path of the Mighty, the Praised."

Qur'an lays the foundation for and regulates all aspects of life and society, more is at stake in the hermeneutics of Scripture in Islam than with most other traditions. Conversely, Christians and other non-Muslims are accused of false interpretation, or indeed of "alteration" (*tahrif*).

An uncompromising monotheism

While all Abrahamic faiths are strictly monotheistic, that is the faithful believe in one God, "no religious community puts more emphasis on the absolute oneness of God than does Islam."[16] Affirmed everywhere in Islamic theology, the short sura 112 of the Qur'an puts it succinctly, taking notice also of the fallacy of the Christian confession of the Trinity:

> Say: "He is God, One.
> God, the Self-Sufficient, Besought of all.
> He neither begot, nor was begotten.
> Nor is there anyone equal to Him."

Hence, the basic Muslim confession of *shahada*: "There is no god but God, and Muhammad is the apostle of God." An essential aspect of the divine unity is Allah's distinction from all else. The common statement "God is great" (*Allah akbar*) means not only that but also that "God is greater" than anything else. Hence, the biggest sin is *shirk*, associating anything with Allah.

In contrast to popular misconceptions, the term *allah*, which predates the time of Muhammad, did not originate in the context of moon worship in Arabia (even though the crescent became Islam's symbol and moon worship was known in that area). Instead, the term derives from Aramaic and Syriac words for God (*elah, alah*). In that light, it is fully understandable that even among Christians in Arabic-speaking areas the term *Allah* is the designation for God. However, to say that etymologically and theologically both Muslims and Christians refer to the same God when they speak of the Divine does not settle the issue of *what kind* of God that is.

The purpose of every Muslim's life is to honor the unity of God and to willingly submit (*muslim*) to it in obedience and gratitude. In light of the centrality and comprehensiveness of the Qur'anic revelation and an uncompromising belief in Allah, it is understandable that, unlike modern forms of Christianity, the Muslim faith encompasses all of life. "Faith does

16. Carman, *Majesty and Meekness*, 323.

not concern a sector of life—no, the whole of life is *islam* [submission]."[17] Hence, the Five Pillars of Islam (profession of faith, prayers, almsgiving, fasting, and pilgrimage) shape all of life.

One of the most well-known ways in Islamic theology to imagine God is the listing of the ninety-nine Beautiful Names of God. Interestingly, there is no unanimity concerning whether *Allah* belongs to that number or is the hundredth one. Indeed, the naming of the Divine is more important for Islamic theology than for Christian theology. Illustrative here is that each Qur'anic sura (save one) begins with the description of God as the "Compassionate, the Merciful."

Although (because of the danger of the *shirk*) Muslims are cautious about applying anthropomorphic designations of Allah, neither are they unknown, including *the* "face of God" ("whithersoever you turn, there is the Face of God," 2:115) or the "hand of God" ("The Hand of God is above their hands," 48:10). Even personal characteristics of Allah are not unknown, even though they are not as prevalent as in the Bible. A leading medieval teacher named Al-Ghazali may at times say that "God is more full of compassion to his servants than the affectionate mother to her nursing child," attributing this statement to the Prophet Muhammad.[18] Similarly to Christianity, Muslim theology of God includes the built-in dynamic between the absolute transcendence of God, because of his incomparability and uniqueness, and his presence and rulership in the world, which is a call for total obedience. Against typical Christian misunderstandings, with his power, uniqueness, and distinction from all that has been created, for most Muslims Allah is also an intimate, protective, personal God.

No need to mention that in its absolute insistence on the unity of God Islam harshly rejects Christian trinitarian monotheism. This of course leads directly to the denial of Christ's incarnation and divinity (4:171).[19] The trinitarian confession is nothing less than blasphemy to Muslims (5:72–76).[20]

---

17. Vroom, *No Other Gods*, 84.

18. Al-Ghazali, *Alchemy of Happiness*, 40.

19. "O People of the Scripture, do not go to extremes, in your religion and do not say about God except the truth: the Messiah, Jesus the son of Mary, was only the Messenger of God, and His Word which He cast to Mary, and a spirit from Him. So believe in God and His messengers, and do not say, 'Three'. Refrain, it is better for you. Verily, God is but One God. Glory be to Him, that He should have a son! To Him belongs all that is in the heavens and in the earth. God suffices as a Guardian."

20. "They indeed are disbelievers those who say, 'Indeed God is the Messiah, son of Mary'. For the Messiah said, 'O Children of Israel, worship God, my Lord and your Lord.

Foundationally, the doctrine of the Trinity is a profound example of *shirk*, as is Jesus's sonship.

Creation and humanity as God's handiwork

All three Abrahamic traditions believe in God, the almighty Creator, who has brought about the cosmos and sustains and guides its life from the beginning to the end. The ultimate meaning of the confession of God as Creator is that the whole universe is ontologically dependent on God. Everything derives from and is dependent on God. The same Creator guides the creation with the help of the laws of creation he has put in place (30:30). Thus, divine purposes are present in creation. While God and world can never be separated, neither can they be equated. God is infinite; the cosmos and creatures are finite.

Similarly to the Bible, the Qur'an describes God as the Creator in the absolute sense; that is, God brought into existence that which was not existent before: "Allah is the "Creator of the heavens and the earth; and when He decrees a thing, He but says to it 'Be', and it is" (2:117). Also, echoing the Bible, Allah "created the heavens and the earth in six days" (11:7).

In the Qur'anic interpretation, not only the human person but also the whole created order is "muslim" ("submission"). The Qur'an teaches that "to God [should] prostrate whoever is in the heavens and whoever is in the earth, together with the sun and the moon, and the stars and the mountains, and the trees and the animals, as well as many of mankind" (22:18). No wonder therefore that all created realities are considered "signs" that reveal the Creator (30:22).[21] Hence, the study of nature may draw us nearer to God (41:53). If all creatures are signs, then "it gives humans the impression that God is within us. If God reveals Himself" through all the created

---

Verily he who associates anything with God for him God has made Paradise forbidden, and his abode shall be the Fire; and for wrongdoers there shall be no helpers'. They are indeed disbelievers those who say, 'God is the third of three', when there is no god but the One God. If they do not desist from what they say, those of them who disbelieve shall suffer a painful chastisement. Will they not turn in repentance to God and seek His forgiveness?; God is Forgiving, Merciful. The Messiah, son of Mary, was only a messenger; messengers passed away before him; his mother was a truthful woman; they both used to eat food. Behold how We make the signs clear to them, then behold, how they are turned away! Say: 'Do you worship besides God what cannot hurt you or profit you? God is the Hearer, the Knower."

21. "And of His signs is the creation of the heavens and the earth and the differences of your tongues and your colours. Surely in that there are signs for all peoples."

beings, "then it is not difficult to get the idea that wherever humans look we can easily feel the presence of God all around and within us."[22]

Similarly to other Abrahamic faiths, so too in Islam humanity is placed in relation to God and in the context of finite, moral life. Although the Qur'an contains no direct statement about humanity being created in the image of God (as there is in the Hadith), the corresponding idea is there. The well-known passage of 30:30 comes close to it: "So set your purpose for religion, as a *hanif*[23]—a nature given by God, upon which He originated mankind. There is no changing God's creation." Here the term *fitrah* is used for "nature," which clearly has resemblance to the image in Christian-Jewish vocabulary. Somewhat similarly to the biblical testimonies, the human being is made of clay in the Qur'an (23:12–14).[24] Not only that, but the one made of clay is also breathed into by the Spirit of God, and therefore even the angels prostrate themselves before him (15:26–30). In accordance with the biblical teaching, in Muslim tradition *fitrah* is universal, not limited to Muslims alone, and is an immutable feature of humanity. As a result, belief in Allah (the confession of *tawhid*) is "natural" to human beings.

All three Abrahamic traditions affirm the dignity of humanity in relation to God. Furthermore, they entertain the idea of humanity as God's viceroy on earth, in Islam typically described in terms of caliph, based on the Qur'anic teaching ("your Lord said to the angels, 'I am appointing on earth a vicegerent,'" 2:30).

The principle of *fitrah* elevates the human person to a unique place among the creatures: "Verily We created man in the best of forms" (95:4). God's blessings and providence have been lavished upon humanity.[25] That said, there is also a realistic acknowledgment of failings and errors of human persons. Indeed, the Qur'anic passage cited just above in this paragraph, continues with this observation: "Then [after creation], We reduced

22. Özdemir, "Towards an Understanding," 12.

23. The exact meaning of the term is somewhat unclear (hence left without English translation here). A number of times it refers to "faith" (of Abraham) and also has the connotation of a nonpolytheistic faith. See Jeffery, *Foreign Vocabulary*, 112.

24. "And We certainly created man from an extraction of clay. Then We made him a drop in a secure lodging. Then We transformed the drop [of semen] into a clot. Then We transformed the clot into a [little] lump of flesh. Then We transformed the lump of flesh into bones. Then We clothed the bones with flesh. Then We produced him as [yet] another creature. So blessed be God, the best of creators!"

25. "And We have given you power in the earth, and have appointed for you therein livelihoods; little thanks you show. And We created you, then shaped you, then said to the angels: 'Prostrate yourselves before Adam!'" (7:10–11).

him to the lowest of the low" (95:5–6). In a number of places the Qur'an speaks of weaknesses, frailties, and liabilities of humanity (see, for example, 10:13).

That said, according to mainline Muslim teaching, human nature is, generally speaking, good—or, at least it is not sinful and corrupted as in Christian teaching. Islam vehemently opposes any Christian notion of original sin and of the catastrophic effects of the fall—although, ironically Adam's "fall-narrative" is recounted no less than three times in the Qur'an (for example, 20), but with a totally different conclusion. As a result, there is no idea of any lostness of humanity and therefore also no need for the Savior in the Christian sense.

Jesus as the prophet next only to the Prophet himself

Unbeknownst to many Christians, Jesus Christ plays an important role in Islamic spirituality and its belief system. Indeed, ironically, one cannot be a true Muslim and ignore Jesus! How so? Because "Islam is the only religion other than Christianity that *requires* its adherents to commit to a position on the identity of Jesus"![26] So much so that "[in] the Islamic tradition, Jesus ('Isa) was a Muslim,"[27] which accounts for titles such as *The Muslim Jesus*.[28]

There are roughly one hundred references or allusions to Jesus (and his mother) in the Qur'an alone, and the commentary literature is rich with allusions and references to him.[29] Alongside 'Isa (Jesus), a number of significant nomenclatures are applied to Jesus in the Qur'an, including the Prophet (e.g., 4:163),[30] Messiah (4:171), and—astonishingly—even God's "Word" and "Spirit" from God (4:171). Jesus is also a miracle-worker, including speaking as the baby from the cradle (19:27–30) and inviting a feast table full of food down from heaven (5:112–14). Most astonishingly, the Qur'an (3:49) testifies that Jesus "will create for you out of clay like the shape of a bird then I will breathe into it, and it will be a bird by the leave

26. Barker and Gregg, "Muslim Perceptions of Jesus," 83.

27. Meshal and Pirbhai, "Islamic Perspectives on Jesus," 232.

28. Khalidi, *Muslim Jesus*.

29. See Ravi, "Comprehensive Listing."; Cragg, *Jesus and the Muslim*, ch. 2; Leirvik, *Images*, 19–25 (and more widely, ch. 2).

30. "We have revealed to you as We revealed to Noah, and the prophets after him, and We revealed to Abraham and Ishmael and Isaac, and Jacob, and the Tribes, and Jesus and Job and Jonah and Aaron, and Solomon, and We gave to David the Inscribed Book."

of God. I will also heal the blind and the leper; and I bring to life the dead, by the leave of God." Particularly important is Jesus's figure as an eschatological prophet; that and his awaited return play a crucial role in Islamic theology (discussed below).

Jesus is put in the line of a number of Old Testament prophets beginning with Moses and Abraham. Indeed, "Belief in Jesus is one of the major principles of faith in Islam, as he is considered one of the five elite prophets; the others are Abraham, Moses, Noah, and Muhammad, peace and blessings be upon them all."[31]

Jesus's teachings, based largely on the Torah, as they are, are highly respected: "From a Muslim perspective, theologically speaking, the essence of the message of Muhammad is consistent with the original ethical and pastoral teachings of Jesus. Any difference is due to the different contexts in which the two men lived."[32]

Furthermore, Mary's role is much more prominent in the Qur'anic presentation. Both of the two main suras that contain the most references to Jesus, 3 and 19, are named after Mary.[33]

Although the Holy Qur'an contains nothing like the New Testament Gospel narratives, there are numerous references to key events in Jesus's life, from conception to earthly ministry to death/resurrection to his eschatological future (Hadith tradition deals in far greater detail with the last theme). It is typical for the Muslim interpretation of Jesus to include references also to legends and gospel materials not ratified by Christians, especially the Gospel of Barnabas.[34]

What about Jesus and the Prophet Muhammad? In the Hadith tradition there is the oft-quoted and highly respectful statement by Muhammad of Jesus: "Prophets are brothers in faith, having different mothers. Their religion is, however, one and there is no Apostle between us (between me and Jesus Christ)."[35] As is well known, Muhammad's own relation to Chris-

---

31. Saritoprak, *Islam's Jesus*, xii. "And verily We sent Noah and Abraham and We ordained among their seed prophethood and the Scripture; and some of them are [rightly] guided and many of them are immoral. Then We sent follow in their footsteps Our messengers, and We sent to follow, Jesus, son of Mary, and We gave him the Gospel, and We placed in the hearts of those who followed him kindness and mercy." Qur'an 57:26–27.

32. Saritoprak, *Islam's Jesus*, 4.

33. "The House of Imrān" (Mary's father's house; sura 3) and "Maryam" (sura 19).

34. For a useful discussion, see Leirvik, *Images*, 132–44.

35. Sahih Muslim, *Kitāb al-Fadā' il*, book 30, ch. 37, quoted in Leirvik, *Images*, 38. For sayings clarifying the relation between Muhammad and Jesus, see Leirvik, *Images*,

tianity and Christian tradition in general, especially in the early phases of his career, was fairly positive and constructive.[36]

That said, it is important to realize that even though Jesus is named a "prophet" in the Qur'an and Muhammad the "seal of the prophets"—thereby making him the highest and the unique prophet—neither one is divine. The reason is that unlike Christian faith, which is determined by belief in Christ, Islam is not based on Muhammad but rather on the Qur'an and Allah. In Islam, only God is divine.

Even the fact that Jesus is a miracle worker (which Muhammad is not), does not imply that therefore Jesus should be lifted up higher than the Prophet of Islam. Rather, the miracles wrought by Jesus are similar to those performed by Moses and other such forerunners of Muhammad. In other words, the most the miracles can do is to confirm Jesus's prophetic status; they cannot confirm his divinity.

Furthermore, even the fact that Jesus is described as sinless in Hadith and legendary tradition, whereas it is not quite certain whether Muhammad was without sin—although in the Shi'ite tradition all imams are!—does not make Jesus superior. Even the unique naming of Jesus as "Messiah" (4:171), a designation reserved only for him, should not be read according to Christian interpretation.

Rather than comparing Muhammad and Jesus with each other, the closest parallel to Christ in Islamic faith could be found between Christ's role as the living Word of God and the divine revelation of the Qur'an. Christ as the creative eternal Word finds a parallel in the Qur'an as the similar divine power.

As has already become clear, the Islamic assessment of the nature, work, and meaning of Jesus differs drastically from the Christian tradition. It is understandable, hence, that because Jesus is so important a figure in Islam, next only to the Prophet Muhammad himself, Christology has also caused continuing conflicts and misunderstandings between the two cousin faiths. All Muslims categorically reject any notion of Christ's divinity

37–38.

36. Robinson, *Christ in Islam and Christianity*, ch. 4.

(4:171[37]; 9:30; 19:35),[38] a corollary of the strict opposition to the Trinity. Even Jesus's virgin birth (19:17–22; 21:91) has nothing to do with divinity. All Muslims also condemn any reference to incarnation in the Christian sense. When it comes to the crucifixion, all Muslims agree that it has nothing to do with the atoning work of salvation, although there are a number of diverse opinions concerning the details. The most common Islamic interpretation is that Jesus of Nazareth was not put to death but rather that another person (for example Simon of Cyrene) was killed. Furthermore, Muslims believe that God "took him [Jesus] away" to heaven to await his return at the end of the ages in order to assist the Mahdi, the main eschatological figure (discussed later in this chapter).[39]

Submission, not "salvation"

On the basis of what has been said so far of the categorical rejection of the doctrine of original sin and fall as well as any notion of the substitutionary atonement by a savior-figure, it becomes clear that Islam's vision of "salvation" is drastically different from that of Christianity. In standard Muslim understanding "'God was *not* in Christ reconciling the world to himself': he was with Jesus withdrawing him to heaven."[40] Indeed, Muslim theology has a hard time intuiting why the justice and fairness of God would ever require a sacrifice and shedding of blood. On the basis of the Qur'anic teaching, it may be legitimate to infer that no one else can "pay" for the sins of others, not even Allah (6:164).

While the difference between the two cousin faiths has to be properly highlighted, it is also important to underline the significant common basis among all three Abrahamic faiths, including the oldest tradition, Judaism. They all place humanity before God and in that light assess what is wrong with us. Furthermore, with all the differences in the interpretation of what

37. "O People of the Scripture, do not go to extremes, in your religion and do not say about God except the truth: the Messiah, Jesus the son of Mary, was only the Messenger of God, and His Word which He cast to Mary, and a spirit from Him. So believe in God and His messengers, and do not say, 'Three'. Refrain, it is better for you. Verily, God is but One God. Glory be to Him, that He should have a son! To Him belongs all that is in the heavens and in the earth. God suffices as a Guardian."

38. "It is not [befitting] for God to take to Himself a son. Glory be to Him. When He decrees a thing, He only says to it, 'Be!', and it is."

39. For details, see Kärkkäinen, *Christ and Reconciliation*, 388–93.

40. Cragg, *Jesus and the Muslim*, 168.

is wrong with us ("sinfulness"), they commonly identify the essence of sin (and "fall") as the deviation of humanity from the Creator. In other words, because sin is ultimately separation from God, it takes God to fix the problem, notwithstanding graced human response and collaboration.

A noted difference between Christian and Islamic soteriology ("the doctrine of salvation") has to do with the emphases in the latter on the human responsibility to submit. Even God is not able to coerce the salvific posture. That said, rejecting the Christian way of salvation based on atonement in Christ is not to deny the presence of grace and mercy in Islam. Even a cursory look at the Qur'an shows the prevalence of the idea of Allah as merciful. Consider this important sura: "Were it not for God's bounty to you and His mercy, not one of you would ever have grown pure, but God purifies whom He will" (24:21). However, in Islam that mercy does not translate into an idea of "justification by faith." Everything is about submitting to the will of Allah, particularly by observing the Five Pillars: confession of the unity of Allah, prayers, fasting, alms, and pilgrimage. "God has prepared . . . forgiveness and a great reward" for those who "submit" and "obey"; obedience includes almsgiving and fasting (33:35).

Where the mercy of Allah comes to the fore is in the completion beyond the balancing act of good and bad as evidenced in this statement (6:160): "Whoever brings a good deed, shall receive tenfold the like of it, and whoever brings an evil deed shall only be requited the like of it; and they shall not be wronged."[41] While one's efforts and good deeds certainly are required to gain access to paradise, God's mercy is also necessary as a surplus. It is in this respect that the numerous references to the merciful nature of Allah—indeed, in the first line of each sura of the Qur'an (save 9)—have to be interpreted.

To summarize, "salvation" in Islam means simply submission to Allah. But the fact that salvation ultimately depends on whether or not one wishes to submit does not mean that believing is thus marginalized. One cannot submit if one persists in ignorance of the revealed will of God. Belief

---

41. Similarly, e.g., 64:17. See also Martindale, "Muslim-Christian Dialogue," 69–71.

WHAT DOES ISLAM ENVISION ABOUT THE "END"?

goes hand in hand with repentance (3:16–19;[42] 19:60[43]) and "the works of righteousness," that is, good deeds (4:57). While deliverance from sin does not have to be excluded from the Islamic vision of salvation, it is fair to say that deliverance from eternal punishment, often depicted as "fire" (2:24) of hell, seems to be at the forefront.

What about the "assurance of salvation"? Although Qur'anic promises to those who believe and do good deeds seem assuring, there are also warnings throughout not to fall away (6:82). Although one may lose salvation, every believer can also trust Allah's "guidance" (an almost technical term in the Qur'an referring to the divine help for believers, as in 4:51; 6:157; and 17:84). Ultimately, Allah is absolutely sovereign in his dealings with humanity.

Like other faith traditions' mystical movements—and unlike the "textbook" official teaching—Sufism focuses on personal devotion and repentance. Sufi mysticism has an amazingly wide appeal among the ordinary faithful, probably influencing deeply more than half of all Muslims. In their spirituality the idea of union with God—theologically a most scandalous idea in light of normal Muslim teaching—is the ultimate goal!

While personal, submission to Allah is also a deeply communal act. Hence, no description of Islam may ignore the importance of the religious community.

Ummah—the Muslim "church"

The term for the Islamic religious community, *ummah*, appears in the Qur'an over sixty times with diverse meanings.[44] The incipient universal vision of early Islam is evident in Qur'an 10:19: "Mankind was but one community; then they differed," obviously implying an original "single *ummah* with a single religion." There is a marked development in the relation of the *ummah* to the religious Other during the Prophet's lifetime, beginning with

---

42. "Those who say: 'O, Our Lord, we believe; so forgive us our sins, and guard us from the chastisement of the Fire,' the patient, truthful, obedient, expenders, imploring God's pardon at daybreak. God bears witness that there is no god, except Him, and the angels, and those of knowledge; upholding justice; there is no god except Him, the Mighty, the Wise. Lo!, the religion with God is submission [to the One God]. Those who were given the Scripture, differed only after the knowledge came to them through transgression among themselves. And whoever disbelieves in God's signs, God is swift at reckoning."

43. "Those who repent and believe and act righteously—such shall enter Paradise."

44. Saeed, "Nature and Purpose," 15–28.

the inclusion of Muslims, Jews, and Christians, based on belief in one God, toward a narrower view limited basically to the followers of the Prophet. A definite limiting took place after his death, and with it a shift toward the presence of more sociopolitical and juridical aspects.

The idea of the superiority of this community was established with appeal to passages such as Qur'an 3:110: "You are the best community brought forth to men, enjoining decency, and forbidding indecency, and believing in God." At times, however, a more hospitable interpretation could also include other God-fearing communities as exemplary.

As is well-known, the *ummah* was split in the early history. The same division has continued since between the Sunni and the Shi'ites. This major division arose over the issue of the Prophet's successor after his death (632 CE). The father of the Prophet's beloved wife Aisha, Abu Bakr, was made the first leader by the majority, but that did not settle the matter. The minority of the community preferred as their leader Ali, the husband of Muhammad's daughter Fatima. Both theological and political issues were involved. Whereas for the majority the leadership choice after the passing of the Prophet belonged to the *ummah* at large, for the rest it was God's choice falling on Ali—with the ambiguous claim that he had both divine endorsement and the Prophet's. While the majority (Sunnis) wanted to stay in the line of Mecca's dominant tribe, the Prophet's own tribe, Quraysh, a minority (Shi'ites) received support from Medina. This led to the final separation by the mid-sixth century. Currently over 80 percent belong to the Sunnis and the rest to the Shi'ites, each side having a big number of denominations.

All Shi'ites share the belief in the divinely ordered status of Ali as the successor to the Prophet (2:124).[45] The largest segment among them, "the Twelvers," has developed a highly sophisticated genetic line of succession from Ali through his two sons (Hasan and Husayn) all the way to the twelfth one. The most distinctive claim has to do with the last imam, who allegedly went into "occultation" (that is, concealment) and whose return they await. All imams in this interpretation possess inerrancy in order to be able to prevent the community from being led astray.

With all the divisions and the major split resulting in even fatal fights and wars, doctrinal differences among Muslims are fairly insignificant in the big picture. Both parties share the same Qur'an, the same prophethood, and the Five Pillars, including prayers, fasting, and other rituals (albeit

45. Haider, *Shī'ī Islam*.

somewhat differently nuanced and practiced). And the Qur'an mandates work for unity: "And hold fast to God's bond, together, and do not scatter" (3:103; see also vv. 4–5).

As already mentioned, obedience and submission to Allah, including willing service and honoring *tahwid*, the absolute unity/oneness of God, shape all aspects of Muslim life, including personal and communal spirituality. Ritual prayer is the most visible form of piety. Muslims ought to pray five times a day at designated times, regardless of their location. Prayer is preceded by ablution and employs a prescribed form and content, mostly recital of Qur'anic verses. Prayer is also the main activity in the mosque;[46] nowadays the Friday afternoon gathering there includes a sermon. Holy Scripture is highly honored and venerated. Since there are no clergy and no theologically trained priesthood, any male in principle is qualified to lead; he is usually chosen from among those most deeply knowledgeable in the tradition. As in other religions, the annual life-cycle follows the religious calendar, starting from the honoring of the date when Muhammad migrated from Mecca to Medina. Friday is not considered a holy day, although it is the day of congregation. Instead, a number of other holy days commemorate significant days in the life of the Prophet and the early *ummah*.[47] Globalization has caused much diversity in rituals and rites, but not in doctrine and prayers.

Similarly to Christianity, but unlike Judaism, Islam is a missionary faith. Its outlook is universal. The Qur'an instructs its readers that "had God willed, He would have made them one community" (42:8). The key verse is well known: "God is our Lord and your Lord. Our deeds concern us and your deeds concern you. There is no argument between us and you. God will bring us together, and to Him is the [final] destination" (42:15).[48] In this light, it is understandable that the earliest Qur'anic passages were not calling people to convert to a new religion; rather, the Meccans were called to "worship the Lord of this House [Ka'ba]" (106:3).[49] Only later, with the rising opposition from the worshipers of local deities, was a decisive break announced and the confession became "There is no god except

46. Mahmutćehajić, *Mosque*.

47. Braswell, *Islam*, 77–80.

48 The "speaker" here is simply the Holy Qur'an, which often uses the "we" formula (not unlike some biblical passages). The meaning of "our" and "you" is somewhat debated with regard to whether it refers to Christians and Jews or just to Christians. Either way, the main thrust of the passage is clear: there is a bond between Muslims and Christians.

49. The Ka'ba is the holiest place in Islam; it is in Mecca.

God" (37:35). We know that in Medina the Prophet with his companions lived among the Jews, and we may safely infer that he obviously assumed that the new faith was in keeping with theirs, as well as with Christian faith (2:40–41). Recall also that at that time the term *muslim* could be applied to non-Muslims, such as Solomon (27:15–44) and disciples of Jesus (3:52).[50] Only when the Jews rejected the Prophet was the direction of prayer changed from Jerusalem to Mecca (2:142).

In keeping with this history is the special status assigned to Abrahamic sister faiths. Between what Muslims call "the Abode of Peace and the Abode of War," a third region was acknowledged, "the Abode of the People of the Book," that is, Jews and Christians.[51] These two traditions enjoy a unique relation to Islam (2:135–37;[52] 5:12, 69), implying that in some real sense the diversity of religions is not only tolerated by Allah but even planned and endorsed, at least when it comes to those who are the "people of the book" (5:48;[53] 48:29[54]).This inclusive tendency notwithstanding, Islam claims to retain a unique place in God's eyes. That is most probably the meaning of the Qur'anic statements that Muslims, in distinction from others, are "God's sincere servants" (37:40). Therefore, ultimately even Jewish and

50. "And when Jesus sensed their disbelief, he said, 'Who will be my helpers unto God?' The disciples said, 'We will be helpers of God; we believe in God; witness that we have *submitted*'" (italics mine).

51. For details, see Watt, *Muslim-Christian Encounters*, ch 2.

52. "And they say, 'Be Jews or Christians, and you shall be guided'. Say, 'Nay, rather the creed of Abraham, a hanīf; and he was not of the idolaters'. Say: 'We believe in God, and in that which has been revealed to us, and revealed to Abraham, Ishmael, Isaac, Jacob, and the Tribes, and that which was given to Moses, and Jesus, and the prophets, from their Lord, we make no division between any of them, and to Him we submit'. And if they believe in the like of what you believe in, then they are truly guided; but if they turn away, then they are clearly in schism; God will suffice you against them; He is the Hearer, the Knower."

53. "And We have revealed to you the Book with the truth confirming the Book that was before it and watching over it . . . ."

54. "Muhammad is the Messenger of God and those who are with him are hard against the disbelievers, merciful among themselves. You see them bowing, prostrating [in worship]. They seek bounty from God and beatitude. Their mark from the effect of prostration. That is their description in the Torah and their description in the Gospel is as a seed that sends forth its shoot and strengthens it, and it grows stout and rises firmly upon its stalk, delighting the sowers, so that He may enrage the disbelievers by them. God has promised those of them who believe and perform righteous deeds, forgiveness and a great reward."

Christian traditions suffer from corruption and misunderstanding of the final revelation.

At her core, the Islam *ummah* is an active missionary community, based on the Qur'anic mandate to reach out to nonbelievers—but with prudence and patience (16:125–27):

> Call to the way of your Lord with wisdom and fair exhortation, and dispute with them by way of that which is best. Truly your Lord knows best those who stray from His way and He knows best those who are guided. And if you retaliate, retaliate with the like of what you have been made to suffer; and yet if you endure patiently, verily that is better for the patient. So be patient, and your patience is only by [the help of] God. And do not grieve for them, nor be in distress because of that which they scheme.

This is often expressed with the Arabic term *da'wah*, literally "call, invocation, or summoning."[55] Combining a universalizing tendency and fervent missionary mandate, Islam's goal of outreach is comprehensive, including ideally social, economic, cultural, and religious spheres. Ideally it would result in the establishment of Shari'a law and the gathering of all peoples under one *ummah*.[56]Although the Qur'an prohibits evangelism by force ("There is no compulsion in religion," 2:256), similarly to Christianity, alliance with earthly powers, militarism, and economic interests were all employed to spread Islam with force and brutality.[57] In other words, not only Christianity but also Islam bears the long legacy of colonialism.

Now, before getting into a big picture of Islamic eschatology, I will briefly consider Islam's relation to science, as it has much to do with eschatology as well.

Islam's struggle with modern science

Catching up with the Western science

As is well known, there was a historical period in early Islam that was characterized by high-level intellectual and scientific activity. Whether it is justified to call it the "golden age" or not, there is no denying the significance

55. Miller, "Da'wah," 4:2225–26.

56. For an exchange between and a Muslim and a Christian about the mission of the *ummah*, see Kateregga and Shenk, *Islam and Christianity*, ch. 12.

57. Miller, "Da'wah," 4:2225.

of the rise of scientific and academic pursuit during the first three or four centuries. It culminated in such great luminaries as Ibn-Rushd (Averroes) and Ibn Sina (Avicenna). Thereafter, what is at times called the "age of decline" followed.[58]

Notwithstanding the accuracy of this kind of broad-stroke reading of history, Western sciences and philosophy are in debt to Muslims. They were the ones to help Christian philosophers to rediscover the writings of Aristotle and his school, and that had a tremendous impact for centuries.

Modern science did not reach major Islamic lands before the nineteenth century. In recent decades, the Islamic world has been at pains to catch up with the West. Not surprisingly, some leading Muslim scholars lament the status of scientific education in their midst. It is noteworthy that among the main developers of modern science one has a hard time in finding a Muslim scholar.

A major challenge to the Islamic world with regard to the adoption of modern academic science is a tight link between it and religion, a phenomenon long abandoned in the West. The Algerian astrophysicist Nidhal Guessoum goes so far as to argue that even school and university science textbooks are little more than "a branch of Qur'anic exegesis."[59] The book by the Iranian physicist and academician Mehdi Golshani titled *The Holy Quran and the Sciences of Nature* is a representative example.

Diverse ways of dealing with science

All that said, not surprisingly there is more than one way to approach the role and status of science and its relation to religion. The following rough typology presented by some Islamic scholars obviously bears resemblance to Christian approaches treated in chapter 3; as do many other religious traditions, Islamic scholars and scientists offer a fairly obvious typology of responses to modern science:

1. Rejection of science because of its alleged opposition to revelation.

2. An uncritical embrace of the technocratic practical results of Western science in pursuit of power- and competence-equality with (as they are perceived) more developed Western nations.

---

58. Abdalla, "Ibn Khaldūn," 3:29–30.
59. Guessoum, *Islam's Quantum Question*, 180.

3. An effort to build a distinctively "Islamic science" based on the authority of the Holy Qur'an and Hadith.

4. An attempt to negotiate between the legitimacy and necessity of contemporary scientific principles and methods while at the same time critiquing the metaphysical, ethical, and religious implications of the scientific paradigm.[60]

Intuitively, the majority of the Muslims follow the first category's approach of opposing science due to its alleged conflict with Scripture and religion. Particularly fierce is the rejection of evolutionism.[61] Astonishingly, it is not rare to find *fatwas* (more or less binding legal-religious rulings) on Darwinian evolutionary theory and on those advocating its ideas.[62] This opposition to science and evolution is not limited to common folk. It is also prevalent among university teachers and students. It is amazing that even among American Muslims, less than half accept evolution. Among the critiques against evolution, the total rejection of human evolution as a part of the rest of creation is the focal point.

There is some real irony related to category #2, namely an uncritical embrace of Western science, particularly for technical, military, and economic benefits. The irony is twofold. First, it of course eradicates the opposition to science—although not for reasons that one would find most worthy, namely intellectual maturity to negotiate between the two. Rather, the openness to science derives from mere utilitarianism. Second, it falsely assumes that science is neutral when it comes to religion and values. This is of course not the case. While it is not for Western science to back up its claims—or oppose scientific investigations and results—using religion, it is also the case that the scientific enterprise is deeply value-driven. Science can and has been used to promote both good and evil. Naïve embrace of sciences ignores this important posture. This has importantly raised valid philosophical-ethical-religious concerns among some leading Islamic theologians.[63]

Totally opposite to category #1 (rejection of science due to its alleged anti-religious undergirding), there is a group of Muslim intellectuals who

60. Kärkkäinen, *Christian Theology*, 113; adapted from Golshani, "Does Science Offer?" 2:96–97.

61. Ayoub, "Creation or Evolution?" ch. 11.

62. See Guessoum, "Islamic Theological Views."

63. Nasr, "Islam and Science," 72.

wish to construct an "Islamic science."[64] Not surprisingly, the Muslim creationist movement exercises wide influence among laypeople in various global locations.[65] Another example of an attempt to construct Islamic science involves the search for "miraculous scientific facts in the Qur'an,"[66] a highly apologetic enterprise. The main problem here, as with Christian fundamentalist creationism-projects, is that the Scripture and religious tradition become the main guide and arbiter of science.[67]

Finally, following the last category in our typology, some leading experts have become convinced that there should in principle be no contradiction between science *qua* science and Islamic faith. That being so, they also reject both the uncritical opposition to science and the desire to build science on religion. They also eschew an uncritical embrace of science and its benefits as something "neutral" and value-free.[68] Obviously, this approach resonates with some key ideas in the Christian science-religion engagement recommended in this project. Yet, it is an emerging phenomenon and it remains to be seen whether authoritative clerics will begin to support and help disseminate such ideas.

After having introduced some key features of Islam as a vibrant and dynamic living religious tradition, including its key doctrines and beliefs, the rest of the chapter delves into a big picture of determinative eschatological beliefs.

Islamic eschatology: main beliefs and distinctive features

Anticipating the "End": signs of the "hour"

In light of the importance of eschatology to Muslims, it is understandable that there is a heightened interest in discerning the signs signaling the awaited "End." This is no different from what has happened in the Christian church, particularly in times of spiritual renewal. In the contemporary world, books, blogs, and talks on "signs of the hour" abound.[69]

---

64. Golshani, "Islam and the Sciences of Nature," 1:77–78.

65. For the Turkish creationist Harun Yahya, see Oktar, "Harun Yahya."

66. See ch. 5 in Guessoum, *Islam's Quantum Question.*

67. See also Nasr, *Need for a Sacred Science.*

68. Guessoum, *Islam's Quantum Question,* 129–35.

69. See, e.g., Salah, "Signs of the Last Hour."

The search for signs is informed and energized by a number of scriptural hints. Just consider the theme of some of the well-known Qur'anic suras such as "The Hour" (22), "The Smoke" (45), and "The Darkened Sun" (82). Not surprisingly, in the Hadith one may find: "Geological, moral, social, and cosmic signs . . . [as well as] the erosion of the earth, the spread of immorality, the loss of trust among the people, and the administration of unjust rulers as some signs of the Hour." In distinction from these "minor" signs, the Hadith lists as "major" ones the "emergence of the Antichrist, the descent of Jesus, and the rising of the sun in the west," which all point to the imminence of the End.[70] The Qur'anic references to trumpets, archangels, earthquakes, and other end-time signs (39:67–69; 81:1–14; 99:1–4) sound quite similar to the New Testament's descriptions in the book of Revelation. There will also be intense suffering by the unfaithful. The rise of the mysterious nations of Gog and Magog likewise plays a role in the eschatological scheme of Islam.[71]

Similarly to Christian tradition, in Islam the (final) hour is unknown to all but God (31:34). As the Prophet stated, "Knowledge thereof lies only with God—and what do you know, perhaps the Hour is near" (33:63). Differently from Hadith and apocalyptic traditions, the Qur'an is more reticent to talk about signs in a decisive manner, signaling that it really is left to Allah when to usher in the final consummation.

Mahdi and Jesus as the major End-time figures

There are two main protagonists in the Muslim eschatological drama, namely the mysterious figure of Mahdi and his deputy Jesus—as well as their antagonist, the Antichrist. What is strange about the figure of Mahdi is that there is no mention whatsoever of him in the Holy Qur'an. Even more mysteriously, neither one of the two main Hadith traditions, that of Bukhari and that of Muslim, contains information about the Mahdi. That said, very importantly all major Islamic denominations universally affirm belief in the Mahdi. Among the Shi'ites, his significance is even more profound.

Notwithstanding this universal support for the expectation of the Mahdi, there are continuing debates concerning a number of issues, including even such foundational questions as whether there is one Mahdi

70. Saritoprak, *Islam's Jesus,* 38.
71. Saritoprak, *Islam's Jesus,* 58–59.

or more than one. Interestingly—particularly in relation to the figure of the Antichrist (about whom more below)—there is also speculation into a possible pseudo- (or anti-)Mahdi. It is understandable that among the various Mahdist movements throughout history, attempts have been made to identify a specific person.[72] From a Christian perspective, it is noteworthy that relationship between the Mahdi and Jesus at times has been so close that particularly in early Islamic history, the two were confused to the point that the expectation of the coming of Mahdi ceased.[73]

But what is not debated is what the Mahdi's main tasks will be at the end. He will defeat the Antichrist and bring justice and peace to the world. The Mahdi will also lead people to truth.

Alongside the Mahdi, Jesus plays an important role in the End-time scenario. Indeed, based on the account above of the profound status and role of Jesus in Islamic faith, the following summative statement by a leading Muslim scholar comes as no surprise:

> Since the early period of Islam, Muslims have read the sayings of the Prophet, referred to as Hadith, about Jesus and the end-time scenario, finding nothing strange about Jesus's praying in a mosque. Muslims see no incongruity between Jesus and the mosque since the Prophet Muhammad and Jesus are considered spiritual brothers. This clearly indicates that Muslims have honored Jesus as a part of their faith and culture. Perhaps for this reason many adherents of Islamic faith name their children 'Isa, the Qur'anic name for Jesus.[74]

Importantly, even though it is not directly mentioned in the Qur'an, it is common to find in Islamic theological manuals a statement that "we believe in the descent of Jesus," a statement having nothing to do with the Christian belief in the descent into hell but rather an assertion of the "second coming."[75] Importantly, the descent of Jesus is considered one of the surest signs of the "hour," the consummation of eschatological events in Islam.

Notwithstanding the lack of direct references to the descent of Jesus in the Qur'an, some key statements about his work and meaning have important eschatological implications. Consider, for example, 3:46 ("He shall speak to mankind in the cradle, and in his manhood, and he is of

72. Goldzliher, *Introduction*, 197–98; Blichfeldt, *Early Mahdism*.

73. Saritoprak, *Islam's Jesus*, 88–89.

74. Saritoprak, *Islam's Jesus*, xiii.

75. Saritoprak, *Islam's Jesus*, xii–xiv.

the righteous"), which can be interpreted to refer to the future ("he *shall* speak") in terms of Jesus's ministry yet unfinished.[76] In the Hadith tradition, Qur'an 43:61 ("And indeed he is a portent of the Hour so do not doubt it but: 'Follow me. This is a straight path.'") has played a role. This passage is in the context of the people of Mecca contesting for the superiority of their gods (or angels?), in response to which the Prophet lifted up the role of Jesus as the sign of "the hour."[77] It is noteworthy that in the Hadith, Jesus is figured as handsome and clean, "symbolic of his pure message and of the mission to be fulfilled." Jesus appears there as the one much loved and supported by the Muslims.[78]

The relationship between the Mahdi and Jesus is close yet somewhat undefined. While, as mentioned, the Qur'an does not directly mention Jesus's "descent" to earth, it is widely attested in the Hadith.[79] According to the standard Islamic interpretation, Jesus of Nazareth was not killed on the cross but was instead "taken up" to heaven by Allah to wait for the return. Then he will fight alongside the Mahdi against the Antichrist and defeat him. Jesus will slaughter pigs, tear down crosses, and destroy churches and synagogues; most probably he will also kill Christians unwilling to embrace Islamic faith.

The picture of the Antichrist is not radically different from that in Christianity. Obviously an archenemy of Jesus, the Antichrist can be seen as the personification of evil (similarly to Satan and Iblis). Although the term itself (*al-Dajjal*) does not appear in the Qur'an, there is wide agreement in Islamic tradition that it contains allusions and indirect references, including the saying attributed to Jesus: "Nay, but verily man is [wont to be] rebellious" (96:6).[80]

Understandably, the Hadith traditions greatly expand and elaborate on the description and influence of the Antichrist: "The antichrist is short, hen-toed, woolly-haired, one-eyed, an eye-sightless, and neither protruding nor deep-seated. If you are confused about him, know that your Lord

---

76. This view was advocated by such influential medieval interpreters as Muhammad Al-Jurjani; see Saritoprak, *Islam's Jesus*, 23 n. 1. A similar interpretation can be offered of Q 19:28.

77. For details, see Saritoprak, *Islam's Jesus*, 27–28.

78. Saritoprak, *Islam's Jesus*, 77.

79. Saritoprak, *Islam's Jesus*, ch. 4.

80. McGinn, *Antichrist*, 111.

is not one-eyed."[81] The Antichrist will fight against the unbelievers until the Mahdi and Jesus come and help defeat his power.

Death and resurrection

For the Muslim, life on this earth is about preparation for eternity. The most important way to prepare is to be obedient and desire to please Allah. Hence, death should be properly kept in mind (23:15; 3:185) as each man and woman has been given a certain life-span (6:2).

What is distinctive about the Islamic conception of death is the experience of torment and pain in the grave prior to judgment and resurrection.[82] The term used in Islam to refer to this period is *barzakh*, "the physical barrier between the Garden and the Fire or between this world and the life beyond the grave, as well as the period of time separating individual death and final resurrection."[83]

Although the Qur'an provides precious few details about what happens between death and resurrection, later traditions have produced fairly detailed accounts. As in Christian tradition, the body decays but the "soul" (or "spirit") continues to exist (see 39:42). According to major Muslim tradition, the deceased person meets two angels—named Munkar and Nakir—who test the faith of the person and help determine one's final destiny. In all Muslim accounts of the afterlife, there is thus an intermediate state that, according to some Muslim theologians, approaches the Roman Catholic idea of purgatory.[84] Muslims also believe in the resurrection of the body as well as (eternal) retribution (sura 75; 36:77–79; among others).

The main theological debate about the resurrection is whether it entails a total annihilation of the person before re-creation, or a reconstitution and renewal. The lack of unanimity is understandable in light of two directions in Scripture itself. Just compare 28:88 ("Everything will perish except His Countenance"), which clearly assumes the annihilationist view,

---

81. Abu Dawud, bk. 37 ("Battles"), #4306.

82. For a detailed account with valuable sources, see Parker, "Torment," 11–17.

83. Smith, "Reflections on Aspects of Immortality in Islam," 92, n. 14, cited (with incomplete bibliographic information) in Parker, "Torment," 12. Qur'an 23:100: "and behind them is a barrier until the day when they are raised." The other two Qur'anic occurrences are: 25:53; 55:20. The term *barzakh* in Arabic means something like a barrier or obstacle.

84. Afsaruddin, "Death, Resurrection, and Human Destiny," 46.

with 10:4: "To Him is the return of all of you. . . . Truly He originates creation, then recreates it," which teaches the other option.

Heaven and hell—salvation and judgment

Consider that a typical list of the basic beliefs of Islam includes "belief in one God, His messengers, His books, His angels, and the day of judgement."[85] The final accounting happens when in the hereafter men and women "return" to their God (32:7–11). Almost every chapter of the Qur'an speaks of or refers to the theme of judgment.[86] Similar to the New Testament, even the evil spirits (*jinn*) will be judged.

The general picture of the day of judgment is very similar to that given in the Bible. Great earthquakes will rock the earth, setting mountains in motion (sura 99). The sky will split open and heaven will be "stripped off," rolled up like a parchment scroll. The sun will cease to shine; the stars will be scattered and fall upon the earth. The oceans will boil over. Graves will be opened, the earth bringing forth its burdens (82). All will bow, willingly or not, before God. After resurrection, each human person is given a "book" that indicates the final destiny (18:49), either heaven or hell.

A debated issue among the Muslim schools is the lot of the (gravely) sinning believer, and no agreement has been reached about this. A related debate asks how the person's good and bad deeds account for the final judgment received. Common to all opinions is the centrality of obedience to Allah or lack thereof; furthermore, it has been widely agreed that only grave sins bring about judgment: "If you avoid the grave sins that are forbidden you, We will absolve you of your evil deeds and admit you by an honourable gate" (4:31).

What about non-Muslims? It seems like the Qur'an teaches a fairly inclusive view of salvation: "Surely those who believe, and those of Jewry, and the Christians, and the Sabaeans,[87] whoever believes in God and the Last Day, and performs righteous deeds—their wage is with their Lord, and no fear shall befall them, neither shall they grieve" (2:62). The implications of this passage are of course widely debated among historical and contemporary Muslim scholars. Echoing the biblical view for those who have never

---

85. Haleem, "Qur'an and Hadith," 25.

86. Fromherz, "Judgment, Final."

87. The Sabaeans (or Sabeans, Sabians; also in 5:69) are an obscure, little-known (Old) Arabic-speaking tribe, also mentioned in the Old Testament (Joel 3:8; Isa. 45:14).

heard the gospel, the Qur'an teaches that "we never chastise until We have sent a messenger" (17:15).

What is not debated is that there are two destinies, as taught in the Qur'an (9:100–102; 7:37–51; and so forth). Hell is a place of great pain and torture. What about heaven? Often depicted in the Qur'an with garden images (sura 37), paradise is a place of great enjoyment, peace, and reunion. The Qur'an offers sensual descriptions, including the pleasures of exquisitely delicious food and drink, as well as sexual relations with divine maidens (often interpreted metaphorically). Particularly splendid and elaborate accounts of paradise ("Garden") can be found in the Hadith. Similarly to the Bible, there are also various levels of reward for the blessed ones.

All in all, eschatology plays a significantly more prominent role in Islam than in the two elder sister faiths. An indication of Islam's eschatological fervency has to do with the rise of contemporary apocalypticism, a phenomenon known also on the fringes of the global Christian church. The following chapter is devoted to this acute topic.

CHAPTER 5

What is the appeal of the catastrophic End of the world (apocalypticism)?

The common Abrahamic roots

IN CONTEMPORARY BIBLICAL SCHOLARSHIP, it is a commonplace to assume that behind, and as an underlying framework of, the New Testament faith is an eschatologically oriented "apocalypticism."[1]

> The word "apocalypse" derives from the Greek *apokálypsis*, "revelation," which is the first significant word of the Book of Revelation: "The revelation of Jesus Christ." This usage in Revelation 1:1 thus gives its name to a literary genre, "apocalypse," and to an ideological phenomenon, "apocalypticism."[2]

Apocalypticism is dualistic in dividing the world between "us" and "them." It looks forward to a sudden, catastrophic divine intervention and considers the current world order both evil and temporary, to give way to the final kingdom of peace. Apocalypticism is deeply escapist. Often linked with violence and the battle of power, apocalyptic literature is filled with fantastic pictures, images, sacred numbers and figures, and so forth.

Like its younger sister faiths, postbiblical Judaism is quite familiar with apocalypticism. Some of the "intertestamental" apocalyptic movements were related to emerging Christian movements.[3] In what ways does

1. Collins, "Apocalyptic Eschatology," 40–55.
2. Arnold, "Old Testament Eschatology," 32.
3. Tabor, "Ancient Jewish," 252–53.

apocalypticism distinguish itself from the "mainline" Israelite eschatology, as evidenced in the Old Testament?

First of all, there are of course some short portions in the Old Testament that are clearly in the genre of apocalypticism. Along with the latter part of Daniel, chapters 7–12, recall passages such as Isaiah 24–27 and Zechariah 9–14. But more broadly speaking, the difference has to do with the heightened role given to the Messiah in the apocalyptic End-time expectations. To understand what this means is to know that by and large the Messiah is not tightly linked to eschatology in the Old Testament, as important as the messianic figure otherwise might be. This changes in apocalypticism during the postbiblical times (1 Enoch, 2 Esdras, and 2 Baruch). There, the Messiah is the one at the forefront of the action. Similarly, in apocalypticism the understanding of history is transformed. Unlike in the Old Testament where Israel's enemies are the target of divine judgment, in apocalypticism cosmic and heavenly powers are also being destroyed. This leads to the apocalyptic "supranationalistic and supraworldly view of God's reign" that also assumes the unity of history—because Yahweh is the one and only ultimate power. This results in a deterministic view of history; everything has been determined beforehand and therefore human initiatives do not matter as much.[4]

What about the role of eschatology in Jesus of Nazareth's proclamation? On the one hand, Jesus's proclamation was thoroughly eschatological, but on the other hand, Jesus did not provide any kind of prophetic timetable for future events. "He did not spell out certain eschatological doctrines, but confronted the people with a radical decision for or against God."[5] This entails a radical departure from apocalypticism, which is prone to setting dates.[6] This is not to undermine the eschatological orientation of Jesus's proclamation otherwise. By and large, Jesus of Nazareth radically reconceived the "intertestamental" vibrant apocalyptic expectation of an imminent divine intervention to judge the enemies of God's people and to save the covenanted ones.

In early Christian centuries, eschatology at large and the apocalyptic flourished. Just think of the work Apocalypse of Peter, probably written in

---

4. Schwarz, *Eschatology*, 53.

5. Schwarz, *Eschatology*, 69.

6. For basic categories and emphases of apocalypticism, see Collins, "Apocalyptic Eschatology," 40–51.

Egypt at the beginning of the second century. While not included in the Bible, it was a well-known End-time vision.[7]

By the time of the establishment of the Christendom—the Christian church's elevation into an imperially favored and sanctioned religion of the Roman Empire in the fourth century—apocalypticism (alongside fervent eschatology at large) waned, although it never disappeared. It rose up over and over again, particularly during the times of revivals and religious renewals. This happened, for example, during the time of the Protestant Reformation in the form of Anabaptist and other movements. Even Luther himself was touched by the apocalyptic expectation of an impending return of Christ, although that belief soon gave way to more practical tasks of the continuing rebuilding of the church.

Somewhat surprisingly, apocalypticism reappeared and refashioned itself beginning in the latter part of the nineteenth century, particularly due to the widespread spiritual revivals and the birth of the modern fundamentalist movement and Pentecostalism. All of those rich spiritual soils fostered the growth of the apocalyptic expectation. Even more surprisingly, following the "secular decade" of the 1960s, what is now called neo-apocalypticism emerged and has since spread mightily among the fundamentalist movements, particularly among the US right-wing Christian communities and, thanks to their global missionary outreach, also throughout world Christianity.

Not only among the Christians but also in Jewish[8] and Islamic[9] contexts, neo-apocalypticism is gaining strongholds, in some quarters alarmingly fast. These are not meaningless religious fads. Rather, they have real-life implications, as with American anti-environmentalist and pro-war forces led by advocates of the American Christian Right.[10] There are global effects as well: an uncritical support for the state of Israel without the expectation of responsibility for fairness and justice; its counterparts can be found among the Iranian Muslim rulers.[11]

I turn now to take a closer look at this development and its eschatological and religious significance, beginning from Christian neo-apocalypticism and then discussing the same in the current Islamic world.

7. Daley, "Eschatology," 92.

8. Gorenberg, *End of Days*.

9. Cook, *Studies in Muslim Apocalyptic*.

10. Tuveson, *Redeemer Nation*.

11. Sells, "Armageddon," 467–95.

Christian neo-apocalypticism

Left Behind

From the ranks of Christian fundamentalist neo-apocalypticism come some of the best-selling titles of the contemporary Christian world, such as *The Late, Great Planet Earth* (1970) by Hal Lindsey[12] and the *Left Behind* series by Tim LaHaye (and Jerry B. Jenkins).[13] While the former book's initial influence was soon overshadowed by the failed predictions of the return of Christ by the author, the latter has exercised unbelievable global influence.

In the honored tradition of apocalypticism, old and new, the Evangelical best-selling author Tim LaHaye and his co-author Jerry Jenkins pose this question to the prospective reader of the *Left Behind* series, which has sold for tens of millions of copies in English and in many translations:

> Are you ready for the moment of truth?
>
> - Political crisis
> - Economic crisis
> - Worldwide epidemics
> - Environmental catastrophe
> - Mass disappearances
> - Military apocalypse
>
> And that's just the beginning . . .
> of the end of the world.[14]

The series begins and is introduced with the idea of "rapture," an invisible first stage of the two-stage return of Christ (a novel idea invented towards the end of the nineteenth century in the English-speaking world, heretofore unknown in the history of the church): "An airborne Boeing 747 is headed to London when, without any warning, passengers mysteriously disappear from their seats. Terror and chaos slowly spread not only through the plane but also worldwide as unusual events continue to

---

12. For details, see Clouse, "Fundamentalist Eschatology," 263–77.

13. See LaHaye and Jenkins, *Left Behind*. For a critical analysis, see Stevenson, "Revelation's Warning."

14. These questions from the back cover copy are repeated in the *Left Behind* promotional materials.

unfold. For those who have been left behind, the apocalypse has just begun."[15]

A short sampling of book titles gives the reader a clear view of the ethos and distinctive features of this apocalyptic fiction writing—which, in the minds of the authors and a growing number of fundamentalist readers represents a *non-fiction* genre and therefore makes it such an influential "eschatological" opinion:

- *Assassins: Assignment: Jerusalem, Target: Antichrist* (1999)

- *Apollyon: The Destroyer Is Unleashed* (1999)

- *The Mark: The Beast Rules the World* (2000)

- *Desecration: Antichrist Takes the Throne* (2001)

- *Armageddon: The Cosmic Battle of the Ages* (2003)

- *The Rising: Antichrist is Born: Before They Were Left Behind* (2005)

In addition to the main series, which is available in books, an audio-drama series, and movies (together with wallpaper, newsletters, logos, timelines, trivia, and so forth), there is also a militaristic parallel project with the telling title, *Apocalypse Burning*:

> Danger and personal crisis on land, sea, and in the air combine with a level of spiritual warfare that is unparalleled in a Christian book. *Apocalypse Burning* is a page-turning thriller that runs side by side with the phenomenal Left Behind series, which has sold in excess of 60 million copies.
>
> First Sergeant Samuel Adams "Goose" Gander is on the front lines, fighting a battle against superior forces. Goose's wife, Megan, is fighting for her freedom in a court case where all the facts seem stacked against her. Meanwhile, Chaplain Delroy Harte believes that the Rapture may have happened but . . .[16]

So, what is wrong with this neo-apocalyptic vision? Or, to put it this way: "What is left out in *Left Behind*?"[17]

15. LaHaye and Jenkins, *Left Behind*, cover copy.

16. Mel Odom, *Apocalypse Burning*, cover copy.

17. This catchy title goes back to my Fuller Seminary colleague, Prof. Dr. Grayson Carter's lecture title.

A constructive critique of Christian neo-apocalypticism

Similarly to its antecedent, the neo-apocalyptic vision of the world is deeply dualistic; it "divides the world into good and evil, demonizes all who are considered enemies, [and] is absolutely convinced of the righteousness of its own cause, and calls for holy warfare."[18] This is what makes the neo-apocalyptic dangerous, both politically and in terms of violence. Particularly concerning is the fact that a common hallmark of the fundamentalist movements in all Abrahamic traditions is the expectation of the terror of Armageddon.[19] It is not that Armageddon is not a biblical concept; it is. But the way it is employed in these movements too often justifies the use of violence on "our" (as opposed to the "other's") side. Furthermore, typically the advocates of neo-apocalypticism consider themselves agents of God's righteous judgment. That has too often led to violence and militarism. To put a human agency in the service of divine judgment is always a precarious move, as the history of all religions regrettably evinces.

Other theological and ethical liabilities of neo-apocalypticism are obvious and not in need of an elaborate analysis. The advocates tend to read Scriptures ideologically as they seek to justify their own cause at the cost of vilifying the counterpart's.

As mentioned, the apocalyptic eschatological timetable is deterministic. Unchecked, it does not lead to the acknowledgment and praise of God's omniscience and omnipotence but rather fatalism. Furthermore, efforts for peace-building, caring for the environment, erasing poverty and injustice, and other ethical pursuit are being ostracized in the expectation of an impending End. Why invest in the world that is to be reduced to ashes? In Christian neo-apocalypticism, there is also the problem of elitism. Rather than being concerned about the salvation of as many as possible, the focus of the eschatological hope is the rapture of a small number of the chosen ones to meet the Lord "in the air" while the world rapidly descends into terror and chaos.[20]

The following summative critique of neo-apocalypticism, particularly as it is being depicted in the Left Behind project, is worth quoting at length:

> [E]vil comes from the outside and consequently leads to the comforting outlook that one side is altogether right and good and the

18. Migliore, *Faith Seeking Understanding*, 334.

19. Clark, *Allies for Armageddon*.

20. See further Migliore, *Faith Seeking Understanding*, 337.

other wrong and evil. This view that people are either all bad or all good justifies the notion that the solution to our problems is the destruction of the wicked in a final triumph of the good that leaves no ambiguity. Such a Manichaean world view enables the use of all sorts of deceitful tricks, violence, and dreadful weapons to accomplish the ends of the "saints." In this same vein, it has been pointed out that the tribulation saints steal, hate, lie, smuggle, blackmail with no sense of remorse, and generally live greedy, materialistic lifestyles at the personal level that seem to be at odds with the separate simple life taught by fundamentalists. And in the realm of social issues, the Left Behind series seems to have a negative slant toward women, world peace, and international humanitarianism.[21]

That said: although the dangers and liabilities of neo-apocalypticism certainly are in need of being exposed, academic theology and established churches should also ask themselves this self-critical question: Why is it that apocalypticism garners such an appeal among the faithful, whether Christians, Muslim, or others? Is there something missing in "mainline" Christianity and theology? What about the intensity of eschatological hope?

With that in mind, I move to consider the theme of apocalypticism among our Muslim brothers and sisters and also seek to compare notes.

Islamic apocalypticism

Versions of the apocalyptic

The apocalyptic worldview is a central Islamic belief and an integral part of its eschatology. As Brent J. Neely and Peter G. Riddell vividly describe it:

> When it comes to the events ushering in the Final Day, the unpredictable energy of Muslim apocalyptic may be compared to the preparation of traditional Arab coffee which is brought to a frothy boil and then allowed to settle back again prior to the next surge: that is, apocalyptic tumult periodically erupts onto the canvas of Muslim society and then recedes, but never disappears, ready to burst out once again at a later time. For some it will be a surprise to discover that a number of scholars attribute the incredible energy and success of the early Islamic conquests to apocalyptic fervour, that is, to the conviction that the end-of-the-world was imminent.

21. Clouse, "Fundamentalist Eschatology," 274.

A certain type of eschatological dynamic and disruptive energy has been unleashed by apocalyptic expectation throughout Islamic history (both Sunni and Shi'i), including considerable "latter-days" agitation associated with the recent conflicts in both Iraq and Syria.[22]

Similar to Christianity, apocalypticism is not confined to only one or some denominations. In one sense or another, it is a *pan*-Islamic phenomenon.[23] On top of that, similar to Christianity, some extreme forms of apocalypticism have arisen that are drawn to millenarian and revolutionary impulses, some of which have received a lot of publicity (particularly those of the jihadist slant).[24]

In line with the general apocalyptic tendency to draw sharp lines between the good and evil, "us" and "them," sinners and saints, "the Qur'an urges those who wish to live in awe and devotion toward Allah to abstain from participation in evil and assiduously refrain from going over to the side of the alternate god, Satan, in the cosmic conflict."[25] Related to this, life is a constant struggle and fight between the good and the evil. Those who are victorious will be richly rewarded, while others will be doomed to judgment. "So we see that Islam followed closely the worldview of apocalyptic Judaism and the manner in which it was articulated in Christianity."[26]

What might be the peculiar and distinctive features of apocalypticism in Islam? According to J. Harold Ellens, there are seven:

1. A "cosmic battle has been in process throughout history in which the Kingdom of Light is arrayed against the Kingdom of Darkness."

2. The human experience is conceived of as a catastrophic process.

3. That men and women "are somehow responsible for acting against the evil in the world led to the view that mundane existence unfolds always under pressure of eternity. Human behavior is judged by a divine expectation."

4. The "resolution to the cosmic conflict and the tragic adventure of life will come by divine intervention."

---

22. Neely and Riddell, *Islam and the Last Day*, 1.

23. Cook, *Studies in Muslim Apocalyptic*.

24. For a basic guide, see Kenney, "Millennialism," 688–716.

25. Ellens, "Ideas," 59 (in-text version; p. 741 in online version).

26. Ellens, "Ideas," 59 (in-text version; p. 741 in online version).

5. In apocalypticism, heaven and earth are effected by cosmic forces, which include angels and demons who conduct warfare on behalf of God or as God's deputies—or, those of God's opponents, the Satan.

6. The "apocalyptic process in history will be resolved on earth and in heaven only by a divinely imposed cataclysmic end."

7. All of that will culminate in final judgment as a result of which there is a division between the condemned and the blessed.[27]

Ellens summarizes the presence of all of these seven features of apocalypticism present in Islam:

> The entire framework of the Qur'an is built around the vision of the cosmic conflict (principle number 1) that causes human history to take on the form of a tragic adventure in a catastrophic process (2). Every Surah of the Qur'an and nearly every strophe of the entire book counsel the faithful that it is imperative to make a conscious and intentional decision to fight on Allah's side in the ordeal of life. It is an ordeal "before the face of God," and so it must be taken seriously as a personal vocation. It is the challenge to struggle against evil (jihad) continuously, inside oneself and everywhere in the outside world (3). . . . The divine intervention (4) that the Qur'an teaches us to anticipate is the action of Allah himself. Allah acts in history in numerous ways. . . . [5] Allah is also present to us in the form of cosmic forces and angel visitants. . . . Angels are Allah's winged messengers (35:1) and they pray for forgiveness for all the inhabitants of the earth (42:5). . . . [6] Throughout the Qur'an there is a consistent flow of cautions and challenges regarding the cataclysmic end toward which history is moving (18:47–49). . . . The final feature of apocalyptic worldviews is the Day of Judgment. The day of divine judgment consigns all the living and the resurrected dead to their eternal destiny (23:101–111).[28]

What about the most radical violent movements in Islam? How would they employ and exploit the apocalyptic tradition? And what might be their liabilities?

---

27. Ellens, "Ideas," 57–59 (in-text version; pp. 740–41 in online version).
28. Ellens, "Ideas," 59–61 (in-text version; pp. 741–43 in online version).

A radical militant Islamic apocalyptic fight: ISIS

The marriage between apocalypticism and political-military rhetoric and recruitment is far from being a novel phenomenon in the history of Islamic religion. Through the centuries it has been used more or less successfully—as "many Mahdi claimants have failed."[29]

Dabiq[30] and *Rumiyah*[31] were recent online magazines published in a number of languages, including English, and used by the Islamic State of Iraq and the Levant (ISL, a.k.a. ISIS) to inspire and energize radical and militaristic movements and their recruitment. The former started in the summer of 2014 and in 2016 the latter took up the mantle. Interestingly, the name *Dabiq*, from a place name in Aleppo, is assumed to have a link with what is described in the Hadith literature as Armageddon. This connection is supposed to refer to the place where the greatest end-time battle between Muslims and Christians ought to take place. The magazine titled *Rumiyah* is a reference to Rome, signaling the desire of radical Islam to conquer and take over the religious, political, and economic power of the world and Western civilization through a reference to the "capital" of ancient and current power structures. Here are some representative samples from these magazines to illustrate the blend of religious and militaristic propaganda in the service of a radical attempt to conquer and take over.

> No. 1, pp. 4–5: Abu Hurayrah reported that Allah's Messenger said, "The Hour will not be established until the Romans land at al-A'maq or Dabiq (two places near each other in the northern countryside of Halab). Then, an army of the best people on the earth at that time from al-Madinah will leave to engage them. When they line up in ranks, the Romans will say, 'Leave us and those who were taken as prisoners from amongst us so we can fight them.' The Muslims will say, 'Nay, by Allah, we will not abandon our brothers to you.' So, they will fight them. Then one third of them will flee; Allah will never forgive them. One third will be killed; they will be the best martyrs with Allah. And one third will conquer them; they will never be afflicted with fitnah. Then they will conquer Constantinople. While they are dividing up the war booty, having hung their swords on olive trees, Shaytan [Satan] will shout, 'The [false] Messiah has followed after your families

29. Ostřanský, *Jihadist Preachers*, 2.

30. Wikipedia contributors, "Dabiq (Magazine)" contains background information alongside listing the published online issues.

31. Wikipedia contributors, "Rumiyah (magazine)" contains background information alongside listing the published online issues.

[who were left behind.]' So, they will leave [for their families], but Shaytan's claim is false. When they arrive at Sham, he comes out. Then, while they are preparing for battle and completing their ranks, prayers are called. So, 'Isa Ibn Maryam [Jesus] will descend and lead them. When the enemy of Allah sees him, he will melt as salt melts in water. If he were to leave him, he would melt until he perished, but he kills him with his own hand, and then shows them his blood upon his spear" [Sahih Muslim]. Shaykh Abu Mus'ab az-Zarqawi (rahimahullah) [may God have mercy upon him] anticipated the expansion of the blessed jihad from Iraq to Sham and linked it to this hadith, saying, "The spark has been lit here in Iraq, and its heat will continue to intensify—by Allah's permission—until it burns the crusader armies in Dabiq" [Ayna Ahlul-Muru'at]. According to the hadith, the area will play an historic role in the battles leading up to the conquests of Constantinople, followed by Rome. Presently, Dabiq is under the control of the crusader backed sahwat [moderate Islamists], close to the frontline between them and the Khilafah. May Allah purify Dabiq from the treachery of the sahwah and raise the flag of the Khilafah over its land.[32]

While the above excerpt is from *Dabiq*, the following one is from *Rumiyah*:

No. 3, pp. 25–26 (Towards the Major Malhamah of Dabiq): The great events unfolding now in northern Sham—in Dabiq and its surroundings—are but signs of the coming malahim [the great end-time battle], inshaallah [if Allah wills]. These great events will force the Crusaders—sooner or later—to accept the terms of the Jama'ah of the Muslims, a truce that is precedent to the Major Malhamah of Dabiq. Today, the old discords are being renewed within the ranks of the enemies of Allah. The Crusaders of the West oppose the Crusaders of the East and their murtadd [apostate] allies oppose one another. The Turks oppose the Kurds, the Sahwat [moderate Islam] of Turkey oppose the Sahwat of Jordan, the Rafidah oppose the Kurds of Iraq, the Kurds of the west oppose the Kurds of the east, and the Nusayriyyah [an extreme Shi'ite group] oppose the Kurds of Sham. "You think they are together, but their hearts are in disagreement. That is because they are a people who do not reason" (Al-Hashr 14).[33] This war of attack and

---

32. Taken from Ostřanský, "Appendix 3: An ISIS 'Apocalyptic Reader." In *Jihadist Preachers*, 270–71. The explanatory notes in the brackets are both from the copied text and my own.

33. Qur'an 59:14 cited in the text.

withdrawal occurring in Dabiq and its surrounding areas—the minor battle of Dabiq—will inevitably lead to the Major Malhamah of Dabiq, even if a withdrawal were to precede it by Allah's decree. Indeed, the Malhamah will come about after that which Allah and His Messenger have promised is materialized, including the treaty between the Muslims and the Romans followed by the Romans' betrayal that leads to the Major Malhamah of Dabiq. Thereafter, will come the certain conquest of Constantinople (and then the city of Rome).[34]

What do we glean from these and similar extreme interpretations? It tells us that any religious tradition can be—and most of them have been—exploited for political, economic, cultural, and other conquests. An obvious question of the relationship between violence and religion emerges. I close this chapter by reflecting on any potential connections and relations between the two religions' apocalyptic tendencies.

An odd bed fellowship:
Muslim and Christian apocalyptic movements

Ironically and counterintuitively, much of recent Islamic apocalyptic shows dependence on Christian sources, some of which have been translated into other languages from English.[35] For example, the theme of the Antichrist, a topic of great interest among both fundamentalist Christians and Muslims, is often aligned with apocalyptic tones. An example of this growing cross-fertilization has to do with a recent report from The Washington Institute's program of "Improving the Quality of U.S. Middle East Policy":

> Washing across the Islamic world is a growing wave of grim and gory literature predicting the aher al-zaman, the Arabic concept for apocalypse that literally translates as the "end of time." This genre is both ancient and modern, as it revisits historic Islamic narratives and incorporates newer, non-Islamic elements. . . . Both Sunni and Shiite Islam contain traditional narratives about the end of days. In the Sunni narrative, Jesus returns to fight the anti-Christ in Damascus, defeats him in Lud, and leads the army of the faithful at the end of time. In the predominant Shiite narrative, the occulted twelfth imam, also referred to as the "Hidden Imam" or

34. Taken from Ostřanský, "Appendix 3: An ISIS 'Apocalyptic Reader." In *Jihadist Preachers*, 274–75. The explanatory notes in the brackets are both from the copied text and my own.

35. Haddad and Smith. "Anti-Christ," 520–26.

Mahdi, will appear in Mecca and lead the Mahdi's Army, defeat-ing the unbelievers. In contrast to these old narratives, the current wave of apocalyptic literature draws heavily from non-Islamic sources. This heterogeneous genre follows the approach of its founder, a minor Egyptian journalist whose 1986 book *The Anti-Christ* incorporated Biblical revelations, Nostradamus's proph-esies, anti-Semitic propaganda, and Protestant evangelicalism.[36]

Particularly significant in these newly converging Christian-Muslim apocalyptic visions is the role of the Antichrist. It is related to the destruc-tion of the unfaithful and unbelievers, both inside and outside. "[Whereas] Apocalyptic Christians foresee the destruction of nominal Christians as part of the ushering in of the drama of the final days, . . . Muslims look to a period of deep devastation of the Muslim community as one of the signs of the end."[37] Furthermore, in Muslim imagination, Israel and America are often depicted as the Antichrist, and therefore as enemies.

On the other hand, fundamentalist Christians tend to see the United States as a "divinely guided" actor in the end-time events, particularly in its support of Israel. In their imagination, particularly as a result of inten-sifying anti-Muslim polemic, a Muslim figure now seems the most likely candidate for the Antichrist![38] No wonder contemporary Muslims "are specifically concerned with what they see as the humiliation of Muslims through Western imperialism and support of Israel, and with Christian dispensationalist triumphalism that seeks the eradication of Islam."[39] In the fight against the West and godless nations, as discussed above, Islamic apocalyptic imagination also centers on the figure of Mahdi.[40]

It is yet to be seen to which direction(s) the forms of Abrahamic neo-apocalypticisms move in the near future, particularly in terms of mutual collaboration. It is also possible that with the growing secularization among both global Muslim and Christian communities, they become more and more fringe movements and begin to lose their appeal to masses. At the time of this writing, however, neo-apocalypticism is alive and well in both Islam and Christianity!

---

36. Filiu and Khalaji, "Rise of Apocalyptic Islam."
37. Haddad and Smith, "Anti-Christ," 505.
38. See Haddad and Smith, "Anti-Christ," 506–7.
39. Haddad and Smith, "Anti-Christ," 512.
40. Haddad and Smith, "Anti-Christ," 526–28.

CHAPTER 6

Why care for the environment when the End of all things is at hand?

Introduction: the eco-catastrophe as a doomsday signal

As MENTIONED IN CHAPTER 3, among the potential "near-future" threats to our globe, alongside nuclear destruction, none other is as urgent as that stemming from environmental pollution. As the Catholic ethicist-theologian Daniel Maguire has reminded us, "if current trends continue, we will not."[1]

The statistics are well-known and readily available, both in popular[2] and scholarly[3] literature, so there is no need for me to go into a detailed explanation of them here. A short note suffices:

> Christians are similar to the rest of society: we value the present more than the future. We selfishly and continually ignore problems related to pollution, landfills, food processing, environmental change, chemical waste, and land mismanagement because they seem irrelevant to our current wants and needs. Environmental problems require lots of time, patience, and perseverance—too much for many churches to handle. Westernized Christianity currently doesn't value the environment, and few Christian

---

1. Maguire, *Moral Core*, 13.

2. Representative, accessible databases include the following: Bradford, "Pollution Facts."; Ukaogo et al., "Environmental Pollution."; Boudreau et al., "Pollution."

3. Consult Exploratorium, "Global Climate Change."

organizations and churches offer educational classes, teaching, and ministries that focus on earth stewardship.[4]

On the more hopeful side:

Imagine if Christians had been on the forefront of protecting our earth, if they actually viewed the world as God's creation, and the animals as God's animals, and the plants as God's plants, and land as God's land. What if the American Church spent millions of dollars fighting to preserve nature instead of investing in divisive culture wars and political lobbying campaigns? What if Christians were viewed as protectors of creation, shielding millions of acres of land, restoring polluted areas, and protecting animals from cruelty and exploitation?[5]

This is a vision that has yet to be materialized.

When eschatological expectation trumps environmental concern

The influence of Christian fundamentalists with their allegedly theologically (read: apocalyptically) based robust anti-environmentalism is staggering, particularly in the USA.

It is impossible to ignore the existence of a powerful, well-financed group of evangelical fundamentalist Christians who deny the scientific evidence for global warming, climate change and the consequent need for urgent action. . . . Their approach to eschatology influences long-term planning on climate issues and has dangerous and destructive influence on other areas government policy making. Evidence from the US and the UK suggests that fundamentalist Christians are engaging in deliberate strategies of influencing government departments and accessing even the legislatures themselves.[6]

But why do Christian fundamentalists end up being anti-environment? The reason is simple: they "feel that concern for the future of our planet is irrelevant, because it *has* no future. . . . They may also believe . . .

4. Mattson, "5 (Stupid) Reasons."
5. Mattson, "5 (Stupid) Reasons."
6. Greene, "Evangelical Fundamentalists." On the fundamentalist rejection of science, see Pigliucci, "Science and Fundamentalism."

that environmental destruction is not only to be disregarded but actually welcomed—even hastened—as a sign of the coming Apocalypse."[7]

As a result:

> Why care about the earth when the droughts, floods, and pestilence brought by ecological collapse are signs of the Apocalypse foretold in the Bible? Why care about global climate change when you and yours will be rescued in the Rapture? And why care about converting from oil to solar when the same God who performed the miracle of the loaves and fishes can whip up a few billion barrels of light crude with a Word? . . . Natural-resource depletion and overpopulation, then, are not concerns for End-Timers—and nor are other ecological catastrophes.[8]

What is fittingly named as "throwaway theology" or "scorched earth theology," advocated by publications such as the aforementioned hugely popular *Left Behind* series focuses only one side of the Christian eschatological hope with the expectation of a total incineration of the earth at the End.[9]

While typically fundamentalists are therefore understandably not keen on following the signs of ecocatastrophe, there is, however, one reason for them to keep their eye on the topic. It has to do with the signs of the rapture, the second coming of the Lord. Says one of their advocates:

> I used to think there was no real need for Christians to monitor the changes related to greenhouse gases. If it was going to take a couple hundred years for things to get serious, I assumed the nearness of the End Times would overshadow this problem. With the speed of climate change now seen as moving much faster, global warming could very well be a major factor in the plagues of the tribulation.[10]

According to a recent research survey, there is a marked difference between the fundamentalist and non-fundamentalist outlook on the world, and this has a significant impact on our topic: for the former, time is "short"

---

7. Scherer, "Christian-Right Views."

8. Scherer, "Christian-Right Views."

9. For a thoughtful reflection, see Merritt, "Is God Going to Incinerate the Earth?"

10. Cited in Scherer, "Christian-Right Views," and attributed to Todd Strandberg without any exact source-information except for a general reference to the https://www.raptureready.com/ website.

and there is a sort of deterministic conviction of the divine timetable set for the world on which the human affairs have no influence.[11]

Even in the political realm—which in the USA is, of course, robustly influenced by the Christian Right—momentous changes have taken place with regard to humans' care for the environment. Just think of this shift: The first Earth Day celebration was established in 1970 with support from the main political parties on the "left" and "right," and enthusiastically endorsed by the Republican Richard Nixon, who also created the Environmental Protection Agency.[12] On the contrary, a few decades later, under another Republican leader, President Donald J. Trump, the almost universally signed Paris Climate Agreement was rejected by Americans.

Fortunately, against the fundamentalist-conservative Christians' support for the departure from the climate act and resistance to climate scientists' unanimous global warnings about an impending natural catastrophe, mainline Protestant denominations, including the Episcopal Church[13] and the Evangelical Lutheran Church in America,[14] as well as the Roman Catholic Church,[15] strongly denounced Trump's withdrawal of the US from the Agreement. Even several major Jewish, Muslim and Hindu organizations condemned the withdrawal from the Agreement.

When environmental concern trumps eschatological expectation

Whereas among Christian fundamentalists the focus on an intense eschatological expectation with an anticipation of an imminent return of Christ, judgment, and an "exit" to heaven imagined as a totally other-worldly reality too often results in the neglect of the environment, on the other end of the spectrum, the problem is the reverse. Among a number of eco-feminists and some other women theologians, some liberationists, post-colonialists, and others, the focus on the protection and flourishing of creation results in either undermining eschatological hope or radically revising it to make it merely this-worldly oriented.[16] When the fundamentalists are asking "Why

11. Barker and Bearce, "End-times Theology," 269.
12. Spencer, "Three Reasons."
13. Curry, "Presiding Bishop."
14. Detweiler, "US Plans to Withdraw."
15. Zauzmer, "Vatican Leaders Dismayed."
16. See Eaton, *Introducing Ecofeminist Theologies*.

invest in the world that will soon face total destruction?" the other camp raises the question of "Why think of some other-worldly events with judgment and destruction when the main concern is the flourishing of nature in this life?" These Christian thinkers, in this case some leading feminists, to put it in somewhat technical theological jargon,

> have refocused eschatology from the distant future ("unrealised eschatology") to the here-and-now ("realised eschatology"). Simultaneously, these feminist thinkers have shifted the thematic centre from humanity, as the apex of creation, to creation itself, with humanity removed from centre stage to a supporting position as an interwoven, interdependent component of that creation. In short, realised eschatology has become the ethical culmination of ecofeminism.[17]

In other words, a marked shift away from spiritual hopes in the afterlife, in the new creation, to concern for the earth in this life has taken place.[18] As one late liberationist wittily put it: "[E]schatology is no longer 'the last things' but 'those things in our midst.'" In keeping with this, "[p]rophecy, then, so intimately connected to eschatological vision and hope, does not involve predicting the future or mapping out the end times, but discerning God's activity in the world now, the meaning of that activity for the community of faith, and the appropriate response."[19] So deeply suspicious are some Christians of holding on to a future-directed eschatological hope that, for them, "[t]he future is envisioned as a return to the pristine past, before human degradation of nature, but with humanity fulfilling its symbiotic potential."[20]

Rightly or wrongly, many women theologians surmise that a major reason for the lack of concern for the environment has to do with deep dualisms rampant in our culture, including between male and female, heaven and earth, as well as spiritual and material. Even more: there is also the claim that the linking of the female with "nature" and physicality, the lower realm of reality, in contrast to the male connection with culture, the higher

---

17. Karras, "Eschatology," 243.

18. See the provocative work by Keller, *Apocalypse Now and Then*.

19. Engel and Thistlethwaite. "Introduction," 14–15, cited in Westhelle, "Liberation Theology," 311–27, 319.

20. Karras, "Eschatology," 243–44.

realm, may also have contributed to humanity's subordination of and "dominion" over the environment.[21]

So: what is the place of environmental care in Christian eschatology?

Although life is much more complex than that, the previous discussion has sought to highlight two kinds of extremes in some quarters of Christian theology in which a constructive balance between the hope for the world to come and the concern for the world (environment) today has been lacking. These two fringe movements, however, do not register at all the mainstream Christian attitude—neither in the past, nor at the moment. So, let us reflect on and respond to the varied critiques against the alleged lack of environmental care in the Christian church and Christian theology.

Let me state as a tentative summative conclusion this much: there is nothing at the heart of Christian eschatology rightly understood that in principle would block the care for nature, which God has created. I submit to you the claim that even the hope for life eternal in the new creation (at times named "immortality") does not necessarily drive Christian eschatology towards indifference to the natural world. Hence, I do not recommend that theologians turn to the hopelessly immanentist, this-worldly eschatologies to save the environment from the fundamentalist dismissal thereof. There is better, radical, middle way for Christians.

This is not to unduly dismiss some justified aspects of the immanentist, this-worldly criticisms against Christian eschatology. No doubt there is much self-criticism to be had among all Christians, and particularly among fundamentalists and conservatives with regard to environmental forgetfulness and even resistance. It is also clear that some of the dualisms mentioned above have contributed to the indifference toward caring for the environment, undermining the significance of such care. Those attitudes have to be corrected. They do not represent the core Christian eschatological vision

As a part of clarifying a proper Christian eschatological attitude toward nature there is a need for a balanced theological critique of the this-worldly theologians' criticism outlined briefly above. First of all, much more nuance is needed in order to do justice to Christian theology at large. Without trying to whitewash the grave misunderstandings and extreme views of

21. One early programmatic essay is that by Ortner, "Is Female to Male?" 67–87.

some Christian groups, also to be noted are the steady support and concern among various churches for the environment as God's good creation. An illustration of this positive force is the growth of theological literature in which creation theology, eschatological hope, and environmental concern are tightly linked together.[22]

Second, a merely this-worldly focus will not succeed in establishing the lasting value of creation. Indeed, if all the efforts of well-meaning Christian environmentalists come to naught with the last breath of men and women, and there is no hope for eternal life, would that be enough? I don't think so. We should be mindful of the simple fact that in all scientific accounts, not only the earth and her life but also the whole cosmos will come to an end; and that in terms of near-future prospects, even if human-made threats such as pollution, waste, and nuclear disaster could be avoided, sooner or later "super"-human asteroid collisions or something similar may totally wipe us out. In that light, how appealing and realistic is merely this-worldly—and therefore, also merely this-earth-focused—vision?[23]

I fail to see the logic in the claim that a "vision of an ecological hope freed from false escapism and content to make common joys abundant and available to us all" should cast off all dreams of an eschatological coming of the kingdom because of the alleged selfish and egoistic implications of its hope for immortality.[24] Of course, any form of eschatological *escapism* should be rejected, but the way to do this is not to omit the ultimate hope for life eternal with the Triune God, who has created this beautiful world and us, in communion with others. How can it be that the lack of hope for the afterlife necessarily leads to concern for the earth; why not "destructive nihilism" instead?[25]

The Roman Catholic eco-feminist Elizabeth Johnson notes in response to her colleagues' merely this-worldly approach to support of environmentalism that: "a solely immanentist end is not the only conceivable possibility, even within an ecological and feminist perspective." Indeed, Johnson goes so far as to argue (in agreement with female theologians from the Global South) that "hope for life with God after death for human persons

---

22. For starters, see Johnson, "Losing and Finding Creation," 3–21; Berry, *The Dream of the Earth*; McFague, *New Climate for Theology*. A useful recent essay (with rich bibliography to which this discussion is also indebted) is Conradie, "What Is the Place?" 65–96.

23. Similarly, see McCall, *Greenie's Guide*, 46–50.

24. Ruether, "Ecofeminism," 30.

25. McCall, *Greenie's Guide*, 71.

and the whole earth not only does not cut the nerve for action on behalf of justice but actually sustains it, especially in violent situations. Furthermore, such transcendent hope, when cast into a nondualistic framework, functions critically and creatively to promote care for the earth precisely because it sees that this world has eternal value."[26] I couldn't agree more with her. I also agree wholeheartedly with the "green" Patriach of the Eastern Orthodox Church, His Holiness Bartholomew. He remarks that regarding ecological concerns "we should turn our attention to the future, to the age to come, toward the heavenly kingdom" with which "we do not imply a sense of escapism or other-worldliness . . . [but rather] a way of envisioning this world in light of the next."[27]

Indeed, it is not at all that a hope for eternal life *necessarily* leads to environmental escapism. Rather, rightly conceived, the hope for life after death brings robust motivation for that work, as detailed below. In fact, "it is hardly possible to motivate people to care for the earth unless they are convinced that there is indeed some future for themselves on earth." On the contrary, it is likely that despair before the impending eco-crisis will most likely elicit resignation and apathy.[28] Hence, there is a need for a dynamic, balanced, eco-theological Christian eschatology.

Towards a green Christian eschatology

While affirming all the valid criticisms against obstructionist and mistaken ways in which the Christian tradition has failed to stand up for defending the integrity and acting for the flourishing of creation, this project boldly propose that genuine hope for the earth is supported by the hope for personal life beyond death and a future for the whole cosmos in new creation.[29] In its widest horizon, a Christian eschatological vision includes not only human and cosmic hope but also hope for nature, the environment. As Moltmann puts it succinctly, Christian eschatology awaits "the redemption *of* the world . . . [rather than] *from* the world" and the "redemption *of* the body . . . [rather than] a deliverance of the soul from the body" because "[t]heir eschatological future is a human *and* earthly future."[30] Christian

26. Johnson, *Friends of God*, 197.

27. Bartholomew, "Opening Address."

28. Conradie, "What Is the Place of the Earth in God's Economy?" 74–75.

29. Brunner et al., *Introducing Evangelical Ecotheology*, ch. 10.

30. Moltmann, *Coming of God*, 259. Emphasis added.

eschatological vision values embodiment precisely because of its hope for future life in a resurrected body, in communion with the triune God and other human persons, in the renewed cosmos. Indeed, it can be argued that to the "communion of saints," inclusively understood, belong also animals and the whole of creation.[31]

This eschatological vision is funded by the conviction that the universe "must make sense everlastingly, and so ultimately be redeemed from transience and decay."[32] This kind of hope-filled expectation provides a solid incentive for working toward preservation of the earth in anticipation of the "new heaven and new earth."

Having been created for the divine destiny, as Vatican II's *Gaudium et Spes* puts it (#22), human persons cannot achieve their fulfillment and goal if physical death and decay are the last word. No merely this-worldly vision can satisfy that yearning; nor is the Christian hope to be seen as in any way antagonistic to the renewal of nature, it includes the whole of creation.

It is clear that the mandate in Genesis 1:26–27 for humanity to act as God's faithful vice-regents does not justify abuse and exploitation. Rather, it is a call to responsible service on behalf of God's good creation. Regrettably the command to "subdue the earth" has too often been taken literally in the Christian tradition. Precisely as the image of God, reflecting the characteristics of the Creator, the human being is placed in the world as a steward, accountable to God. Rather than superiority, humanity should exhibit solidarity with the creation to which it also belongs. Indeed, says Orthodox theologian John Zizioulas, humanity is called to exercise priestly vocation on behalf of creation, and the "human being is not fulfilled until it becomes the 'summing up of nature,' as [a] priest referring the world back to its Creator."[33] There is a continuity between the human and nature, and Christ died and was resurrected not merely for humans but for nature as well.[34]

As detailed above, too often it is claimed that the Christian eschatological hope would lead to the dismissal of the hope for the rest of creation. This is not the case. The Canadian female theologian J. M. Soskice rightly

---

31. Johnson, *Friends of God*, 242 and passim.

32. Polkinghorne, *God of Hope*, 148.

33. As paraphrased by Fisher, *Human Significance*, 152, with quotation from Zizioulas, "Preserving God's Creation," 2.

34. Consider the section title "§5 THE RESURRECTION OF CHRIST AND NATURE: THE NATURAL PROBLEM" in Moltmann, *The Way of Jesus Christ*, 252.

notes that if "there is no hope of the triumph of God's justice on earth, [there is] no point in praying that God's kingdom will come and [God's] will be done on *earth* as it is in heaven."[35] That is because we will be "redeemed *with* the world, not *from* it."[36] Rightly, the American philosopher Kevin Corcoran reminds us that "we human beings have been made from the mud and dirt—God-blessed, God-loved, and God-embraced mud and dirt—and made for life in an equally earthy environment."[37] God's kingdom includes this whole world inasmuch as "God's reconciling, redemptive, and restorative activity takes place within the natural, material world. This is the theater of God's redemptive activity, the theater of God's kingdom."[38]

Eschatological consummation: an integrated comprehensive vision

With these words, the Holy Father Francis began his groundbreaking "green" encyclical:

> "LAUDATO SI', mi' Signore"—"Praise be to you, my Lord". In the words of this beautiful canticle, Saint Francis of Assisi reminds us that our common home is like a sister with whom we share our life and a beautiful mother who opens her arms to embrace us. "Praise be to you, my Lord, through our Sister, Mother Earth, who sustains and governs us, and who produces various fruit with coloured flowers and herbs." [39]

The pope laments that "this sister," nature, "now cries out to us because of the harm we have inflicted on her by our irresponsible use and abuse of the goods with which God has endowed her." This is because we humans have taken onto ourselves the role and mandate as "lords and masters, entitled to plunder her at will." This sinful violence in our hearts and attitudes has put the earth in great danger and so now she "groans in travail" (Rom 8:22). Relatedly, we have forgotten the simple fact that we humans are also dust of the earth and that our sustenance depends on nature's resources (#2). As a Christian response to the looming earth catastrophe, the Roman

35. Soskice, "Resurrection and the New Jerusalem," 57.

36. Moltmann, *The Spirit of Life*, 89, emphasis in original.

37. Corcoran, "Thy Kingdom Come," 67.

38. Corcoran, "Thy Kingdom Come," 67.

39. Francis, "Laudato Si. On Care for our Common Home." References in the main text (in parenthesis) in this section are to this document.

pontiff outlines what he calls "The Gospel of Creation" (ch. 2). In a powerful manner, Francis reminds us that creation is "more" than bare nature, as it is God's handiwork and God indwells it through the Spirit: "God is intimately present to each being, without impinging on the autonomy of his creature, and this gives rise to the rightful autonomy of earthly affairs. His divine presence, which ensures the subsistence and growth of each being, 'continues the work of creation'"[40] (#80). Funded by a holistic, comprehensive eschatological vision, the pope further teaches:

> The ultimate destiny of the universe is in the fullness of God, which has already been attained by the risen Christ, the measure of the maturity of all things. . . . The ultimate purpose of other creatures is not to be found in us. Rather, all creatures are moving forward with us and through us towards a common point of arrival, which is God, in that transcendent fullness where the risen Christ embraces and illumines all things. Human beings, endowed with intelligence and love, and drawn by the fullness of Christ, are called to lead all creatures back to their Creator. (#83)

The papal encyclical is in keeping with the teaching of St. Paul in Romans 8:19–24, in which the apostle tightly links the hope for personal, communal, and cosmic consummation:

> For the creation waits with eager longing for the revealing of the sons of God; for the creation was subjected to futility, not of its own will but by the will of him who subjected it in hope; because the creation itself will be set free from its bondage to decay and obtain the glorious liberty of the children of God. We know that the whole creation has been groaning in travail together until now; and not only the creation, but we ourselves, who have the first fruits of the Spirit, groan inwardly as we wait for adoption as sons, the redemption of our bodies.

Indeed, this wide-ranging cosmic framework is the proper take on the main Christian symbol of eschatology, namely, the kingdom of God. The kingdom of God—the Triune God's generous, fair, and holy rule—should not be reduced merely to individual hope or even the future hope of the whole people of God. Christian hope of the eschatological consummation includes *the whole of God's creation*, "the integration of the real history

---

40. This last short citation is attributed in the *Encyclical* to Aquinas, *Summa Theologiae*, [part] I, q[question]. 104, art. 1 ad 4.

of human beings with the nature of the earth."[41] In the Christian vision, "[a]ll creatures on this earth find their way to one another in the community of a common way, a common suffering and a common hope."[42] This kind of hope-filled balanced and dynamic eschatological expectation provides a superior incentive for working toward preservation of the earth in anticipation of the "new heaven and new earth." This holistic and "earthly" eschatological vision is masterfully expressed by the American Anabaptist theologian Thomas A. Finger: "Since the new creation arrives through God's Spirit, and since it reshapes the physical world, every theological locus is informed by the Spirit's transformation of matter-energy."[43] Christ's resurrection through the life-giving Spirit is already a foretaste of the "transformation of matter-energy" in new creation, "a transformation of the present nature *beyond* what emergence refers to."[44]

What about the Islamic view of the issue under consideration? Would it be capable of combining the care for the nature and the expectation of the coming of the End?

Nature and creation in an Islamic eschatological perspective

Generally speaking, as Muslim scholars freely admit, a track record and awareness of seeking to balance concern for today's environment and tomorrow's End has not been the hallmark of the youngest Abrahamic faith. This posture is, to cite S. H. Nasr, a leading American-based conservative Muslim scholar, a part of "general indifference to the environmental crisis."[45] That said, he himself has been on the forefront of beginning the work towards articulating an Islamic theology and ethics of environment.[46] It remains to be seen what the results and the impact of that work might be.

This tells us that there are resources in Islam that are worth highlighting and rediscovering for the sake of environmental care. A foundational resource, no different from the theologies of the other two Abrahamic sister faiths, is this: because in Islam "every individual creature or being has its

41. Moltmann, *God in Creation*, xi.

42. Moltmann, *Way of Jesus Christ*, 273.

43. Finger, *Contemporary Anabaptist Theology*, 563.

44. Russell, *Cosmology*, 37, emphasis in original.

45. Nasr, "Islam, the Contemporary Islamic World," 86.

46. Nasr, *Man and Nature*.

own ontological existence as a sign of God, and by its very being manifests and reveals His majesty and mercy, . . . every creature deserves attention and consideration for its relation to the Divine."[47] This theological conviction is significant when thinking of ecology and environment. It can be linked with another ancient Islamic notion—that of "balance." As with the heavens that are sustained "by mathematical balance," human beings and their actions likewise should be balanced. That is, human nature and actions should be straightforward and honest in relation to each other and natural resources.[48]

Now, these foundational theological resources prompt the question as to their role and nature in relation to humanity. It is important to hear what Muzaffar Iqbal is arguing, as that is something similar to what Christian theology contends as well: "Unlike the worldview created by modern science, the Qur'ānic view of the elements of the cosmos does not make them subservient to humanity; rather they remain in the service of their Lord, Who created them and set on tasks for His Purpose." While natural resources of course benefit humanity, they are not commodities to be used indiscriminately for the sake human well-being.[49] This foundational teaching is closely related to Islam's view of humanity in a special relation to the Creator. While not daring to use the Jewish-Christian notion of the "image of God" for fear of compromising the absolute difference between Allah and the created order, the term *fitrah* is used. It denotes something akin to the conception of the image of God. The *fitrah* affirms "religion true to the primordial nature of humankind" and the men and women as God's servants. Hence, the environmental message based on the Qur'anic teaching is "part of the instinctive nature of humankind and need not be instilled, but rather awakened."[50]

No wonder Nasr and some other leading Muslim scholars have rightly critiqued the one-sided technocratic use of nature in the modern West—and I would add, in Muslim lands as well—for its neglect and undermining of the spiritual, theological, and moral dimension of the crisis. This criticism, which is also useful for Jews and Christians, is in keeping with the conviction in Islam that even the environmental crisis can be attributed

47. Özdemir, "Towards an Understanding," 11.

48. Comments in *The Holy Qur' an*, trans. Yusuf Ali, 5177–78, cited in Özdemir, "Towards an Understanding," 13.

49. Iqbal, "In the Beginning," 2:413–14.

50. Chishti, "Fiṭra," 67.

ultimately to "the loss of a relationship between humans, the natural realm, and Allah." To put it in Islamic language: when the way of the *Sharī' a* is forgotten, dire consequences even to nature may follow.[51] It is very important to note that the meaning of the widely debated term *Sharī' a* has little or nothing to do with the image in popular media of the desire to suppress rights of women or enforce moral codes on the population. In its original meaning in tradition, *Sharī' a* is something like the ethics of the Torah or of the Sermon on the Mount. Sure, it is a moral code, but not externally, nor implemented by force—anymore than Torah or Jesus's teachings are supposed to be enforced.[52]

Adnan Z. Amin summarizes some of the theological, philosophical, and spiritual resources supporting ecological values in Islam:

> The traditional concern of Islam for social justice and care for the poor, the orphaned, and the widowed has a broader relevance that embraces concern for the natural environment as well. Protection of land and proper treatment of biodiversity are now being advocated by Islamic scholars and teachers. In addition, the unity of all reality *(tawhīd)* and the balance of nature *(mīzān)* as recognized by Islam constitutes an important basis for religious ecology and environmental ethics. Islamic teachings on land management hold great promise for protection of fragile ecosystems, namely, valuing sacred precincts *(harām)* and setting aside land for the common good *(himā)*.[53]

In keeping with this conviction is the 2015 "Islamic Declaration on Climate Change" as a part of the United Nations Climate Change initiative.[54]

Now, it is true that so far I have mentioned nothing about the relation of the emerging environmental concern in Islam in relation to the eschatological End. The reason is that in my research I was not able to identify such sources. And I will note below (in chapter 9) that the focus on a sudden catastrophic End in judgment in Islamic theology may also thwart the inclination to see continuity between life now and in the afterlife. This in turn

51. Chishti, "Fitra," 69–71.

52. As a non-specialist in Islam, I am not arguing that *Sharī' a* may also carry other meanings and that even the Muslim experts were not disagreeing about its meaning and use. I am simply using this term in this particular discussion in the way Chishti and some others as Muslims are using it.

53. Amin, "Preface[to *I&E*]," xxxiii–xxxiv.

54. United Nations Climate Change, "Islamic Declaration." See also Al-Jayyousi, "How Islam Can Represent a Model."

may undermine a key motivation to work for the environment in anticipation of the consummation. It is safe to say, however, that while the details of the theological negotiation will be left to Muslim scholars and clergy, this brief discussion leaves the door open for combining a robust work for the betterment of God's creation with an intense eschatological expectation.

A related issue in Christian theology—similarly to other Abrahamic faiths—has to do with the relevance and usefulness of working towards social and economic justice as well as equality between all human beings in light of the coming End. This is the topic for the next chapter.

CHAPTER 7

Why care about justice and poverty when the End of all things is at hand?

Is eschatological expectation blocking social concern?

The liberationist critique of religious eschatology

MOVING FROM THE TOPIC of eschatology and environment to eschatology and justice is a seamless transition. These two domains belong together, as brilliantly captured in the title of a book by a leading Latin-American liberationist Leonardo Boff: *Cry of the Earth, Cry of the Poor*.[1] Much of what was discussed in the previous chapter is relevant in this context as well, although I will not repeat it here.

Similar to the issue of the environment, there is a long-held opinion according to which the more intense the eschatological anticipation, the less imagination and work there is toward social, economic, and political injustice. The question is raised: how useful for the sake of liberation and reconciliation of people is the expectation of God's coming shalom?

A quick look at some representative works by liberationists of various stripes easily reveals the marginal role, and at times even the omission, of the doctrine of last things. Consider the senior American black theologian J. Deotis Roberts's essay in the *Cambridge Companion to Black Theology* (2012): "Dignity and Destiny: Black Reflections on Eschatology."

---

1. Boff, *Cry of the Earth, Cry of the Poor*.

Notwithstanding the title, the writing speaks of anything but eschatology![2] Another senior black liberationist, James Cone, devotes only six pages to eschatology in his programmatic *Black Theology of Liberation*.[3] A promising collection of essays titled *Liberating Eschatology* (1999), in honor of the leading American feminist theologian Letty M. Russell, has very little to say of eschatology—except for the essay by the male theologian Moltmann! Or, take this recent widely used textbook promoting a robust liberationist approach by the Grand Old Man of Hispanic/Latino theology, Justo L. González: *Mañana: Christian Theology from a Hispanic Perspective*. It has not even a paragraph, let alone a chapter, on the End!

A central claim among a diverse group of liberationists is simply this: a momentous shift has to be attempted from the expectation of a divine intervention at the end of history with cataclysmic events as taught in Christian tradition towards a this-worldly, mostly humanly engineered change of conditions of living and flourishing. Note this programmatic statement by a group of liberationists:

> Hence, eschatology is no longer "the last things" but "those things in our midst." The stress is on a God acting in history and on the need to discover God's direction for abundant life in the midst of our ambiguous and conflict ridden history. Prophecy, then, so intimately connected to eschatological vision and hope, does not involve predicting the future or mapping out the end times, but discerning God's activity in the world now, the meaning of that activity for the community of faith, and the appropriate response.[4]

It is interesting that some liberationists have traced the roots of the this-worldly eschatologies as far back in history as the renowned eighteenth-century philosopher G. W. F. Hegel. Famously, he "believed himself loyal to the genius of Christianity by realizing the Kingdom of God on earth. And, since he transposed the Christian expectation of a final consummation into the historical process as such, he saw the world's history as consummating itself."[5] In other words, rather than waiting for the ultimate

---

2. Roberts, "Dignity and Destiny," ch. 15.

3. Cone, *Black Theology*, 135–42.

4. Engel and Thistlethwaite, "Introduction," 14–15, cited in Westhelle, "Liberation Theology," 319.

5. As described by Löwith, *Meaning in History*, 57–58, cited in Westhelle, "Liberation Theology," 313.

divine intervention after Christian tradition, the "End" is now conceived in terms of this-worldly and humanly engineered process.

Although the marginalization of the ultimate eschatological coming of the God's kingdom brought about by the Triune God is in need of a critique, no theological movement should dismiss the important and necessary critique against *abuses* of eschatology in the hands of many Christians as an excuse for neglecting social concern. One just wishes that the liberationist critique would be more nuanced and constructive. Consider this one from Cone, in many ways of a justified critique, which is also badly in need of correction:

> An eschatological perspective that does not challenge the present order is faulty. If contemplation about the future distorts the present reality of injustice and reconciles the oppressed to unjust treatment committed against them, then it is unchristian and thus has nothing whatsoever to do with the Christ who came to liberate us. It is this that renders white talk about heaven and life after death fruitless for blacks.[6]

This claiming all "white talk" about eschatological hope to be fruitless for blacks is an indication of the lack of nuance. It makes liberationists ignore the fact that while there are some—too many, indeed—Christians and movements to whom it may apply, there is an equally large number of Christian constituents whom the critique does not concern at all. All that said, except for the lack of nuancing, the statement's main message is worth endorsing. But it would be more powerful and impactful had it included the necessary nuances!

Now a question emerges: What might be a *constructive* liberationist proposal? In other words, what is the *content* and *substance* of liberationist eschatology? Let me invite two liberationists into a conversation: Rosemary Radford Ruether, a leading American feminist liberation scholar, and James Cone, the Grand Old Man of black liberation.

Following them, I will respond to some of the valid critiques and challenges posed by liberationists, and then, at the end of this chapter, attempt to outline a constructive Christian liberative vision of the End.

---

6. Cone, *Black Theology*, 137.

A feminist and black theology's vision of the "End"

Prefacing her summative statement on a feminist eschatology as "brief and tentative," Rosemary Radford Ruether writes that

> the Christian symbol of future hope, the reign of God on earth, provides a vision of "what ought to be" in human-human and human-earth relations, against all distortions into violence and oppression. It provides us with the paradigm of who God is for us and with us and thus the foundations of our hope. This hope has nothing to do with an assurance of continuing progress in history nor of divine intervention to defeat God's enemies. Rather, hope is an insurgent power of resistance, a refusal to accept the dehumanizing oppression of ourselves or others and the counter-dehumanization of others, including those who are dehumanizing us and others. Insurgent hope not only sustains resistance, but also sparks continual creativity to turn death and destruction into a means of new life.[7]

Rather than immortality in any traditional sense, she continues, the feminist envisions the dissolution of individual, personal existence into some kind of universal matrix of being: "Everything that lives and dies goes back into this matrix and is reborn in and through it. Our dreams and accomplishments live on through the collective memory of our communities through which insurgent hope is continually reborn."[8]

Ruether's merely this-worldly focused conception of eschatology as a means of liberation and resistance is of course to be applauded for its liberative potential. At the same time, similar to what was mentioned with regard to kindred approaches to environmental work, it only lasts for the time being. This feminist vision fails to do the work eschatology has done in Christian theology from its inception, namely to provide hope both for this world and the world to come.

Having lamented above the marginal space devoted in Cone's *A Black Theology of Liberation* to the doctrine of last things, I also wish to register some important contributions, in addition to what was already mentioned above. Cone rightly observes that the question of death, the anticipation of "the certainty of nonexistence[,] understandably places us in a state of anxiety" and that therefore, the issue of the End is necessary for any theological and religious ideology. This is a needed corrective to those well-meaning

7. Ruether, "Eschatology," 339.
8. Ruether, "Eschatology," 339.

liberationists who tend to push away the whole topic of eschatology as something harmful to liberative efforts. Black eschatology claims that death, as much as it is also a matter of the future, is also a daily experience for these oppressed folks. "They see death every time they see whites." Black theology "rejects as invalid the attempt of oppressors to escape the question of death." In other words, black theology does not allow for the white oppressors (as they are called in the book) to try to evade their finitude by immersing themselves into all kinds of luxuries and hobbies. White people should face the certainty of nonexistence![9]

Where Cone's violent—yes, violent!—rhetoric becomes counterproductive and has to be rejected is when he claims that "Christ does not die to 'save' them [the white oppressors] but to destroy them so as to recreate them, to dissolve their whiteness in the fire of judgment, for it is only through the destruction of whiteness that the wholeness of humanity may be realized."[10]

Having assessed what he calls *white* eschatologies, counterintuitively in his constructive proposal James Cone turns first to two white European male theologians and philosophers of the past generations, namely Rudolf Bultmann (known for his "demythologization" program of the New Testament texts—that is, while historically not true and therefore in need of being purified from the mythical content such as miracles, the biblical texts are still valuable for human existence as inspiration) and the existentialist philosopher Martin Heidegger. Reflecting the basic orientation of feminists and many other liberationists, Cone endorses this radically revised orientation to eschatology in which, "apocalyptic speculations on non-earth reality" are carved out and in which "eschatology . . . must focus on human beings as they exist in their existential situation, in which the meaning of history is located in the present moment of decision." True, the black theologian notes, even such this-worldly, "non-eschatological" eschatology (as I call it here) still lacks a liberative impulse, but it can be streamlined into it.[11]

Happily, though, this is not all that Cone recommends. He notes that in the absence of an anticipation of a future, the poor, the oppressed, and the marginalized have little for which to hope. Therefore, he also turns to Moltmann's theology of hope, which focuses on the empowering hope of Christ's resurrection. While holding tightly to the need to work towards

9. All citations in this paragraph so far are from Cone, *Black Theology*, 136.

10. Cone, *Black Theology*, 134.

11. Cone, *Black Theology*, 137–38.

rectifying current socio-political issues, the Bultmannian this-worldly approach is put in a dynamic and corrective relationship with what I consider a rightly conceived future hope: hope in which "heaven" is no longer an excuse for the oppressed to resign under the force of the oppressed, waiting for the reward in the thereafter. Cone concludes:

> Without a meaningful analysis of the future, all is despair. . . . If we really believe that death is not the last word, then we can fight, risking death for human freedom, knowing that the ultimate destiny of humankind is in the hands of the God who has called us into being. We do not have to worry about death if we know that it has been conquered and that as an enemy it has no efficacy. Christ's death and resurrection have set us free.[12]

Although it is still somewhat unclear to me what exactly the content of Cone's ultimate eschatological consummation may imply and particularly in what ways the consummation might effect the wider communal and cosmic dimensions, no doubt his refusal to let a this-worldly orientation take over his theology is pointing in the right direction.

Now to a constructive, liberative eschatology that has the potential to inspire and empower work for equality, justice, and human flourishing at both the personal and the communal levels.

Eschatological hope as the catalyst for liberation and reconciliation

The kingdom of God as the paradigm for hopeful liberative work

While, again, acknowledging the tendency of some traditional theologies to have a sort of "exit-mentality"—that is, a tendency to use hope for the future as an excuse to overlook present social concerns—this project argues that "only in the kingdom of God will human society find the consummation that is freed from all self-seeking and mutual oppression."[13] As much as human efforts towards reconciliation, justice, and equality may achieve, ultimately reconciliation of peoples and societies requires the reconciliation of the basic relationship between the individual and society. That may finally happen only at the eschaton. As the late Wolfhart Pannenberg

12. Cone, *Black Theology*, 141.
13. Pannenberg, *ST* 3:523.

108

explained: "The rule of God's righteous will means that to each of us will be given our own and that none of us can arrogate to ourselves any more. Strife regarding the amount that is specifically due to each will thus be ended, and with it the suffering caused by the feeling that others and the social 'system' have unjustly deprived us."[14] To expect this kind of final reconciliation to take place in this world is to fall into the trap of unrealistic dreams.

Another way of arguing for the importance of the eschatological coming of the kingdom as the ultimate victory of justice for all men and women, past and present, is to remind us of the inevitable limitations of merely this-worldly ideologies. Just think of atheist Marxism-Leninism, whose utopian vision of the equality of all did not come even close to materializing itself. Not only that, even if it were ever to happen by earthly means, equality would only relate to that particular generation, not to the countless generations that have passed away. This kind of fulfillment can never compete with the Christian vision in which *all* men and women, having been created into the image of God, may expect a just and gracious balancing of the scales. Hence, the need for a future orientation of eschatological hopes. Only by connecting the fulfillment of human society's destiny of equality, peace, and reconciliation with the coming of God's righteous kingdom can the "reconciliation of the individual and society in the concept of fulfillment of human destiny" happen.[15]

The conviction that this ultimate reconciliation can only happen in the new creation brought about by the Triune God does not have to lead the church into passivity, let alone apathy. On the contrary, this conviction empowers, directs, and guides all good efforts. Having been drawn graciously into the coming of God's kingdom, God's fair and loving rule, the church already in this life is aligning itself with kingdom values. The Christian community is joining the work for liberation and justice precisely because it knows that in so doing it participates in the work of the Trinitarian God. The Brazilian Roman Catholic liberationist Leonardo Boff put it well: "The historical process anticipates and paves the way for definitive liberation in the kingdom. Thus human forms of liberation acquire a sacramental function: They have a weight of their own, but they also point toward, and embody in anticipation, what God has definitively prepared for human beings."[16]

14. Pannenberg, *ST* 3:584.

15. Pannenberg, *ST* 3:585–86 (585).

16. Boff, *Liberating Grace*, 152. Here, I am indebted to Schwarz, *Eschatology*, 156.

Deeply involved in this liberative work, the church also acknowledges the fact that without the hope for the final eschatological consummation brought about by the Triune God, "human efforts are at best patchwork, bandages on the wounds of a hurting world."[17] Consider here the parallel with the healings and exorcisms the Lord Jesus performed during his earthly ministry. As important as these cures and deliverances were for the people in need, it was also the case that none of them produced a lasting solution. Soon, the healed person would catch another disease and the delivered person would become trapped in a new form of slavery. Only with the reference to the future, to the ultimate solution, could hope for the defeat of the powers of sickness, evil, and decay be sustained. Let me say it again: rather than fostering passivity and apathy, Christian hope for God's future inspires commitment to liberation.

While it has been established that liberation in the present age and the coming of God's kingdom belong together integrally, it is also essential for us to understand that in so doing they should not be subsumed under each other, otherwise theological reductionism follows. This is wisely diagnosed by another South American liberationist, the late Argentinean Methodist José Míguez Bonino: "When the cause of Jesus Christ . . . is totally and without rest equated with the cause of social and political revolution, either the Church and Jesus Christ are made redundant or the political and social revolution is clothed in a sacred or semi-sacred gown."[18] To limit the scope and goal of God's eschatological consummation to merely immanent, this-worldly fulfilment is to limit the scope and potential of the divine promise for making all things new. Commensurately: to neglect the work for human persons' this-worldly needs with the reference to the "sweet by and by" means violating the Golden Rule and Christian love.

Consider carefully the balanced instruction from the Roman Catholic document titled "Eschatological Hope and the Commitment for Temporal Liberation" by the Sacred Congregation for the Doctrine of the Faith in its *Instruction on Christian Freedom and Liberation* (1986). While the document advises the faithful to make a careful distinction between the eschatological consummation and work for the betterment of this world, or, as it put it, "between earthly progress and the growth of the kingdom," it also hastened to remind us that the eschatological "hope does not weaken

17. Schwarz, *Eschatology*, 371.

18. Míguez Bonino, *Doing Theology*, 163. For this I am indebted to Ross, "Christian Mission," 89.

commitment to the progress of the earthly city, but rather gives it meaning and strength . . . for man's vocation to eternal life does not suppress but confirms his task of using the energies and means which he has received from the Creator for developing his temporal life."[19]

A radical balance should be sought between two extremes, which can be expressed in the following slogans: "Why invest on the earth when only heaven counts?" and "Why do we need heaven when only earthly matters count?"[20] A solid liberative eschatology "allows the Christian to bring both hope and realism to engagement with contemporary social challenges. An ultimate eschatological horizon that inspires and provokes engagement with current challenges is combined with recognition that whatever is achieved will be partial, provisional, and penultimate."[21]

While human work and efforts to improve the world have their intrinsic value, theology's task is also to issue a self-critical note to the effect that "all human activity, constantly imperiled by man's pride and deranged self-love, must be purified and perfected by the power of Christ's cross and resurrection."[22] Only in the eschaton does liberating eschatology achieve its ultimate goal.

Having established the necessary connection between an anticipation of the coming consummation of God's promised kingdom and the need for a continuing work for the improvement of living conditions in this world, particularly with regard to those who are the weakest among us, it is useful to wrap up this chapter by widening the horizons of what might be a truly holistic and comprehensive vision of Christian liberation, flourishing of life, and *shalom*.

The most comprehensive framework of liberation and flourishing

One of the terminological candidates for signifying a most holistic and comprehensive framework of Christian vision of liberation is "reconciliation." Although this theologically pregnant term can also be used in more technical sense, denoting an aspect of Christ's atoning work or relating to

19. Sacred Congregation for the Doctrine of the Faith. Ratzinger, "*Instruction,*" #60.

20. Boff, *Was kommt nachher?* 26–28 (I have translated freely from the German those phrases that appear as subheadings).

21. Ross, "Christian Mission," 91.

22. Paul VI. *Gaudium et Spes.*

the mending of relations between humanity and the Triune God or between human persons, in current mission theology it has also taken on
an all-embracing and broader meaning. The term that comes closest to it
when used in this manner is the Hebrew term *shalom*, widely used in the
Old Testament to mean well-being, peace, fulfilment, and consummation
in every respect. Similarly, reconciliation is the work of the Triune God,
which brings fulfillment to God's eternal purposes of creation and salvation
through Jesus Christ (Col. 1:19–20; 2:9).[23]

Originally "reconciliation" was a secular concept, one used in antiq-
uity, particularly in international diplomacy, and subsequently adopted by
Christians as a theological theme grounded in Christ. Hence, to the Christian vision of reconciliation also belongs the church's missional mandate in
working toward peace and easing conflicts.

Reconciliation encompasses "spiritual" and sociopolitical aspects at
the personal, communal, and global levels. It speaks of the multidimen-
sional nature of salvation, encompassing inclusivity, equality, and peace. At
its core, reconciliation is about restoring broken relationships and effecting
a new-covenant-based relationship of mutual love and commitment.

Another way of expressing the widest possible vision of salvation—
what the late seminal South African missiologist David Bosch called
"comprehensive salvation"[24]—is to speak of creation as the first salvific act,
of political liberation as "self-creation of man," and of "salvation . . . [as]
re-creation and complete fulfillment."[25] This does not mean, the Peruvian
liberationist Gutiérrez reminds us, making the church serve a short-term
worldly cause of good will. Rather, it means linking God's work in history
with the redemption and renewal brought about by the coming of the new
creation.[26]

Ultimately, in its broadest and most comprehensive sense, *missio Dei*
(God's mission) extends to the whole of creation, or, as *Together towards
Life* from the WCC's Commission on World Mission and Evangelism, put
it:

> God did not send the Son for the salvation of humanity alone or
> give us a partial salvation. Rather the gospel is the good news for
> every part of creation and every aspect of our life and society. It is

23. Langmead, "Transformed Relationships," 6.

24. Bosch, *Transforming Mission*, 399–400.

25. Gutiérrez, *Theology of Liberation*, 153–60.

26. Gutiérrez, *Theology of Liberation*, 160–68.

therefore vital to recognize God's mission in a cosmic sense and to affirm all life, the whole *oikoumene*, as being interconnected in God's web of life.[27]

(#4) What about the Islamic vision of justice and the End?

Not unlike other Abrahamic faiths, the importance of justice and fairness, similar to the need for the follower of Islam to pursue them, is based on God's nature. A well-known Qur'anic passage reminds us that "Surely God shall not wrong so much as the weight of an atom; and if it be a good deed, He will double it and give from Himself a great wage" (4:40). Because Allah is the source and origin of justice, the same principle is also infused into the creation itself. To live in keeping with that principle of justice (often named "balance" in English renderings) pushes the Muslims to replicate it in daily life (55:7–9):

> And He has raised the heaven and set up the balance,
> [declaring] that you should not contravene with regard to the balance.
> And observe the weights with justice and do not skimp the balance.

Anyone even casually familiar with the Jewish Torah recognizes something familiar here.[28] In the following long citation, Nazir Khan summarizes the many implications of these foundational Qur'anic principles regarding justice, equality, and fairness:

> One's relationship with God must manifest in the way one deals with others, and thus there is tremendous emphasis on upholding the rights of all creation—from one's family, to one's neighbors, to all human beings, to animals and the environment . . . A verse of the Qur'an cited routinely at the end of the Friday sermon states, "Verily God commands justice, excellent conduct, and caring for one's relatives, and He forbids all forms of immorality, evil and transgression. He admonishes you so that you may take heed" (Qur'an, 16:90). The Qur'an admonishes human beings to always arbitrate every matter with justice (Qur'an, 4:58), and to remove every bias in upholding justice even if it requires taking a stance against one's own interests: "O you who believe, be persistently standing firm in justice, as witnesses before God, even if it be

---

27. World Council of Churches, "*Together towards Life.*"

28. Useful current works discussing the topic of justice and related issues in Islam include Kamali, *Freedom, Equality and Justice*; Rahemtulla, *Qur'an of the Oppressed.*

against yourselves or your parents and relatives" (Qur'an, 4:135).
So important is the notion of impartiality to justice that the Qur'an
advises, "Let not the hatred of others towards you prevent you
from being just. Be just, that is closer to piety" (Qur'an 5:8).[29]

All Abrahamic traditions affirm the inviolable dignity of the human
person because of having been created by God.[30] They all endorse the
equality of both sexes and all races. As a result, all men and women share
the same divine destiny. That they have not always followed these theological principles is no reason to undermine them.

Islam teaches: "And of His signs is the creation of the heavens and the
earth and the differences of your tongues and your colours. Surely in that
there are signs for all peoples" (30:22).[31] The technical term "sign" is a way
to speak of nature as a whole and of human nature as something signifying
God, the Creator.

When it comes to gender, the picture is more complicated, notwithstanding the general Abrahamic faith's conviction mentioned above.
Women are supposed to be equal to men and, like men, it is their faith and
character (rather than sex) that matters. But on the basis of some Qur'anic[32]
and later teachings, there is also a justification to be found in Islam for
enforcing the submission of women. The matter of how to negotiate that
dilemma—one not unknown to other Abrahamic faiths—is best left to
Muslim theologians.

29. Khan et al., "Divine Duty." This entire collection published by the Yaqeen Institute for Islamic Research (Irving, TX) is an excellent resource for contemporary scholarly
discussion of themes related to justice by leading Islam experts (https://yaqeeninstitute.
org/collections/justice-in-islam/).

30. Kamali, Dignity of Man.

31. Oftentimes, 49:13 is also taken as a paradigm of equality: "O mankind! We have
indeed created you from a male and a female, and made you nations and tribes that you
may come to know one another. Truly the noblest of you in the sight of God is the most
God-fearing among you. Truly God is Knower, Aware."

32. 2:223: "Your women are a tillage for you; so come to your tillage as you wish; and
offer for your souls; and fear God; and know that you shall meet Him; and give good tid-
ings to the believers." 2:228: "Divorced women shall wait by themselves for three periods.
And it is not lawful for them to hide what God has created in their wombs if they believe
in God and the Last Day. Their mates have a better right to restore them in such time if
they desire to set things right; women shall have rights similar to those due from them,
with justice; but their men have a degree above them; God is Mighty, Wise."

A huge problem for Islam, similarly to Judaism[33] and Christianity, is the relation to war, particularly "holy war." As is well known, it is not only the definition of holy war, as important as it is, but also the meaning of the widely used term *jihad* that continues to divide the opinions of Muslims, whether in reference to "the greater jihad," a personal struggle to overcome temptations, or to a "lesser jihad," a call to a holy war. True, the Qur'an contains unambiguous rules for holy war: spiritual guidance should be pursued from Allah and going to war should be only the very last resort and the leaders should be spiritual leaders, not only or primarily military ones. It is also widely taught that the enemies should be given an opportunity to accept Islam first or at least be willing to give alms (an option reserved for those belonging to sister Abrahamic faiths).[34] Furthermore, there is growing number of contemporary reformists who, like Christians and Jews, are speaking for nonviolence. Importantly, there are also significant Muslim leaders, including religious leaders, who believe that a peaceful democratic model of society likewise fits with the principles of Islam.[35]

Similar to what was concluded at the end of the previous chapter dealing with the relationship between eschatology and environment, it is fair to state that Islam has a solid scriptural and theological foundation for pursuing justice, equality, and fairness. But as to how that would work out in relation to the intense eschatological expectation of the sudden divine intervention, I have found little information.

Having now discussed a number of issues relevant to eschatology, from sciences' conjectures of the End, to Islam's eschatological vision, to apocalypticism in these two sister faiths, to the issues of environment and justice in an eschatological perspective, the rest of the book focuses on two large clusters of topics at the heart of traditional doctrines of the last things. These include, first, death, judgment, resurrection, and the 'intermediate state,' and second, religious ends for the both the blessed and the condemned ones.

33. See Dobkowski, "'Time for War.'"
34. Troll et al., *We Have Justice.*
35. Sachedina, *Islamic Roots.*

CHAPTER 8

What happens to us after death?

Death as the "final enemy"

The ambivalence towards death in our current culture

DIFFERENTLY FROM OUR CURRENT times when death is pushed to the margins, in ancient times people lived with the feeling of an impending closure to physical life—with a hope for future blessedness mixed with fear and anxiety. You may have heard the ancient saying *memento mori*, meaning "Remember you will die" (literally "remember to die"), hence, a call to be mindful of the end of your life. It was typical particularly for monks to remind themselves of their mortality on a daily basis. And it is a common tradition to believe that this reminder was whispered into the ear of a ruler or war hero returning home to a cheering crowd. But as I said at the outset, things have changed in our times. As the Eastern Orthodox thinker David Hart Bentley observes with regard to the above-mentioned injunction:

> This is not, one would think, something we generally need to be told; at least, as a purely practical counsel, it would seem to lack any genuine urgency, given that most of us really have very little say on the matter, and all of us will certainly prove equal to the task when the occasion presents itself. And yet, in point of fact, though we may be unique among animals in our awareness of our own mortality and in our ability to anticipate and reflect upon our own deaths, to die is something we do need, in some sense, to be reminded to do—and not merely because our deaths belong to the future (which is notoriously difficult to remember), nor

116

merely because in moments of great elation we are liable (like the general at his triumph) to forget that all glory is fleeting, that all joy is transient, and that Fortune's wheel never ceases turning. We cannot easily remember to die because death runs contrary to the whole orientation of human consciousness. And this is true even for those far advanced in years, for whom the prospect of death is no longer something distant and fantastic.[1]

Not surprisingly, indicative of the ambivalence towards death particularly in the modern cultures of the Global North—differently from many locations in Africa, Asia, and Latin America, including notably Muslim mainlands there and beyond—the book by the anthropologist and philosopher Ernst Becker, *The Denial of Death*, became a best-seller. Even though one of the chapters in the book is titled "The Terror of Death" (2), it argues that modern men and women seek to ignore it, and that even the most hopeful constantly think of ways to overcome it.[2]

Be that as it may, it is ironic that, on the one hand, the human species is the only one capable of anticipating death. "An animal dies a less 'deathly' death than we do."[3] (For the pet owners: Sure, a dog or a cat may get scared immediately prior to being killed, for example in the veterinary's office, but as far as we know, no animal has the capacity for self-transcendence, that is, to "step outside" one's own immediate situation and reflect on one's mortality; even for the pets, the fear is an instant instinctual reaction.) On the other hand, this same human species, endowed with the capacity to consider the phenomenon, its meaning, and its implications to one's life of mortality, typically refuses to acknowledge it, or—as most of us do currently—basically seeks to avoid it altogether. Even with the dramatic extension of human life-span, particularly in "developed" countries, the topic of death is kept out of the purview of public discourse and everyday conservations.

Why death?

That said, interest in the phenomenon of death has not escaped contemporary culture. A great deal of academic research is being conducted to gain a

---

1. Hart, "Death, Final Judgment," 476.
2. Becker, *Denial of Death*.
3. Rahner, *Foundations of Christian Faith*, 439.

better understanding of what happens in the processes of death. Indeed, a whole new field of study called thanatology has emerged.[4]

> Thanatology is the study of dying, death, and grief. This study encompasses thoughts, feelings, attitudes, and events. Contributors to the growing knowledge of death-related phenomena include social, behavioral, and biomedical researchers as well as economists, health-care providers, historians, literary critics, philosophers, and theologians.[5]

The keen scientific interest in issues related to thanatology is accentuated with the long-term debates about what constitutes death.[6] According to the 1981 US Uniform Determination of Death Act, death is defined in terms of "either (1) irreversible cessation of circulatory and respiratory functions, or (2) irreversible cessation of all functions of the entire brain, including the brain stem" (§1).[7]

Although debates about what exactly constitutes the death of the human person (and also that of other species) continues among scholars, at the general scientific level there is no uncertainty about the necessity in all species of coming to the end of the lifespan. If not for other reasons, then as long as the resources of the cosmos are limited, its consumption and hence population also has to be limited. In other words, it cannot increase *ad finitum*. More than that: in the kind of world in which we live, death is not only inevitable but also, and, ironically, *desirable* from the evolutionary-ecological point of view. Why so? Because not only the continuation but also the development of the life of species requires the coming to an end of the current ones. Generations have to follow each other.

Be that as it may, an essential related question has to do with this seemingly simple question: is death, then, "natural" for the human being? This is a difficult question to answer. I side with Bentley Hart that "[s]imply said, death can never be wholly and unequivocally 'natural' for us, precisely

---

4. For basic issues and methods, see Meager and Balk, *Handbook of Thanatology*. For the Association for Death Education and Counseling of the Thanatology Association, see https://www.adec.org/. A current academic journal is *Advances in Thanatology*, published by the Foundation of Thanatology, Center for Thanatology Research and Education. Degree programs and certificates in thanatology have been established in some institutions, such as Marian University (Wisconsin): http://www.marianuniversity.edu.

5. Advameg, Inc. *Encyclopedia of Death and Dying*.

6. Sumegi, *Understanding Death*, 9–14.

7. The National Conference of Commissions on Uniform State Laws, "*Uniform Determinations*."

because we are conscious of it; hence—quite unnaturally—it has a meaning for us, even if we think that meaning to be no more than the end of all meaning." The reason why death seems so "unnatural," as inevitable as it may be, is this:

> The horizon of human awareness is one of indeterminate futurity, an openness that aims *naturally* beyond nature; we have projects, plans, expectations, ambitions, ideas that cannot be contained within the close confines of the present. . . . To be human is to possess—consciously, that is—a future and to be able to turn one's will and imagination toward it. Death, therefore, must always come as an interruption for us, a guest anticipated but never properly prepared for and always arriving out of season.[8]

Towards a theology of death

Alongside scientific and cultural viewpoints, there is also the question of the role and meaning of religion-at-large with regard to death and hope for an afterlife. On the one hand, it is understandable that hope for life after death is deeply embedded in human evolution, as evinced in the custom of burials going back at least to the (Middle) Paleolithic age (300,000 to 50,000 years ago).[9] On the other hand, some scholars argue that

> Strange as it may seem, the textual, historical, and archaeological evidence clearly shows that the religious impulse in human society has no clear connection at all with hope in an afterlife. Systems of faith vary, of course, from culture to culture and from land to land; but, when we examine the beliefs of early civilizations anywhere in the world, we find that only a small minority of them had any concrete notion of a meaningful life beyond this life, and practically none imagined that—if there were such a life, in any meaningful sense—it was open to any but a very special few.[10]

At the moment, I am not quite sure how to resolve these two obviously different kinds of assessments of religion's role with regard to death and particularly with regard to the hope for life thereafter. So for now I tentatively venture this much: from a theological perspective, it seems obvious

8. Hart, "Death, Final Judgment," 477.
9. Lieberman, *Uniquely Human*, 162–63.
10. Hart, "Death, Final Judgment," 478.

that a key function of religion is to provide hope for life beyond this current life. There are virtually no known religious traditions in the world without "eschatological" visions and conjectures.

This takes me to theological reflection on death and the hope for an afterlife. At first it might strike some readers as odd to hear me complain about the lack of a theology of death, that is, a careful biblical-theological reflection on the nature, meaning, and implications of death. When compared to many other topics such as sacraments, liturgy, sin, salvation, and, say, Trinity, much more theology has been written. But why does it matter? Because unless we know how to die, we are probably not well-equipped to navigate the complexities of life. "A major aspect of any theology of death, then, is that it must also be a theology of life."[11] With that in mind, let me attempt a brief outline of a theology of death.

From a theological perspective, this truth is uncontested: only God who is infinite has no limits such as the limits of a finite life-span. All finite beings, that is, *creatures*, owe their life to the Creator. Hence, unlike the "uncreated" Creator, they do not have the resources to sustain their lives forever. Even in the new creation, in heaven, life eternal donated to the believers is just that—a *donated* life, a gift. Even there the mortal creature does not (technically speaking) become inherently immortal—although, by God's grace and continuing provision of life-energy the creature may never taste death again.

To acknowledge the finite nature of creaturely life is not yet to pass judgment as to the nature of death. Theologically speaking, it can be either "neutral" or negative vs. positive. John Hick surmised that among the earliest Christians physical death was not necessarily considered a tragedy because of "so vivid a sense of the reality and love of God, and of Christ as having overcome death." Only with the consolidation of a Pauline theological outlook, as established authoritatively by Augustine much later, did death come to be seen as an enemy and a punishment for sin.[12] Be that as it may, there is no denying that throughout the centuries, at least until the time of modernity, even physical death has been attributed to original sin and the fall, and therefore it has been conceived as something negative and tragic. With the rise of evolutionary theory, as explained above, physical

---

11. Davies, *Theology of Death*, 15.
12. Hick, *Death and Eternal Life*, 207.

death came to be linked with the "natural" corruptibility of all creaturely life. Hence, in that perspective physical death is a "natural" event.[13]

In other words, there is no denying that death is "natural" in the sense that all individuals of all species must die to make room for the next generation. Hence, we have to reconsider the ancient and widely held view among Christians, even to our current times, that had there not been the fall, humanity would have never tasted death.

Is this myth of "everlasting life" in pristine paradise really taught in the Scripture? And is it a defining Christian doctrine? First of all, notwithstanding exegetical disputes concerning the earliest chapters in Genesis— narratives cast in a poetic-mythic genre—the plain reading of Genesis 3 tells us that the failure of the first human couple to obey God's command can hardly be taken as the reason for physical death. Adam and Eve disobeyed and they were not hit with physical death but rather were expelled from the Garden, from the intimate closeness to the Creator. In order to negotiate this dilemma, modern theology rightly made a distinction between (at least) two kinds of deaths, namely "natural" (physical) death due to the creaturely nature of finite life and the death of "judgment" that manifests intensification of the personal feeling toward death in light of the possibility of being cut off from the life of God.[14]

All that said, the idea of death as "natural"—while true—has to be handled with care and qualified theologically. As inevitable as death might be for the finite human person, it is also against the nature of human beings, endowed as we are with the drive to continue and support life. No wonder biblical testimonies do not beautify death, nor speak of it in positive terms. Indeed, as Paul put it, death, while inevitable, is seen as an "enemy" (1 Cor 15:26). This is in keeping with the Old Testament view of death as a separation from God (Ps 88:5). The human person fears and shuns death. The Catholic catechism puts this seemingly paradoxical statement in perspective: "Even though man's nature is mortal[,] God had destined him not to die."[15]

Christian faith has to live in this dynamic tension between the willingness to acknowledge the inevitable coming to an end of finite creaturely life, on the one hand, and on the other hand the hope for final overcoming of death and corruption in the eschaton as a result of which life eternal, as

---

13. See further, Kärkkäinen, *Creation and Humanity*, ch. 15.

14. See further, Kärkkäinen, *Creation and Humanity*, ch. 15.

15. Libreria Editrice Vaticana, "*Catechism*."

a gift from the Eternal God, can be hoped for. In Christian eschatological vision, death, as the last enemy, will be destroyed. Life everlasting will be the last word.

Death for the Christian can therefore be regarded as both "finality and transition."[16] On the one hand, physical death is a final closure. Life for each deceased is over. On the other hand, that is not yet the whole story. Moltmann puts it succinctly: "God's relationship to people is a dimension of their existence which they do not lose even in death."[17] He reminds us of the important statement of Luther's: "Accordingly, where and with whomever God speaks, whether in anger or in grace, that person is surely immortal. The Person of God, who speaks, and the Word point out that we are the kind of creatures with whom God would want to speak eternally and in an immortal manner."[18] In other words, even death cannot separate the human person created in the image of his or her Creator and the possibility of life eternal in communion with God. God meets us "on the other side" and we are reminded of that fact: "Just as . . . [a human being] cannot bring forth being of himself, so neither can he hurl it back into sheer nothingness."[19]

This takes us on to the complicated issue of what happens "after" physical death and "before" the final consummation culminating in the resurrection of all.

Is there an "intermediate" state between death and final consummation?

Why should we intuit an "intermediate" state?

It is possible to conceive the "transition" from this life to life to come in more than one way when it comes to the question of whether there is a "gap" between physical death and the final consummation, physical resurrection, and new creation. But before we get to that, why in the first place, intuit any kind of "intermediate state"? The biggest theological reason, addressed in the introduction to this book, has to do with the careful negotiation between the personal and communal/cosmic consummation: each human person's final fulfillment is contingent on the emergence of the new

16. Schwarz, *Eschatology*, 296.

17. Moltmann, *Coming of God*, 76.

18. Luther, *Lectures on Genesis*. 76.

19. Ratzinger, *Eschatology*, 156; cited in Schwarz, *Eschatology*, 277.

heaven and new earth in which resurrected bodily life is possible. On the other hand, communal consummation is nothing but the sum of the consummation of all persons. If God is the Creator of the whole cosmos, as Christian faith confesses, then only with the redemption and renewal of the whole cosmos can the promise of "making things new" be evinced.

That said, contemporary theology has rightly been reserved about talking about the intermediate state, at times to the point of virtually dismissing it. Why? Because of the scarcity of biblical allusions, let alone teaching on the topic. Similarly, there is very little solid teaching and discussion of the topic in Christian historical traditions. For example, there is not even a hint of the intermediate state in the creeds. Even if that is due to the lack of debates, that fact alone suggests its marginal role in evolving Christian thinking. The Genevan Reformer John Calvin therefore appropriately adds this word of caution:

> Moreover, to pry curiously into their intermediate state is neither lawful nor expedient (see Calv. Psychopannychia). Many greatly torment themselves with discussing what place they occupy, and whether or not they already enjoy celestial glory. It is foolish and rash to inquire into hidden things, farther than God permits us to know. Scripture, after telling that Christ is present with them, and receives them into paradise (John 12:32), and that they are comforted, while the souls of the reprobate suffer the torments which they have merited goes no farther.[20]

That said, with all the reservations, it seems as if there is no legitimate reason to undermine, let alone deny unduly, the idea of the intermediate state. Paul J. Griffiths puts it well:

> This [intermediate state] is an almost universal idea among Christians because it is so widely believed that there will be a last judgment involving the return of Jesus Christ to earth, the bodily resurrection of all the dead, and the final and decisive separation of the righteous from the unrighteous, the members of each then going to their appropriate final destiny. If this idea is coupled with the obvious fact that this return, final judgment, and general resurrection have not yet happened, then the thought that there is an intermediate state for those who die before the last judgment is inevitable.[21]

---

20. Calvin, *Institutes*, 3.25.6.
21. Griffiths, "Purgatory," 431.

At the same time, Griffiths also reminds us of what was mentioned above, namely that "[i]maginations of this intermediate state . . . have been enormously varied in their details."[22]

Varied visions of the "in-between"

The most traditional Christian vision of the intermediate state, founded on the classical body-soul dualism (a theological anthropological intuition according to which the human person is composed of two "substances," namely the physical/material and the mental/spiritual), takes it for granted that following the moment of physical death the soul continues its existence until judgment and resurrection while the body decays in the grave. In traditional language, those on the way to final blessedness wait in the "bosom of Abraham," paradise (Luke 16:19–31; 23:43), the "waiting room" of heaven. For those on the way to perdition, the eternal place of punishment is Gehenna (Mark 9:43), and they spend their intermediate state in Hades (Acts 2:31).[23]

The theological problems—or, at least, challenges—have to do with a couple of issues to which I will return with more details below: the body-soul dualism presupposed by this view is mightily challenged and revised by more recent theological and philosophical accounts of the nature of human nature. Many question the idea of a prolonged disembodied state of existence (in which the body is separated from the soul) because the foundational Christian view of the human person, as a creature of God, is holistic and embodied, awaiting bodily resurrection in the new creation. A related problem with the traditional view has to do with the following issue: many also wonder if the soul's experiences—if there are any—during this intermediate state would make the "person" that meets God at the last judgment a different one from the one at the moment of physical death.

Traditional anthropological dualism also supports the Roman Catholic Church's official doctrine of purgatory,[24] a doctrine widely and regularly misunderstood by non-Catholics (and, unfortunately, also by some poorly-versed Catholics): "All who die in God's grace and friendship, but still

22. Griffiths, "Purgatory," 431.

23. For details of the traditional view, see Erickson, *Christian Theology*, 1183–84.

24. Reliable, up-to-date, and well-documented recent presentations include: Griffiths, "Purgatory," 427–45; Cevetello, "Purgatory," 824–29. For a solid monograph, see Fenn, *Persistence of Purgatory*.

imperfectly purified, are indeed assured of their eternal salvation; but after death they undergo purification, so as to achieve the holiness necessary to enter the joy of heaven."[25] The primary scriptural reference here is the apocryphal 2 Maccabees 12:43–45:

> He then took up a collection among all his soldiers . . . to provide for an expiatory sacrifice. In doing this he acted in a very excellent and noble way, inasmuch as he had the resurrection of the dead in view; for if he were not expecting the fallen to rise again, it would have been useless and foolish to pray for them in death. . . . But if he did this with a view to the splendid reward that awaits those who had gone to rest in godliness, it was a holy and pious thought.

Obviously this passage is open to more than one interpretation! Be that as it may, the Catholic tradition teaches that the cleansing that takes place after death is through penal suffering, as opposed to the cleansing that happens in this life by performing works of satisfaction. Since no works can be done after death, passive suffering is the only way. And because the Catholic tradition is more open to the power of prayers for the dead, it is understandable that the means by which the saints in purgatory may be assisted is by prayer, alongside the celebration of the mass and good deeds. Protestants need to be reminded that the "merits" accrued by the living on behalf of those in purgatory do not imply "salvation by works." Similarly to the Protestants, Roman Catholics teach that one is saved only by grace through faith in Christ. The merits are meant to alleviate and hopefully shorten the time of suffering in the process of cleansing. Recall that only those who are already saved may receive the benefits, not those on the way to perdition.

It is also essential for Protestants to understand, as the citation above from the Catechism mentions, that purgatory in Catholic teaching is not a "second chance." Rather, the person on the way to blessedness but in a need of cleansing will undergo sufferings. Those damned have no opportunity to change their eternal destiny in purgatory.[26]

---

25. Libreria Editrice Vaticana, "*Catechism.*" (#1030). Purgatory has been part of the traditional Catholic doctrine before it was formally ratified at the Council of Florence (1439).

26. Libreria Editrice Vaticana, "*Catechism.*" (#1031): Purgatory "is entirely different from the punishment of the damned."

Even if I, as a Protestant theologian, do not include purgatory as part of my eschatological menu, I do not have any dogmatic reasons to reject it for Catholics.[27] I think that behind the doctrine of purgatory are intimations that are well worth all Christians pondering, even if they, like myself, might not be willing to subscribe to the doctrine of purgatory itself. As I argue in the next chapter, we do not have to think of eternity—life in the new creation—as static timelessness. Rather, even in a perfect state, as Christian tradition allows us to imagine, saints may grow into a more perfect conformity. If so, why is it that this may not happen before the final consummation? It was no less a teacher than St. Paul who taught us in 1 Corinthians 3:13–15 that all believers will enter eternity through cleansing fire (comforting us that even if most, or even all, of our building is burned, we still be saved "as if through the fire"). This seems to leave the door open for progress and development. And why not? Life, the greatest gift of the Creator, is dynamic and evolving. Note what Moltmann suggests: "God's history with our lives will continue to go on after our deaths until that completion has been reached in which a soul finds rest."[28] Indeed, argues the Methodist philosopher Jerry Walls, even those who reject the doctrine of purgatory have to face the challenge of negotiating "the problem of sin and moral imperfection that remains in the lives of believers at the time of death."[29] And the noted late science and religion expert, quantum physicist, and Anglican priest John Polkinghorne adds: "We may expect that God's love will be at work, through the respectful but powerful operation of divine grace, purifying and transforming the souls awaiting resurrection in ways that respect their integrity."[30]

Alongside these two traditional views, there are also ways of negotiating the intermediate state that either makes it a null matter or a matter of "unconscious" existence. An example of the latter is an ancient theory known as "soul-sleep," which suggests that the soul waits in a state of unconsciousness until the final state. While never a dominant doctrine, it has been quite widely held by both Roman Catholic and Protestant traditions. This view has been affirmed from the time of Pope John XXII of the thirteenth century through the Wittenberg Reformer Luther and the

27. Just consider Calvin, "Psychopannia," 414–90, which clearly speaks of continuous progress before the final judgment day.

28. Moltmann, "Is There Life after Death?" 252.

29. Walls, *Heaven*, 53–62 (53).

30. Polkinghorne, *God of Hope*, 111.

Anabaptists of the sixteenth century, all the way to the Seventh Day Adventists (and the Jehovah Witnesses). The key evidence has been the numerous biblical references to "sleep" as a metaphor for death (1 Kgs 2:10; John 11:11; Acts 7:60; 1 Cor 15:6; 1 Thess 4:13–15).[31] The standard theological observation—many would say rebuttal—is that metaphors such as "sleep" are just that, namely *metaphors*, and are not meant to be taken literally. Be that as it may, whether this theory holds or not, it seems like some kind of an idea of interval between one's physical death and the consummation is needed, whether one is aware of that (as with the assumption of an existence of soul apart from the body) or not (as in this soul-sleep theory).

A total denial of the idea of any gap between my physical death and the consummation comes from some few scholars such as W. D. Davies, a Welsh New Testament scholar of the past generation.[32] In his study on Paul's indebtedness to Rabbinic Judaism (former rabbi that Paul was), Davies writes about "instantaneous resurrection," in light of 2 Corinthians 5:1–10. Other Pauline passages, particularly that in 1 Corinthians 15, the longest and most detailed one of which clearly refers to future resurrection, Davies simply pushes aside, noting that he believes that Paul changed his mind in the later writing. A more theologically sound attempt to ignore the intermediate state is the argument that death, as the boundary between time and eternity, places us in a realm in which we already experience what will be our eternal destiny.[33] The biggest question in the minds of Davies' critics is obvious: even with a critical approach to Scripture, one surely is not allowed simply to pick and choose which passages to endorse and which to ignore! And with regard to all who reject the intermediate state in one form or another, the overriding argument is that the lack of any gap seems to frustrate the universal and all-encompassing divine plan to bring to consummation to all people at the end.

How to negotiate the relationship between the personal and communal consummation

The basic reason why the question of the intermediate state is debated and complex is because the Bible does not give a coherent picture of what

31. For details, see Grenz, *Theology*, 590.

32. Davis, *Paul and Rabbinic Judaism*, 310–18.

33. This has been argued, for example, by the British scholar Stephen Travis. For his and like-minded views and documentation, see Garrett, *Systematic Theology*, 765–66.

happens after physical death. There are passages, such as Philippians 1:20–24, that seem to imply some type of continuation of personal life after death. Other passages can be read as supporting immediate entrance into blessedness at death (2 Cor 5:8; 1 Thess 5:10). The biblical data also includes a number of references to what became the "soul-sleep" view in tradition (Dan 12:2; Luke 8:52; 1 Cor 15:51; 2 Pet 3:4). Whereas "sleep" entails inactivity, some passages seem to imply conscious activity (particularly the parable in Luke 16:19–31).[34] It seems as if all of these diverse biblical testimonies and metaphors imply that as final and inevitable as physical death is, it is not the last word; rather, God is. Furthermore, they tell us that the "intermediate" state is just that, namely *intermediate*, temporary, rather than the final eternal blessedness. The final consummation is still to come.

A guiding principle for the negotiation between the personal and communal—and ultimately, even the cosmic—eschatological consummation is the continuity-in-discontinuity schema, which I will detail below with regard to the hope for resurrection. Briefly: for an eschatological hope to make sense, there has to be some kind of continuity between life and its conditions "down here" (on this earth) and the new creation "up there," or else, any talk about the embodied resurrected life hardly makes any sense. On the other hand, there has to be discontinuity enough for life in the new creation to be "more" than just prolonging the lifespan, as it were. The surplus of the life to come needs to be substantial enough to be worth looking forward to with eager expectation. Hence, the earthly "body" (that is, the whole human person) has to undergo a radical change, without losing the person's identity of which, as we understand human life, relationality and community are essential parts.[35] Hence, in line with traditional Christian intuition it seems fitting to expect some kind of gap between my physical death and consummation so that the final judgment, resurrection, and transition to new creation is a communal process. That this is said from the perspective of time-bound earthly existence—which likely is very different and limited in light of the eternity of God, which after all does not experience the sequence of time (past, present, and future)—does not necessarily make it any less true, as all theological statements are drawn from our own experience and life conditions.

A promising way, on the one hand, to acknowledge the difference between earthly time and divine eternity is to imagine that God in his

---

34. Grenz, *Theology*, 593–95.

35. For a detailed discussion, see Kärkkäinen, *Creation and Humanity*, 289–98.

eternity can be found on both sides of death. This means that whereas we time-bound humans enter eternity individually, it is only at the end that we receive the final consummation in communion with all others.

Be that as it may—namely, whether in the final analysis there is something like an "intermediate state" and, if so, what kind of existence that might be—because we are "constituted by relation to God,"[36] even death cannot separate us from God and God's love (Rom 8:38–39). Hence, the deepest meaning of what Christian theology calls an intermediate state is simply "God holding us fast until the resurrection."[37]

Speculatively, one may also intuit that provided we are kept by God during the intermediate state, then the biblically based intuition of some kind of connection between the living and the dead (Heb 12:1–2) becomes meaningful. Hence, theologically it is not only permissible but also appropriate to reserve a place, for example, for prayer for the dead. Similarly, there is no reason to exclude their prayer for us.

However the theology of death and the intermediate state are conceived, Christian tradition agrees that the belief in the resurrection of the body is hope for defeating death in the new creation. Resurrection is the focus and center of Christian hope, a topic to which we turn next.

"I believe . . . in the resurrection of the body"

The basis and condition of Christian faith: Jesus's resurrection

In no uncertain terms—in a section in the New Testament that is widely considered to represent the oldest Christian tradition, 1 Corinthians 15—the apostle Paul puts forth an argument upon which hinges both the credibility of Christian proclamation and the reality of Christian hope for afterlife (vv. 13–19):

> But if there is no resurrection of the dead, then Christ has not been raised; if Christ has not been raised, then our preaching is in vain and your faith is in vain. . . . If Christ has not been raised, your faith is futile and you are still in your sins. Then those also who have fallen asleep in Christ have perished. If for this life only we have hoped in Christ, we are of all men most to be pitied.

36. Johnson, *Friends of God*, 194.

37. Grenz, *Theology*, 597.

Paul's claim is not without challenges for its novelty among religions, including Jewish faith on the foundations of whose messianic hopes the belief in the resurrection rests. First of all, even though religions know of myths of deities and divine figures rising and dying, those are all "temporary" visits to the world of humans. No wonder the gentile audience of earliest Christian preachers found the claim to the one-time decisive resurrection of Jesus the Christ incredible (Acts 17:32). Even in the Old Testament and Judaism, the resurrection of one single person, including the Messiah, before the resurrection of all at the end is not known. In other words, early Christianity revised radically its mother religion's hopes—and made it the basis for the future resurrection of all. Furthermore, Paul and other New Testament writers' focus on the *bodily* rather than merely "spiritual" or "ideal" (as in, an idea rather than as a historical event) resurrection was found highly contested among their contemporaries.

Differently from the early centuries, by the time of the Enlightenment and its critical principle, the whole rationality of any appeal to someone rising from the dead became an almost nonsensical idea with no reasonable basis. Building on that contestation, contemporary (to us) critical scholarship finds a number of objections to the idea of Jesus's resurrection—and by implication, to his followers' resurrection, including the future generations of followers such as us. These objections can be summarized under three main groupings of rebuttals: there is no access to historical knowledge that would validate Jesus's resurrection; there is no analogy for (i.e., an event comparable to) such a resurrection; and there is no hard-core evidence.[38] How might we consider these rebuttals?

Concerning the first one, which surmises that rather than having an access to the factual historicity of Jesus's resurrection, we only have an access to his disciples' belief in it, in other words, human hopes and perhaps even hallucinations:[39] The obvious counterargument is that this view represents a typical positivistic[40] objection, according to which things such as raising people from the dead do not happen—and therefore, they are claimed to be

38. Wright, *Resurrection*, 16–20.

39. Bultmann, "New Testament and Mythology," 36–41.

40. According to logical positivism, a philosophical movement from the beginning of the twentieth century, only empirically tested claims can be taken as true and only those kinds of events can be expected to happen. (Indeed, they went further, saying that only claims that can be empirically tested have a claim to be meaningful utterances. If a claim cannot be empirically tested it is neither true nor false, but utterly devoid of propositional content.)

non-events. This objection to resurrection ignores the fact that on the basis of the New Testament authors' eye-witness reports, we may have access to the public nature of the first followers' testimonies, particularly the empty tomb whose validity contemporaries did not contest (notwithstanding a wide rejection of its alleged theological implications) and a big number of reports of first-hand witnesses regarding their personal encounter with the risen Lord (indeed, Paul even speaks of several hundreds of them, including an account of a number of well-known early followers of Jesus).[41]

Second, what about the charge that there is no analogy to resurrection (first presented by David Hume and subsequently, at the turn of the twentieth century, made a programmatic statement by Ernst Troeltsch), according to which the resurrection is a unique event, with no parallels, and hence incredible.[42] The counterargument reminds us that being a one-time event does not in itself necessarily disqualify it from being a historical event; as far as we know, the Big Bang only happened once and yet we consider it a reasonable assumption notwithstanding the lack of analogy. Jesus's resurrection by definition—if he is God-Man as Christian tradition affirms—cannot even in principle have an analogy; his resurrection was a unique world-changing event.

Third, the objection to the lack of any reliable evidence for the resurrection ignores many factors that, while hardly sufficient in themselves, may be taken as supporting the possibility of the event. Alongside the reference to the empty tomb tradition and to the testimonies of hundreds of contemporaries, is the surprising and counterintuitive rise of the Christian church—whose founder was publicly executed, a shameful event marked by disgrace. With that in mind, it is hard to understand the emergence and rapid spread of this new (originally Jewish) sect apart from a firm belief in the resurrection of Jesus Christ.

What I mean to say with this brief consideration of modern rebuttals of the claim to Jesus's resurrection is that while it is of course impossible to provide insurmountable, indubitable evidence for it, its truthfulness can be rationally defended. In other words, even though Christ's resurrection is a tenet of faith (as recounted in Christian creeds), it not merely a matter of "blind" faith, something totally apart from historical investigation and rational reasoning.

41. Brown, *Virginal Conception*, 92–124.
42. Troeltsch, "On the Historical."

Back to the foundational role of Jesus's resurrection as the basis for our own future hope. Paul taught that Jesus was "designated Son of God in power according to the Spirit of holiness by his resurrection from the dead" (Rom 1:4). Indeed, the titles denoting the divinity of Jesus Christ, such as Lord (*kyrios*) and Son of God, derived ultimately from belief in the raising from the dead and the completion of Christ's salvific work (Rom 4:25) and the eschatological bodily resurrection hope, as explained above. But not only that, as very important as it is. Beginning with the early theology of the church, and building on the gradual definition of New Testament traditions (such as Colossians and Ephesians), Christ's resurrection (and ascension) also came to be understood in cosmological terms, as the basis for the renewal of the whole world. Indeed, in several early theologies, "the resurrection was based on a strong understanding of God as Creator, and this led to a strong sense of God's purposes for this material creation and its goodness."[43] Early teachers firmly rejected opposing pagan notions, such as the deeply dualistic Gnosticism, which posited a radical separation between evil matter (the physical) and good spiritual reality. Instead, building on the implications to the whole created order of Christ's resurrection, Christian tradition came to await new heavens and new *earth*! The resurrection of Jesus Christ on the first Easter morning provided the "first fruit," an anticipation of the coming new creation, in which the power of entropy, ultimate decay and death, is overcome. The whole of the cosmos anticipates the new creation in which all of creation will participate (Rom 8:18–25). Out hope participates in, and is set within the wider context of this cosmic hope.

"How are the dead raised? What kind of body do they have?"

Having affirmed the foundational role of Christ's resurrection as the basis of our hope for eternal life, Paul raises the two-part question of the heading above (15:35). And what a question it is! No doubt it is among the "big questions" of our faith. It has engaged the best minds of Christian thinking from the beginning and its urgency is no less felt in light of the challenges of contemporary neuroscience and the philosophy of the mind.[44]

Rather than delving into sophisticated speculations, the highly learned apostle seeks to illustrate the nature and possibility of the eschatological

---

43. Wilkinson, *Christian Eschatology*, 103.

44. For starters, consult Baker, "Persons and the Metaphysics," 168–75.

hope for the resurrection of the body with reference to nature. A seed is sown, it dies and is buried, before sprouting and maturing into the kind of plant it is supposed to be. Christ and his resurrection is the "first fruit," which anticipates and guarantees the rest of the harvest.

> So is it with the resurrection of the dead. What is sown is per-
> ishable, what is raised is imperishable. It is sown in dishonor, it
> is raised in glory. It is sown in weakness, it is raised in power. It
> is sown a physical body, it is raised a spiritual body. If there is a
> physical body, there is also a spiritual body. (1 Cor 15:42–44)

What is raised up has both similarity and dissimilarity with the seed. Switching into the Adam, the first man ("from the earth") and Christ, the last man ("from heaven") analogy, Paul explains:

> The first man was from the earth, a man of dust; the second man is
> from heaven. As was the man of dust, so are those who are of the
> dust; and as is the man of heaven, so are those who are of heaven.
> Just as we have borne the image of the man of dust, we shall also
> bear the image of the man of heaven. (vv. 47–49)

The same dynamic between the sameness and difference—call it continuity *versus* discontinuity—was evident in the risen Lord and his encounter with the first eye-witnesses. On the one hand, due to his "new-ness"—and in defeating the expectations of the disappointed followers—the disciples did not recognize the Risen One on the way to Emmaus. On the other hand, after the breaking of bread, their eyes were opened and they saw who Jesus was (Luke 24:31). Or think of the narrative in the last chapter of John's Gospel. On the one hand, the risen Christ seemed not to be hindered by the closed doors (at least as the face value reading of the text clearly implies) when he joined the scared disciples in hiding. On the one hand, totally against what is characteristic of "ghosts," he later showed doubting Thomas his wounds. And later still in the same chapter (John 21), he eats fish—he, the one who already in his earthly ministry had promised to have the kind of food and drink that satisfies the insatiable hunger and thirst of those who believe!

As mentioned, this problem of continuity *versus* discontinuity be-tween this life and the hoped-for bodily resurrection was not unfamiliar to the earliest theologians. Even if their incisive solution may not satisfy us, the formulation of the issue and the attempts to resolve it are well worth acknowledging. One such well-known effort in patristic theology goes something like the following: after the body decays at death, God on the last day will reassemble it from the last constitutive material particles available and rejoin it with the soul that did not die. The fathers were aware of obvious problems, such as death by cannibalism or at sea when there was no trace of the deceased person's material body available, and they sought creative solutions to such problems, the details of which do not have to concern us here.

A more sophisticated way to negotiate the issue comes from the Angelic Doctor Thomas Aquinas, the zenith of medieval philosophical-theological brilliance. Significantly modifying the body-soul dualism (although not totally abandoning it), he devised an account of the nature of human nature, an account typically named "hylomorphism." Thomas followed the philosopher Aristotle's conception of the soul as the "form" (or actuality) of the body in which rather than a separate entity, soul is more like a life principle, "that aspect of the person which provides the powers or attributes characteristic of the human being."[45] In this developed view, the soul functions somewhat similar to the architect's plan or drawings for a building: although no house can be built without a plan, nor would it do to think of the plan alone as something "separate" from the building. Only when the 'form'—in this case, the pattern in which building materials and various elements of construction—is put in place, does what we call a building emerge. This hylomorphic intuition is not plagued by the more concrete "compositional" accounts of the human nature characteristic of most fathers. It points to something similar to what the current scientific account means when speaking of "information" (DNA) and energy in the emergence of human nature with its many complex functions.

In contemporary theology, notwithstanding the continuing influence of body-soul dualism, particularly among more traditional and conservative Christians, a turn to a holistic account of the nature of human nature, including a rediscovery of the centrality of a human's bodily aspects, has taken place. This has everything to do with how we conceive of death and resurrection. Among contemporary theologians, no one has provided as nuanced a theology of death as the late Roman Catholic theologian Karl Rahner. Rather than the traditional (Catholic) idea of death being the separation of the soul from the body, he considers "death as an event concerning

---

45. Murphy, *Bodies and Souls*, 13; see Murphy's lucid exposition for details and original sources.

Death and resurrection in Islam[58]

Life under the shadow of death

As briefly mentioned in chapter 4, life on this earth for the Muslim is but preparation for eternity, at the core of which is obedience and a desire to please Allah. Indeed, it is the life to come that is "real"—or: more real—than the short lifespan on earth, as the Holy Scripture teaches: "And the life of this world is nothing but diversion and play. But surely the Abode of the Hereafter is indeed the [true] Life, if they only knew" (29:64). Whereas life on earth is only temporary, the afterlife lasts forever: "Nay, but you prefer the life of this world, whereas the Hereafter is better and more lasting" (87:16–17). Hence, death should be properly kept in mind (23:15).

> Every soul shall taste of death; you shall surely be paid in full your wages on the Day of Resurrection. Whoever is moved away from the Fire and admitted to Paradise, will have triumphed, the life of this world is but the comfort of delusion. (3:185)[59]

As a result, the awareness of the coming to an end of life, to be followed by judgment and the final destiny, hangs over the faithful's life.

> The knowledge of a future life beyond death, the quality of which will be determined by the moral quality of one's life on earth, has served to instill in Muslims a constant awareness of both the precarious nature of this existence and the urgent need to prepare for that future one. . . . The Qur'anic idea of continued existence and eternal life in the hereafter functions not only as a consolation for believers, in view of the tribulations inherent in life on earth, it is also intended as an incentive for humankind to believe, to perform good deeds, and to reap the reward.[60]

Or, to put it another way: "An indication of the centrality of the afterlife within the overall Qur'anic narrative is that almost every act forbidden or condemned by the Qur'ān, as well as every deed commended and encouraged by it, is done . . . with a view to the consequences of that action or behavior for a person's fate in the next life."[61]

---

58. See Kärkkäinen, *Community and Hope*, 52–64.
59. Afsaruddin, "Death, Resurrection, and Human Destiny," 43–44.
60. Hamza, "Afterlife," 1:159–60.
61. Hamza, "Afterlife," 1:160.

Similarly to older Abrahamic traditions, death is inevitable: "Every soul shall taste death. Then to Us you shall be returned" (29:57). To every person has been determined his or her life-span "term" (6:2).[62] This life is single and unique, and there is no way to return to earthly life after death.

Although the Qur'an unequivocally affirms the reality of death, it provides precious few details about what happens at and after death. Suffice it here to summarize the main Qur'anic points:

> [I]n S[ura] 56:82 we are told that the soul of the dying person comes up to his throat, and in S 6:93 death is described as a kind of flooding-in process [*ghamarāt al-maut*] at which time angels stretch forth their hands and ask that the souls be given over to them. Exactly what happens after that the Qur'an does not say, although the traditions describe the succeeding events elaborately. Again, the only clue in the Qur'an as to whether or not the dead have any degree of consciousness is the indication in S 35:22 that the living and the dead are not alike, and that while God can accord hearing to whomever He wills, the living cannot make those in the graves hear them.[63]

It is left to later traditions to develop fairly detailed accounts that, similarly to Christian tradition, are subject to debates and concerning which denominational differences exist.[64] What Christian theology calls "soul," is represented in Islamic theology as *nafs* (soul) or *ruh* (spirit). These two terms—"soul" and "spirit"—are not clearly distinguished, and more often than not they are confused. When a distinction is made, then it is often thought that while "the rational soul [*nafs*], which directs the activities of the body, perishes at physical death . . . the life-infusing soul or spirit [*rufs*] continues and awaits the coming of the Hour."[65]

In other words, death means the separation of soul from body. Ibn Qayyim clearly supposes the conscious state of the departed soul: "when he begins to move to another world, he sees, hears, and speaks, by some means which, we, the living, do not perceive."[66] The soul can also be recognized as

---

62. Q.6:2: "It is He Who created you from clay; then He decreed a term. A term is stated with Him . . ."

63. Smith and Haddad, *Islamic Understanding*, 32.

64. See further Smith and Haddad, *Islamic Understanding*, 32–33.

65. Smith and Haddad, *Islamic Understanding*, 19–20 (20).

66. Layla, "The Soul's Journey after Death," 2.

Firm belief in resurrection

Death, as irrevocable as it is, however, does not have the last word in Islam, an affirmation shared with other Abrahamic faiths. Muslims believe in the resurrection of the body: "Then indeed after that you die. Then on the Day of Resurrection you shall surely be raised" (23:15–16). Sura 75 is titled "The Rising of the Dead." It begins with the saying that "Nay! I swear by the Day of Resurrection" and ends with the rhetorical question that the same God who created the human being in the first place (as male and female) "Is not such able to revive the dead?" (v. 40). Similarly, in response to the question "'Who will revive the bones when they are rot?'" another sura gives a firm answer: "Say: 'He will revive them Who originated them the first time, and He is Knower of all creation" (36:78–79). Many other passages teaching the resurrection can be found in the Holy Book (41:39; and so forth). In sum:

> The promise, the guarantee, of the day at which all bodies will be resurrected and all persons called to account for their deeds and the measure of their faith is the dominant message of the Qur'ān as it is presented in the context of God's *tawḥīd*. One can find testimony of this assurance on almost every page of the Qur'ān.[76]

According to the mainstream teaching, Muhammad (who is, recall, not a divine figure in Islam but rather the conduit of divine teaching) will be the first among the resurrected ones. A related important tradition teaches that major prophets follow in his footsteps. "The stress on the importance of Muḥammad's resurrection before the other believers is related not only to his recognized stature as the seal of the prophets, but also to the general understanding of his role as intercessor for his community."[77]

Debates similar to those of Jewish and Christian philosophers during history concerning the nature of the resurrection can be found among Islamic scholars. These debates were particularly vivid in medieval times. The main question had to do with this issue—not unknown in Christian tradition either: whether resurrection entails annihilation or reconstitution.

The main Qur'anic word *ma'ad* literally means "to return," but that in itself does not provide a definite hermeneutical key. The difficulty in this debate, particularly in Classic Islamic thought, has to do with varying ways of negotiating what appear to be two kinds of orientation in the Holy Qur'an. Take a look at these two defining verses:

76. Smith and Haddad, *Islamic Understanding*, 63.
77. Smith and Haddad, *Islamic Understanding*, 73.

- 28:88 "Everything will perish except His Countenance. His is the judgement and to Him you will be brought back."

- 10:4: "To Him is the return of all of you: God's promise, in truth. Truly He originates creation, then recreates it that He may requite those who believe and perform righteous deeds, justly."

As the face-value reading of the texts clearly point in different directions and to different interpretations, the two major theological schools (introduced above in chapter 4), namely the (mainline Sunni) Asharites and the Mu'tazalites, argued for different positions. What can be called an annihilationist view (meaning that before the resurrection of the body the deceased will more or less perish) was advocated by the Asharites. The Asharite position seems to point to the typical reading of the first of the two texts and philosophically is known as "occasionalism." For our purposes, it suffices to define occasionalism in the following way: occasionalism is the view that every event in the world is directly caused by God rather than by creatures. Despite how things appear, created substances, including you and me, are not the efficient cause of anything that happens. For example, you clap your hands and there is a clapping sound. You might imagine that the sound is caused by your clapping your hands together, but it is not. In reality, according to occasionalism, God directly caused you to clap your hands and directly caused the sound. And because of God's fidelity, he makes sure that the two events occur together. But, despite how it looks, the clapping hands are not the cause of the sound. Hence, creation is not eternal but totally contingent. As a result, it makes complete sense that the human being, a contingent creature, is liable to annihilation before the new creation. Furthermore—but this is a more complicated and complex issue—there was a tendency among the Asharites to downplay, and perhaps even to deny, a physical resurrection in favor of a "spiritual" one in which the "soul" and "spirit" are integrally linked. That said, some leading Asharites, including even the celebrated al-Ghazali—who, alongside Asharite tradition, also represents mystical and perhaps also other orientations—stuck with belief in the resurrection of both body and spirit.[78]

Indeed, in his most well-known treatise, *The Incoherence of Philosophers*, al-Ghazali devotes a whole chapter (the last one, 20) to refute the false view according to which resurrection is not physical in nature. He challenges and refutes a well-known philosopher's view (Avicenna,

78. Stieglecker, *Die Glaubenslehren des Islam*, ##1388–96, 757–61.

righteous standard of God. Theologically this can be expressed in the following way: "Eternity is judgment . . . [because it] brings the truth about earthly life to light." That, however, does not mean the annihilation or destruction of creatures, because God, the Judge, is also Creator.[85] With that in mind, those who have placed their hope in God and God's promise of eternal life, seek to "live at each moment in accordance with the eternity of God to which we are aiming."[86] This is because judgment is not only a matter of distant future, it is a daily process: "Whenever, consciously or unconsciously, we choose good, we enter already by anticipation into eternal life; whenever we choose evil, we receive a foretaste of hell."[87]

Who will be the judge? According to the New Testament teaching, it is basically God, the Father (Matt 6:4; Rom 3:6; 1 Cor 5:13). At the same time, there are also occasional references to Jesus as judge. But in his case, texts mention on the one hand that Jesus judges no one (John 3:17), but on the other hand that he serves as judge (John 5:22). This means that both salvation and condemnation can be expected from the one who became one of us; Jesus is our advocate at the throne of judgment (1 John 2:1).[88] Furthermore, in keeping with the trinitarian faith, even the Spirit of God is assigned the role of judgment. The Spirit "will convince the world concerning sin and righteousness and judgment: concerning sin, because they do not believe in me; concerning righteousness, because I go to the Father, and you will see me no more; concerning judgment, because the ruler of this world is judged" (John 16:8–11).

Because God is the judge, the standard thereof is the righteous will of God as revealed in Jesus's teaching and the divine Word more widely (John 12:48; Luke 12:8–9). Briefly put, "the message of Jesus is the norm by which God judges even in the case of those who never meet Jesus personally," not of course in relation to the response to the gospel (which is impossible in that case), but in keeping with the direction in which Jesus's message points.[89] We can trust that the divine judgment is fair and balanced. The one who sits in the judgment seat is the loving and caring Father, the crucified Christ who bears the marks of suffering and death, and the compassionate Spirit, the Comforter. This judge is fair and his judgment is in proportion

---

85. Pannenberg, *ST* 3:610.

86. Schwarz, *Eschatology*, 393.

87. Ware, *Orthodox Way*, 135.

88. Pannenberg, *ST* 3:613–14, on the basis of Ratzinger, *Eschatology*, 205–6.

89. Pannenberg, *ST* 3:614–15 (615).

to our opportunities and resources (Luke 12:48). Ultimately, we can be confident that "the final judgment is not a judgment of our merits, but of our response to God's grace which he has extended to us in Jesus Christ."[90]

Judgment in Islamic tradition

Consider that a typical list of the basic beliefs of Islam includes "belief in one God, His messengers, His books, His angels, and the day of judgement."[91] This reminds us again of the importance of the theme of judgment in this youngest Abrahamic faith. Indeed, without any exaggeration it can be said that almost every chapter of the Qur'an speaks of or refers to the theme of judgment.

Above we noted that the first time the human person will be tested happens immediately following physical death and that there might be suffering and punishment for sin already in the grave. This means that— rightly and properly understood, we can speak of a two-stage judgment, with an initial (at death) and a final (at the eschaton) stage. Hence, rather than speaking of "two judgments," it is best to speak of a process of judgment culminating in the final and ultimate judgment.[92]

Again, not surprisingly, there is a lot of commonality between the Christian and Islamic vision of the day of judgment—going back to the Old Testament idea of the "day," a technical term referring to the end of times when evil and evil people(s) will be condemned and Yahweh's righteousness established. Commensurately, all three Abrahamic traditions refuse to give any kind of precise dating of the coming day, only its *inevitability* in the future is strongly affirmed.

Simply consult the following two suras for a typical description of the day of judgment, the first one of which is 82, titled as "the Cleaving," indicating gloomy and sinister events:

> When the heaven is split open, and when the stars are dispersed, and when the seas are burst forth, and when the tombs are overturned, a soul will know what it has sent ahead and left behind. O man! What has deceived you with regard to your generous Lord? Who created you, then made you upright, then proportioned you, assembling you in whatever form He will? No indeed! Rather you

90. Schwarz, *Eschatology*, 391.
91. Haleem, "Qur'an and Hadith," 25.
92. So also Smith and Haddad, *Islamic Understanding*, 64.

deny Judgement. Yet lo! there are above you watchers, noble, writers, who know whatever you do. Indeed the pious shall be amid bliss, and indeed the profligates shall be in Hell-fire, entering it on the Day of Judgement, and they shall not be absent from it. And what would show you what the Day of Judgement is? Again, what would show you what the Day of Judgement is? [It is] a day when no soul will be of any avail to another soul, and the [absolute] command on that day will be God's.

And sura 99 is ominously titled "Earthquake":

When earth is shaken with its [final] quake, and the earth brings forth its burdens, and man says, "What is wrong with it?" On that day it shall relate its chronicles, for its Lord will have inspired it. On that day mankind shall issue forth in separate groups to be shown their deeds. So whoever does an atom's weight of good shall see it, and whoever does an atom's weight of evil shall see it.

Not unlike in Jewish and Christian eschatologies, Muslims believe that at the moment of judgment everything about the person's life written in God's book will be taken up by the divine Judge. This is clearly implied in the Holy Qur'an (18:49): "And the Book shall be set in place. And you will see the guilty apprehensive of what is in it, and they will say: 'O woe to us! What is it with this Book that it leaves out neither small nor great, but [instead it] has counted it?' And they shall find all that they did present. And your Lord does not wrong anyone." On the left hand of God, so the tradition assumes, are the deeds of the condemned and in the right hand the book for each blessed. Indeed, based on 17:13, a general belief is that this book recording the deceased person's life will be attached to his or her neck at the moment of death: "And We have attached every person's omen upon his neck and We shall bring forth for him, on the Day of Resurrection, a book which he will find wide open."[93]

Furthermore, Islamic expectation is that the day of judgment is a period of great cosmic conflict when the forces of Satan—led by the Antichrist and represented by the wars of Gog and Magog—combat the forces of God, led by the Mahdi and Jesus.[94]

In light of Islam's robust focus on the justice of Allah, there is no doubt about the rightness and accuracy of the divine judgment. The Holy Qur'an affirms it frequently: "And God created the heavens and the earth with the

93. Smith and Haddad, *Islamic Understanding*, 76.
94. Peterson, "Eschatology."

truth and so that every soul may be requited for what it has earned, and they will not be wronged" (45:22). This righteous and truthful judgment operates in the context of "balance" (*mīzān*) to which many scriptural references can be found. "In the singular it has been interpreted as the principle of justice and occasionally even the books through which the principles of justice are clarified. As such it is also easily seen as the instrument of justice, the means by which human responsibility ordained in this world is assessed in relation to the next." Underlying this term (balance) is of course weighing. A typical Muslim belief is that a couple of angels (usually Jibril and Mikhael) do the work of assessing the quality of one's life and faith in order to determine the end result.[95]

Not only is judgment necessary and inevitable because of the righteous and just nature of Allah; there are also benefits to judgment seen from the perspective of human life and destiny. First, the anticipation of judgment helps one pursue a good life and avoid evil. Even though men and women ideally would obey God just for the sake of it being a right and holy thing to do, more often than not they do so in order to avoid punishment and gain benefits—which, of course, presupposes the reality of resurrection and judgment at the eschaton. Second, the belief in resurrection and retribution may well encourage us to take care of the poor and other marginalized and needy in the hopes of an eternal reward. Third, the only way for the underprivileged and exploited to hope for justice is to look for resurrection and divine retribution. There is no way that could even come close to happening in this life. Finally, so the logic goes, without the hope in resurrection, human life would be miserable because the human person lives longer than other creatures and is capable of suffering and worrying about the future. Having nothing to hope for, the long life—often filled with suffering and misery—might be too much.[96]

95. Smith and Haddad, *Islamic Understanding*, 77.
96. Stieglecker, *Die Glaubenslehren des Islam*, ##1383–87, 755–57.

CHAPTER 9

How should we envision the final consummation—of ourselves and of the whole world?

For orientation

THIS LAST CHAPTER IMAGINES the final consummation of eschatological expectations in both the Christian and Muslim visions. While not identical, the religious expectations of these two Abrahamic sister faiths are far closer to each other than, say, between (all three) Abrahamic and Asiatic faiths' visions of the End.

A defining and distinctive feature of Christian eschatology—as detailed in the introduction chapter above—has to do with the tight linking together of the personal, communal, and cosmic consummation. While in Islam there is also a connection between the personal and communal levels, theirs is far more individualistic and the role of the cosmic consummation—so it seems to me—has been left open or has not been developed.

As I discuss below, another defining feature of Christian and Islamic expectations has to do with the way the transition from "here" to "there" is envisioned. Even though Christian tradition knows an annihiliationist "quick" move from time to eternity, there is also the balancing and challenging vision of a more gradual transformative process in which this world and the coming world are linked together, allowing for both discontinuity and continuity. Everything good and valuable in this world will be carried forward, so to speak, to the next one, even if everything evil and harmful will be judged and purged.

Because of the limitations of the human mind, namely that we are able to take up only one issue at a time for a focused discussion, the first part of the chapter will zoom in on the personal destiny of both the saved and condemned, and the second part on the wider communal and cosmic renewal.

Christian interpretations of the religious ends for the condemned

Hell and its rebuttals

The most traditional belief in all religions concerning those who will miss the final bliss is hell. Basically all living faiths envision hell as an unparalleled suffering and penalty. As is well-known, Islam has a rich tradition of hell.[1] Even Asiatic faiths such as Buddhism and Hinduism affirm hell; however, differently from mainline Abrahamic interpretations, as for them hell is not the ultimate destiny.[2]

Although interpretations of what hell is and whether it exists in the first place vary,[3] no one denies the presence in the biblical canon of frequent references to it (Isa 66:15–16; Jer 7:30–34; Joel 3:1–2; Matt 13:42, 49–50; 22:13; and Synoptic parallels; 2 Thess 1:9; Jude 7; Rev 14:10–14). The Greek transliteration of *gehenna* derives from the Hebrew *ge hinnom*, a valley south of Jerusalem where children were sacrificed to Molech in fire (2 Kgs 16:3; 2 Chr 28:3; 33:6) and in which, as a consequence, a coming divine judgment of Judah would take place (Jer 7:30–34).

As common as the belief in hell is across the Christian tradition, there is no single Christian understanding of hell. What might be called the "traditional" understanding includes the following features:

- it is for punishment for sins during earthly life;

- it is a final judgment from which there is no escape;

- at least a portion of all men and women will end up in hell;

- the condemned in the hell are conscious of their extreme suffering; and

- a long-standing debate has to do with whether hell is eternal (never-ending) or temporary.[4]

1. Thomassen, "Islamic Hell," 401–16.

2. Braarvig, "Buddhist Hell," 254–81; Jacobsen, "Three Functions of Hell," 385–400.

3. Crockett, *Four Views on Hell*.

4. An excellent, accessible discussion of all the main aspects of the doctrine of hell is

As common as the idea of two destinies, heaven and hell, has been and still is in Christian tradition, it is important to note that it was not the focus of early Christian eschatology. Rather, those early Christians theologians "portrayed an optimistic certainty concerning salvation and focused much more on heaven as a desirable state to reach."[5] Note that even the early creeds do not mention hell. Only in the aftermath of Christianity becoming a state religion with huge mass conversions (coupled with an increase of nominal Christianity) does it appear that hell gained more prominence. In the beginning of the second Christian millennium, an intense interest in the topic emerged.

Not surprisingly, beginning with modernity, the whole idea of eternal punishment in hell has faced significant rebuttals, so much so that some scholars speak of the disappearance of hell altogether.[6] With that in mind, it is surprising that as recently as beginning from the 1960s, a number of studies and discussions of the topic have seen the light of day.[7]

What might be the typical objections in contemporary theology to hell?

> For a conscious creature to undergo physical and mental torture through unending time . . . is horrible and disturbing beyond words; and the thought of such torment being deliberately inflicted by divine decree is totally incompatible with the idea of God as infinite love; the absolute contrast of heaven and hell, entered immediately after death, does not correspond to the innumerable gradations of human good and evil; justice could never demand for finite human sins the infinite penalty of eternal pain; such unending torment could never serve any positive or reformative purpose precisely because it never ends; and it renders any coherent Christian theodicy impossible by giving the evils of sin and suffering an eternal lodgment within God's creation.[8]

Without necessarily undermining many of these weighty theological objections, the advocates argue that it is impossible to get around the extensive biblical witness. Importantly, there are some scholars, including the leading British New Testament scholar C. F. D. Moule, who acknowledge

---

Walls, *Hell*.

5. Schwarz, *Eschatology*, 399–404, here 399–400.

6. Mohler, "Modern Theology," 15–42.

7. Buenting, *Problem of Hell*.

8. Hick, *Death and Eternal Life*, 200–201.

hell as the biblical teaching even if (in the case of Moule) he himself supports universalism.[9]

What about annihilationism?

In response to the traditional conception of eternal judgment, particularly among evangelicals in the English-speaking world, an alternative vision of the religious end has emerged in recent decades. This vision is called either annihilationism or conditional immortality. While not synonyms, for the sake of this conversation they can be taken as such.[10] As the former nomenclature implies, it teaches that the "impenitent wicked will cease to exist after (or soon after) the last judgment."[11] Note that annihilationists disagree over whether the damned will be annihilated immediately after the judgment or after a possibly prolonged period in hell. And the term "conditional immortality" suggests that only the saved will receive eternal life, as a gift, whereas the condemned will simply cease to exist. In other words, eternal life is conditioned on faith in God, the Creator who gave life in the first place.

What is annihilationism's appeal? Annihilationists consider their view to be supported by the biblical witness. There is no denying frequent allusions that seem to imply the destruction, coming to an end of the godless (Ps 37:9–10; Mal 4:1; Matt 3:10–12; Phil 3:19; 2 Thess 1:9; 2 Pet 3:7; Rev 20:14–15). On the other hand—and this is the routine counterargument of the opponents—there are also biblical passages which seem to be best understood in terms of the eternal nature of hell (Matt 25:46; Rev 14:9–11; 20:10; among others). Debates continue and are not likely to be resolved.

Another key concern for annihiliationists and their opponents is the interpretation of the term "eternal" (*aionios*), an issue mentioned above. Whereas tradition, in keeping with the face-value commonsense understanding of the term, took "eternal" to mean never ending, in modern theology the pendulum has swung in favor of "final" (as in final judgment) or "a very long time" rather than never ending. That said, in recent decades a growing number of scholars have returned to the idea of eternal as

---

9. See Moule, *Meaning of Hope*, especially 46.

10. Fudge, *Fire That Consumes*; Pinnock, "Conditional View," 135–66.

11. Pinnock, "Annihilationism," 462.

everlasting.[12] Related to this it should be noted that the idea of just passing out of existence may not be a more gracious alternative than hell.[13]

A radical departure from the traditional doctrine of two destinies, either in terms of hell or annihilation reserved for the reprobate, is the diverse family of universalisms, which intuit some kind of blessed end to all.

The appeal and diversity of univeralism(s)

The term "universalism" or "universal salvation of all" means what the term clearly implies, namely that at the end, even if there is a temporary time spent in hell for those in a need of purification, all men and women will be saved. Even though, as with many other terms (such as "postmodernism" or "pluralism"), we ought to speak of universalisms in the plural for the simple reason that there are more than one type of universalism,[14] here is a fairly standard definition:

> Universalism . . . is the religious doctrine that every created person will sooner or later be reconciled to God, the loving source of all that is, and will in the process be reconciled to all other persons as well. There will thus be, according to this doctrine, a final restitution of all things in which all of the harm that people have done to themselves and to others will be canceled out, and all broken relationships will be healed. But *Christian universalism* . . . is more specific than that; it is the Christian doctrine that the death and resurrection of Jesus Christ is the divinely appointed means whereby God destroys sin and death in the end and thus brings eternal life to all. As St. Paul himself put it, "in Christ God was reconciling the world to himself" (2 Cor. 5:19).[15]

From of old, alongside the idea of the salvation of all men and women, universalism was also at times interpreted to mean the restoration of all things (Greek: *apokatastasis panton*) (or as it was put in the definition above: "the restitution of all things"). This term comes from the New Testament passage of Acts 3:21[16] (which happens to be its only occurrence in the

12. Bauckham, "Universalism," 52.

13. Grenz, *Theology*, 640–41.

14. See, e.g., Murray, "Three Versions of Universalism."

15. Talbott, "Universalism," 446.

16. "Repent therefore, and turn to God so that your sins may be wiped out, so that times of refreshing may come from the presence of the Lord, and that he may send the

canon) and its meaning is not clear. What the *apokatastasis* came to mean was not only the salvation of all men and women but also of "everything," whatever that may mean. This was the formulation of the first major advocate of universalism, the early third-century Origen. According to this disputed and also revered Christian teacher, all things will be restored to their original state at the end and all things will be subjected under the lordship of Christ. Not surprisingly, he appealed often to 1 Corinthians 15:22–28.

> For as in Adam all die, so also in Christ shall all be made alive. But each in his own order: Christ the first fruits, then at his coming those who belong to Christ. Then comes the end, when he delivers the kingdom to God the Father after destroying every rule and every authority and power. For he must reign until he has put all his enemies under his feet. The last enemy to be destroyed is death. "For God has put all things in subjection under his feet." But when it says, "All things are put in subjection under him," it is plain that he is excepted who put all things under him. When all things are subjected to him, then the Son himself will also be subjected to him who put all things under him, that God may be everything to everyone.

To the "restoration of all things" in Origen, most commentators surmise, belongs the expectation that not only hell will be destroyed but also that Satan will be "saved."[17]

Although universalism, or a strong universalist orientation, were present beyond Origen among some few major early theologians (such as Gregory of Nyssa),[18] it encountered broad opposition, notwithstanding that many early theologians hoped for the possibility of postmortem salvation.[19] The leading teacher of the church in the Christian West, St. Augustine, firmly rejected universalism. One of the key reasons for his opposition had to do with his doctrine of double predestination, according to which some will be saved while others, perhaps the great majority, will be damned.[20] The strict rejection of universalism, including *apokatastasis*, be-

---

Messiah appointed for you, that is, Jesus, who must remain in heaven until the time of *universal restoration* that God announced long ago through his holy prophets" (Acts 3:19–21; emphasis added).

17. Origen, *First Principles* books 1 and 3 are the best places to trace his somewhat complicated argument for universalism; as a beginning, read bk. 1, chap. 6.

18. Tsirpanlis, "Concept of Universal Salvation," 1131–44.

19. Trumbower, *Rescue for the Dead*.

20. Augustine, *City of God*, 21.

came the normal church doctrine with the affirmation of two, rather than one, destinies.[21]

Even though occasional support for universalism emerged throughout the centuries, particularly beginning from the post-Reformation period, not before the modernity full scale endorsements reappeared. Not surprisingly, in the theology of the "father of modern theology," the liberal Friedrich Schleiermacher, universalism (based on his revised doctrine of election) played an important role. Even though he affirmed two destinies, Schleiermacher intuited them only as temporary. At the end, even damnation will not last forever.[22]

Undoubtedly, behind Enlightenment and liberal theologians' desire to revise or totally reject the traditional belief in the two destinies was the general modernist resistance to what they saw as the repulsive nature of eternal hell. In the aftermath of the introduction of biblical criticism, which divested the traditional idea of the Bible as the Word of God (as well as doctrinal criticism with its target on all major Christian doctrines), modern theologians felt as if they had the freedom to formulate theological opinions different from, often times in direct contradiction to, pre-Enlightenment tradition's self-confinement in the received opinions.

Universalisms come in many forms. A dramatic indication of widely differing motifs and reasons behind universalisms is the "church father of the twentieth century," Karl Barth, with his Christocentric universalism. Indeed, in direct opposition to his former liberal teachers, who built on Schleiermacher's legacy, the Swiss Reformed theologian sought to restore the centrality of Jesus Christ to all theology, not least to salvation of men and women. In his robustly reworked theology of election, Barth famously argued that all dealings of God with the humanity (and the world) were filtered through Christ, who is both the "Elected Man" and the "Electing God." Rejecting the traditional Augustinian-Calvinist "double predestination," he spoke of the "dual treatment" of this Elected One, both as the one who was rejected (on the cross) on our behalf and as the one who was vindicated (in resurrection) on our behalf. As a result, so Barth surmised, Christ's rejection and vindication mean that no one else will be rejected any more.[23] While vacillating in his response to the critics, both conservative

---

21. McDermott, "Will All Be Saved?" 232–43.

22. Schleiermacher, *Christian Faith*, 548–51, 720–22.

23. Barth. *Church Dogmatics*, II/2, 163.

and liberal, it is clear that Barth ended up affirming a kind of universalism—and perhaps against his own will!

Among living theologians, no one has offered a more conceptually sophisticated, carefully nuanced, and powerfully appealing defense of universalism than Jürgen Moltmann. Its main argument is something like the following:

- divine judgment "serves the universal establishment of the divine righteousness and justice";

- God is able and willing to overcome human resistance to the offer of salvation;

- indeed, at stake is "confidence in God: what God wants to do he can do, and will do," or else, ultimately each human person's salvation or damnation were left in his or her own hands;[24]

- "if *the double outcome of judgment* is proclaimed, the question is then: why did God create human beings if he is going to damn most of them in the end, and will only redeem the least part of them?"[25]

The most likely candidates to endorse universalism are religious pluralists of various sorts. Building on modernity's idea of the "common essence" of religions that leads to "rough parity" of all faiths, they strongly oppose any idea of lifting up any particular religion as the only salvific or true one. The pluralistic universalism of the late philosopher of religion John Hick is the most well-known. Indeed, he began to espouse universalism even before becoming a pluralist, as evident in his widely debated work *Evil and the God of Love* (1966). In it, he rejected hell on the basis that it is incompatible with the establishment of theodicy—a loving God's capacity to overcome evil in the world that God has created good (the details of which we will not explore here).[26] After the turn to pluralism, a number of other reasons further drew him towards a firm rebuttal of two destinies. In his monumental *Death and Eternal Life* Hick argued that "since man has been created by God for God, and is basically oriented towards him, there is no final opposition between God's saving will and our human nature acting in freedom."[27]

---

24. Moltmann, *Coming of God*, 243–46, here 243, 244.
25. Moltmann, *Coming of God*, 239–40.
26. Hick, *Evil and the God of Love*, 341–45.
27. Hick, *Death and Eternal Life*, 254.

Yet another dramatic illustration of the ever-widening diversity of advocates of universalism and their arguments in favor of it has to do with its growing appeal even among the conservative segment of Christianity, namely evangelicals. Particularly some American and British evangelicals, despite their opposition to liberal theology and religious pluralisms, have counterintuitively endorsed universalism (even if the overwhelming majority of their fellow believers reject the doctrine categorically).[28] The best known among these evangelical universalists is Thomas Talbott, who supports it particularly with an appeal to divine love, which he understands as incompatible with eternal judgment.[29]

Having now presented the main options for intuiting the final destiny of the damned—hell, annihilationism/conditional immortality, and universalism(s)—I attempt a contemporary constructive statement. Rather than delving into detailed pro- and con-arguments of each of the opinions (a discussion that can be found in standard textbooks, particularly in those focused on eschatology), the following section seeks to develop an alternative in critical and sympathetic dialogue with the views engaged here.

The possibility of eternal damnation and "optimism of salvation"

The possibility of hell and eternal damnation

There is no denying the fact that, according to Christian tradition, a conviction shared by two other Abrahamic cousins, "The *possibility* of hell stands in stark contrast with the *reality* of heaven."[30] While we can have an "unshakable hope," as Rahner puts it, in God's capacity to bring about the salvific plan prepared for the human race, "we neither can nor must say anything about the end of an individual who suffers final loss except that a person who is still living in history and who is just not exercising his freedom must reckon with this possibility seriously."[31]

As repulsive and horrific as the prospects for imagining anyone—anyone, even the bloodiest murderer—to be destined to spend eternity in hell

28. McDonald, *Evangelical Universalist*; Bell, *Love Wins*.

29. Talbott, *Inescapable Love of God*. Talbott himself does not speak use the name "evangelical universalism" to describe his position, but it does not seem inappropriate.

30. Novello, *Death as Transformation*, 1; citing Hayes, "Hell," 459.

31. Rahner, *Foundations of Christian Faith*, 435.

might be, a total denial of that possibility runs directly against the biblical witness; it would also be a rejection of the mainstream Christian tradition. That said, the biblical attestation is more complex than that. On the one hand, there are a number of passages that warn us of the possibility of eternal damnation (Matt 18:8–9; 25:41; Mark 9:43–48; Luke 16:26) and, on the other hand, there are also passages that seem to point in a different direction (Rom 5:18; 11:32; 1 Cor 15:22, 28; 1 Tim 2:4). The best way to handle the biblical data is not to pit one sort of passages against the other but to listen to both. At the same time, it seems reasonable to conclude that in Scripture "the tenor is not one of universal homecoming but of a twofold outcome of human history, namely acceptance and rejection." Hence, the "universalistic message would contradict the New Testament's insistence that our response to the gospel determines our final destiny."[32]

This means that God's love and desire to save all men and women will not overrule human responsibility, based on Christian creation theology. As limited and fallible as human will might be (a topic widely and deeply debated throughout history), very few theologians were ready to strip off the human being created in God's image as totally free from responsibility. As the Roman Catholic liberationist Leonardo Boff claims, the "human person has absolute value: he can say *no* to God. He can decide alone for his future which centers around himself and his navel."[33] Another Catholic, Rahner, elaborates on this: "we Christians see man as a free being who can decide against God forever. Hence we also have to extend into the future what we experience in the present as our capacity to be free, and . . . we have to say something about the possibility that man's freedom might suffer absolute loss in its final and definitive state, that is, the possibility of 'hell.'"[34] John Polkinghorne, the British physicist-priest says the same in other words: although "God's offer of mercy and forgiveness is not withdrawn at death," it is also the case that "no one will be carried into the kingdom of heaven against their will by an empowering act of divine power."[35]

This, however, is not to determine how many or few men and women might be assigned to hell, nor to make a decision about what kind of painful state hell would be. In this respect, the recent scholarship and literature has helped theology gain a more balanced and proper view of hell:

32. Schwarz, *Eschatology*, 346.

33. Boff, *Was kommt nachher?* 75, my translation.

34. Rahner, *Foundations of Christian Faith*, 435.

35. Polkinghorne, *God of Hope*, 136.

First, physical punishment and suffering are not an integral or necessary part of the doctrine. Metaphors such as "gnashing of teeth" and similar in the Bible are just that, *metaphors*. Second, punishment does not have to be the leading motif (although it is certainly an aspect in biblical testimonies): the logic of hell may be supported by other forms of justice (such as restorative [ones]), the integrity of the divine nature, the irrevocability of human freedom, and so forth. Third, the position that hell will be "densely populated" should not be the default position; rather, our desire and prayer should be that as few as possible would be found there. Fourth, making hell an absolutely unending form of damnation to all that may end up there does not necessarily follow. And finally, although normally one's eternal destiny is sealed at the moment of death, one could also imagine some kind of possibility of purification and preparation before final consummation.[36]

Hell is of course closely linked with the theology of judgment discussed above. Building on our conclusion therein, namely that ultimately judgment means entering divine eternity, I find Rahner's nuanced and sophisticated statement highly instructive:

> Eternity as the fruit of time is an entrance into God's presence either in an absolute decision of love for him, love for his immediacy and closeness face to face, or in the finality of closing oneself against him in the consuming darkness of eternal godlessness. Revelation presupposes God's power to enable every person, no matter what his everyday earthly life looks like, to have enough spiritual and personal eternity in his everyday life so that the possibility for eternity which is found in a spiritual substance is in fact actualized as eternal life. Scripture does not know of any human life which is so commonplace that it is not valuable enough to become eternal, and this is its high optimism.[37]

Even then, the utterly complex question of the relationship between divine love and hell emerges, a question that has been pondered for millennia without any easy answers. While I do not think there is any kind of comprehensive response to be had on this side of the eschaton, I find highly significant the argument of some Eastern fathers. They surmised that "God did not create hell: it was created by humans for themselves. The source of eschatological torment is the will of those humans who are unable to

---

36. Kärkkäinen, *Christian Theology*, 581.
37. Rahner, *Foundations of Christian Faith*, 440–41.

partake in God's love, to feel God's love as a source of joy and blessedness."[38]
The Orthodox Bishop Kallistos (Ware) further explains: "Christ is the judge;
and yet, from another point of view, it is we who pronounce judgment upon
ourselves. If anyone is in hell, it is not because God has imprisoned him
there but because that is where he himself has chosen to be. The lost in hell
are self-condemned, self-enslaved; it has been rightly said that the doors of
hell are locked *on the inside*."[39]

Hopeful optimism

To argue for what can be named as "optimism of salvation"[40] is neither to
deny the possibility of hell as eternal damnation nor to endorse universalism. The arguments in favor of universalisms are weighty and not easily
dismissed; yet, they are not persuasive enough to swing the pendulum in
favor of the stated universalism, let alone *apokatastasis*. The universalist
arguments include

- the power of divine love to win, even over and against human
  resistance;

- the "nonreality" of evil, that is, ultimately only God, the goodness,
  lasts; and finally,

- human aversion to the whole idea of eternal punishment.

Reasons that I do not find the universalist arguments convincing enough to
endorse that view include these:

- It is impossible for me to assume that in granting freedom to the human person, which in turn entails responsibility, God would simply
  overrule it (as limited and as fallible as the use of will might be in
  itself). The human person has been given the chance, as horrible as
  that may be, to choose against his or her Creator.

- The "point of no return" argument teaches that although God is
  patiently waiting for repentance, physical death constitutes a final
  boundary mark. While this is not to deny the possibility of progress in

---

38. Alfeyev, "Eschatology," 113–14.

39. Ware, *Orthodox Way*, 135.

40. Pinnock, *Wideness in God's Mercy*, ch. 1.

the afterlife, particularly in the new creation, neither is it to endorse the "second chance."

- It seems to me warranted to think that the argument from justice simply entails the separation between those who aligned their lives with the will of God (as imperfectly as that may have happened) and those who intentionally and willfully deviated from it. It simply sounds repulsive to intuit that the worst criminals and murderers end up receiving the same destiny as pious and loving Christians.

While other arguments against universalism can be found, these are the foundational ones to my mind. It is safe to say that as a stated, dogmatic position, universalism is not in keeping with mainstream Christian understanding.

That said, resisting universalism and maintaining openness to the possibility of eternal damnation does not have to lead one to a loss of hope for the salvation of many, even most men and women. One of the most important biblical passages to that effect is Matthew 8:11–12, a saying attributed to no one else but Jesus of Nazareth: "I tell you, many will come from east and west and sit at table with Abraham, Isaac, and Jacob in the kingdom of heaven, while the sons of the kingdom will be thrown into the outer darkness; there men will weep and gnash their teeth." The passage is widely—and in my judgment, correctly—interpreted as stating that those who take for granted their entrance into God's kingdom, be they Israelites or Christians, may face condemnation, whereas pagans (non-Jews) or non-Christians may be included.[41] In other words, those who were counted out were let in while at the same time the "privileged" might have found themselves left behind.

To differentiate between universalism and what I call the optimism of salvation, I find useful the distinction between "strong" and "hopeful" universalism: whereas the former teaches "universal salvation," the latter suffices to *hope* that as few as possible find themselves in eternal punishment.[42] "Hopeful universalism" comes closest to what I advocate here as optimism of salvation with the caveat that I do not find the term "universalism" useful here because it stretches the term's meaning in an unhelpful manner. Rather, I prefer the expression "optimism of salvation" that derives from

---

41. Pannenberg, *ST* 3:616; he draws a parallel between this passage and 1 Pet 3:19–20 in this regard.

42. Parry and Partridge, *Universal Salvation?* xx–xxii.

the late Canadian Baptist Clark Pinnock. It is based on his understanding of God as "unbounded generosity." Says Pinnock: "The God we love and trust is not One to be satisfied until there is a healing of the nations and an innumerable host of redeemed people around his throne (Rev. 7:9; 21:24–26; 22:2–6)."[43] This attitude speaks of hospitality, a "hermeneutic of hopefulness,"[44] as opposed to the "fewness doctrine," according to which it is certain that only a small number of people will be saved.[45]

This is the most, I think, that we can safely say on the basis of Christian tradition. The Orthodox Bishop Kallistos (Ware) puts it succinctly: "Our belief in human freedom means that we have no right to categorically affirm, 'All *must* be saved.' But our faith in God's love makes us dare to *hope* that all will be saved. . . . Hell exists as a possibility because free will exists."[46]

Before engaging the discussion on the destiny of those to be saved, let us delve into the details of the Islamic view of judgment and eternal loss.

Judgment and hell in Islam

The previous chapter discussed the importance of judgment in Islam. It reminds us of the urgency for every Muslim to avoid hell at all costs and to seek to secure a place in heaven.

All Muslim traditions agree on the traditional Abrahamic teaching on two destinies, heaven and hell.

> And the first to lead the way, of the Emigrants and the Helpers, and those who follow them by being virtuous, God will be pleased with them, and they will be pleased with Him; and He has prepared for them Gardens—with rivers flowing beneath them to abide therein forever: that is the supreme triumph. And among those around you of the Bedouins there are hypocrites, and among the townspeople of Medina, who are obstinate in hypocrisy. You do not know them but We know them, and We shall chastise them twice, then they will be returned to a terrible chastisement. And [there are] others, who have confessed their sins, they have mixed a righteous deed with another that was bad. It may be that God will relent to them. Truly God is Forgiving, Merciful. (Q 9:100–102; see also 7:37–51; and 75:20–25, among others).

43. Pinnock, *Wideness in God's Mercy*, 18–20.
44. Heading in Pinnock, *Wideness in God's Mercy*, 20.
45. Pinnock, *Wideness in God's Mercy*, 13–14, 17.
46. Ware, "Dare We Hope for the Salvation of All?" 215.

Not surprisingly, Islamic tradition has unusually rich traditions about hell.[47] A general description goes something like this:

> The Qur'ān mentions various names for Hell. Along with Gehenna (*jahannam*, Q 7:41, passim), the most frequently used is Fire (*nār*, Q 4:56, passim); also common are other words connected with heat. The Qur'ān also gives a broad picture of the topography of Hell. It is an underground prison, always burning. The damned will enter humiliated, while Hell roars like a volcano (Q 68:7–8). Various punishments await the damned, who may be chained, forced to wear fiery garments, or pushed into the void, while boiling and stinking water is poured over them. They will also be forced to eat from trees—such as the cursed tree of Zaqqūm (Q 37:62, passim)—which bears fruits that torment them. Every attempt to improve their condition or to get help from believers will prove futile . . . .[48]

In sum: it is a place of pain and torture, as graphically described both in the Qur'an and in later tradition.[49] As mentioned above, "fire" symbolism is the most common, although the official nomenclature is "Jahannam." It derives from Hebrew term *gehinnom*, originally a valley outside Jerusalem (Hinnom Valley), a place connected with judgment and perhaps even with human sacrifices.[50]

> The Qur'an depicts Jahannam as an infernal dwelling or refuge with seven gates (counterparts for the seven heavens) awaiting unbelievers, hypocrites, and other sorts of sinners (4:140; 15:43–44). It will be the fiery abode of jinns and satans, as well as humans (11:119; 19:68), including polytheists and "people of the book" (98:6).[51]

According to mainline Islamic teaching, not only the infidels but also the believers will enter hell. The main scriptural evidence routinely invoked is 19:71 "There is not one of you but shall come to it [hell]. That is an inevitability [already] decreed by your Lord." But unlike the believers who will, so to speak, pass it, the ungodly will stay there. Here the verse following the above-cited forms the Qur'anic basis: "Then We will deliver

---

47. Thomassen, "Islamic Hell," 401–16.

48. Tottoli, "Afterlife."

49. See Afsaruddin, "Death, Resurrection, and Human Destiny," 48–50.

50. For a short overview, see Campo, "Hell," 442–43.

51. Campo, "Hell," 442.

those who were wary and leave those who did wrong crouching therein" (v. 72).[52] There is an additional nuance to the doctrine of hell in the mainline (Sunni) interpretation, namely that whereas hell is eternal for condemned non-Muslims, for Muslims it is temporary.

Alongside the belief in all people first entering hell (although only the condemned staying there), a couple of other important deviations from the Christian intuition of hell are the following. First, "In contrast to Christian views, hell is not governed by Satan (Iblis), but he is consigned there for punishment in the end-times."[53] Second, there is a common vision of the condemned passing over a bridge to hell. While not directly taught in the Holy Qur'an, it is a widely held tradition. The idea of a couple of angels welcoming (or perhaps guarding) the bridge is often related to this ancient Islamic belief. Indeed, as mentioned above, it is not only the condemned but also the saved who will pass the bridge, though that only the former will fall into hell.

Furthermore, as implied above, it is widely believed that for some who fall into hell, it might not be their final destiny. Unlike those totally condemned, these people might have enough faith and have done sufficiently many good works to mitigate their final destiny, but on the way to heaven, cleansing and purging is needed.[54] If so, then there is a parallel with the Roman Catholic doctrine of purgatory.

How would a Muslim ensure the place among the saved and so avoid the horrors of hell? The standard answer to this all-important question is simple and non-controversial across the variety of Islamic traditions and denominations: believe in the unity of God (*shahada*) and pursue good deeds (including avoiding grave sins: "Surely those who believe, and . . . [whoever] performs righteous deeds—their wage is with their Lord, and no fear shall befall them, neither shall they grieve" [Q 2:62]).[55]

---

52. Klein, *Religion of Islám*, 91–92.

53. Campo, "Hell," 443. That said, even the Christian tradition does not speak with one voice about the role of Satan in relation to hell. Whereas the idea of Satan governing hell is well-established in Christian tradition, just consider the rich imagery of Satan ruling in hell in medieval tradition, early theology also interpret Satan as *condemned* there; support for the latter idea can be found in the NT.

54. The two passages most often invoked as the basis for the bridge are 36:66 and 37:23–24. But even a casual look at them makes one wonder about their relevance to this developed doctrinal idea. For details, see Smith and Haddad, *Islamic Understanding*, 78–80.

55. For details of Islamic soteriology, see ch. 8 in Kärkkäinen, *Spirit and Salvation*.

While there is no debate about the basis of salvation, long-time debates have been conducted around the issue of gravely sinning believers, concerning which no unanimity was reached among the (medieval) schools. While there is a consensus about "grave" (or major) sins resulting in condemnation in hell, disagreements relate to *how many* kinds of sin count as "grave" and which sins those are. There is a range of opinions between seven grave sins all the way up to over forty! Even the two major scriptural passages routinely invoked here fail to give any kind of precise solution: 4:31 merely gives a warning and promise: "If you avoid the grave sins that are forbidden you, We will absolve you of your evil deeds and admit you by an honourable gate" and 42:37 only mentions "grave sins and indecencies."[56]

A related debate concerns the balance, if any, between final judgment and one's deeds, good and bad. All schools agreed that grave sins (notwithstanding the above-mentioned debates about their exact nature and number) will send one to hell. That is not debated (see again the above-quoted scriptural passage from 4:31). But disagreements arose about any possibility for switching one's destiny with enough good works to alleviate the otherwise inevitable final judgment due to grave sins. The most conservative and strictest groups, such as the Mu'tazilites, were of the opinion that even the good deeds will not undo the condemnation resulting from grave sins, particularly *shirk*—associating God with anything non-God—the worst and most serious sin in all of Islam. Similarly, they opined that there is no cure for *kufr*, unbelief and reluctance to submit to God's authority. On the other side of the debate, the mainstream Asharites and some other major Sunni traditions maintained belief in the balancing of good and evil deeds. An important scriptural passage was 99:7–8: "So whoever does an atom's weight of good shall see it, and whoever does an atom's weight of evil shall see it." These schools opined that rather than a semi-automatic process in which one grave sin inevitably cancels out of the merit of the good deeds, Allah has the wisdom and capacity to balance the scales. Particularly when repentance and intercession are there, even the grave sinner may have hope.[57]

What about non-Muslims? While a complex and complicated issue, on the basis of some important Qur'anic passages, one of which was cited

---

56. For an accessible account, including a listing of potentially grave sins, see Wiki-Shia contributors, "Grave Sins."

57. Smith and Haddad, *Islamic Understanding*, 22–24.

above in another context, it seems likely that at least other Abrahamic cousins may have hope of avoiding hell: "Surely those who believe, and those of Jewry, and the Christians, and the Sabaeans,[58] whoever believes in God and the Last Day, and performs righteous deeds—their wage is with their Lord, and no fear shall befall them, neither shall they grieve" (2:62). A similar kind of clearly defined openness is echoed with passages such as 17:15: "Whoever is guided, is guided only to [the good of] his own soul, and whoever goes astray, goes astray only to its [his soul's] detriment. No burdened soul shall bear the burden of another. And We never chastise until We have sent a messenger." The passage seems to imply that unless the person has had an opportunity to hear the true message of Islam, that person will not be condemned; only those who willfully missed the opportunity will meet that fate.[59]

Heaven and new creation: the ultimate Christian vision

The dynamics of the transition from "here" to "there": on the way to new creation

A wide and complex issue to be dealt with on the way to imagining the destiny of those to be saved has to do with the transition of creation from this earthly time and existence to the new creation (heaven). While the transition of each individual to be saved was discussed above in the context of the resurrection of the body, the focus here is in the total vision of the transition from this world to the new one. There are a number of dynamics or dynamic couplets at work. Here, I first list the four dominant ones and then take up one at a time:

- "already"—"not yet"
- continuity *versus* discontinuity
- time *versus* eternity
- destruction *versus* transformation

The basis dynamic of Jesus's preaching concerning the coming of the kingdom of God is routinely expressed in terms of the "already" and "not yet" couplet. On the one hand, Jesus proclaimed that with his coming God's righteous rule had already arrived and its signs were healings, freedom

58. An ancient people in the Southern part of Arabia.
59. Saritoprak, *Islam's Jesus*, 51–53.

from under the oppressing powers, pronouncement of forgiveness of sins, and those outside the people of God joining the community. On the other hand, he consistently referred to the final, ultimate establishment of the kingdom when all sorrows, tears, injustice, and even death and decay have been defeated.

This same dynamic forms the framework for the Christian eschatological expectation. This saves Christian spirituality from escapism, as we already live in the anticipation of the final consummation, having already had "tasted the . . . the powers of the age to come" (Heb 6:5).

Another, related dynamic at the heart of Christian eschatological expectation has to do with the relationship between continuity and discontinuity. On the one hand, there needs to be some kind of continuity between the life-conditions on this earth and the world-to-come in order for the personal, embodied life to make sense. The reason is that Christians hope for eternal life in a resurrected body. Whatever the exact nature of the renewed body may be, it is an *embodied* existence. On the other hand, there also needs to be a radical discontinuity, or else we do not have much for which to wait. The most dramatic manifestation of the discontinuity has to do with the defeat of death and decay. As impossible as it may be for us to imagine the lack of death—of which aging and deterioration of our bodies and minds over the years are signals—it is the biggest enemy and obstacle to a life eternal.

The continuity-discontinuity dynamic also relates to the laws of nature in new creation. Notwithstanding long-term debates among the scientists and philosophers about what we mean when speaking of the laws of nature—whether they are "laws" that truly regulate life in this cosmos or whether they are merely after-the-fact observations based on the seeming regularity of nature's events—it is clear that they need to be transformed in order to allow a renewed life in new creation.

Yet another closely related dynamic has do with a proper understanding of the single most important eschatological symbol or concept, namely "eternity." The meaning of that term is of course closely related to the concept of "time." And, as I note below, after the advent of relativity theories and quantum physics, time cannot be spoken of independently of space. They are closely interrelated and hence, a preferred contemporary nomenclature is time/space or space/time.[60]

Our understanding of "time" is indebted to Augustine, although his notion is also in a need of revision. Augustine correctly intuited that time is

60. Goosen, *Spacetime and Theology*, ch. 3.

a created entity. In other words, with the creation of the cosmos, God also created time.[61] This correct insight, however, was coupled with another, problematic conception: if time has its origin in God, then God somehow must exist "outside" of time. This idea places God "outside" of time and that easily leads to a problematic juxtaposing of eternity and time, namely that either one thinks of God's eternity as something "timeless" or one thinks of it as an unending time. Both of these conceptions of eternity (based on the above-mentioned problems in the conception of time) lack substance. A mere extension of time, even to an extremely long duration, hardly brings fulfillment or consummation. Similarly, a "timeless" existence hardly strikes one as dynamic and living!

Rather than imagining God "outside" time, it is better to imagine that in his omnipresence and deep engagement with the world, God transcends (space-)time. Incarnation alone shows evidence that God can exist in space-time—but as the almighty Creator, God can certainly not be contained within them. In that sense, we can say that God is both "in" and "outside" simultaneously!

With regard to the question of the "timeless" eternity, it is far better to conceive eternity, on the one hand, as the source of earthly time and, on the other hand, as the fulfillment and bringing to completion of all that is lacking in earthly time, particularly the defeat of death and decay. In sum, we can speak of eternity as the ultimate fulfillment of God's new creation. The scientist-theologian R. Russell's conception of eternity as the "boundless temporality of the trinitarian God" summarizes this brilliantly.[62] Hence, "we find God on both sides of the fence, both as eternal and as temporal."[63] Imagining a renewed time-space environment in the new creation assumes that if "in this universe, space, time and matter are all mutually interlinked in the single package deal of general relativity . . . [then it] seems reasonable to suppose that this linkage is a general feature of the Creator's will. If so, the new creation will also have its 'space' and 'time' and 'matter.'"[64] In other words, there is both some real resemblance with the old but also a radical transformation to make possible life in physical resurrection never tasting death. The current life without this divine transformation is not fit for God's eternity (1 Cor. 15:50).

---

61. Augustine, *City of God*, 11.6.
62. Russell, *Time in Eternity*, 5.
63. Peters, "Trinity," 263–64, here 264.
64. Polkinghorne, *God of Hope*, 117.

In sum:

> eternity comes to be in time as time's own mature fruit, an eternity which does not really continue on beyond experienced time. Rather eternity subsumes time by being liberated from the time which came to be temporarily so that freedom and something of final and definitive validity can be achieved. Eternity is not an infinitely long mode of pure time, but rather it is a mode of the spiritual freedom which has been exercised in time, and therefore it can be understood only from a correct understanding of spiritual freedom.[65]

This kind of conception of time gives us the needed resources to imagine the final eschatological redemption that makes possible final reconciliation and peace with the "entry of eternity into time."[66] As I explained in chapter 8, God's eternity not only brings fulfillment but also judges all that does not match up to the standard of eternity.

This dynamic Christian vision stands in stark contrast to a widely held Islamic eschatological doctrine with a "focus on a sudden, even instantaneous transformation in which the earth and heaven are rent, scattered, or melted away, and each human soul stands to hear the judgment on its eternal destiny."[67] That annihilationist vision does not leave much hope for this world.

The final all-important dynamic has to do with the ancient debate between whether the transition from time to eternity will bring total destruction, annihilation of the world, or whether there is a way to think of the transition in terms of a transformation? Two well-known biblical passages serve as the templates and show the dynamic that has elicited and inspired this continuing debate. Both of these biblical passages find many supporting teachings in various parts of the Bible:

> But the day of the Lord will come like a thief, and then the heavens will pass away with a loud noise, and the elements will be dissolved with fire, and the earth and the works that are upon it will be burned up. (2 Pet 3:10)

> For the creation waits with eager longing for the revealing of the sons of God; for the creation was subjected to futility, not of its

65. Rahner, *Foundations of Christian Faith*, 437.
66. Pannenberg, *ST* 3:603.
67. Sells, "Armageddon," 469.

own will but by the will of him who subjected it in hope; because
the creation itself will be set free from its bondage to decay and
obtain the glorious liberty of the children of God. We know that
the whole creation has been groaning in travail together until
now; and not only the creation, but we ourselves, who have the
first fruits of the Spirit, groan inwardly as we wait for adoption as
sons, the redemption of our bodies. (Rom 8:19–23)

Whereas the passage from 2 Peter clearly envisions a sudden, catastrophic
dissolution—burning to ashes—of the cosmos before its renewal, the
metaphor of painful child-bearing paints a picture of a gradual process in
Romans 8. Both of these perspectives belong to the biblical teaching and
should not be pitted against each other, nor artificially harmonized. Rather,
we need to have a dynamic and tension-filled negotiation.

Historically speaking, it is instructive to note that even among the
Protestant Reformers no unanimity was reached on this issue. On the
basis of the Petrine teaching (supported by passages such as Rev 20:11;
21:1),[68] Lutheran theologians (particularly during the post-Reformation
"orthodoxy") emphasized annihilation. The Reformed (Calvinists) instead
highlighted the Romans 8 type of gradual transformation and God's faithfulness as Creator to creation. In the words of Moltmann: "The eschatological transformation of the universe embraces both the identity of creation
and its newness, that is to say both continuity and discontinuity. All the
information of this world remains in eternity, but is transformed."[69]

My tentative conclusion is this: indeed, there is much in the "old creation" to be annihilated, particularly decay and the effects of sin and fall.
That said, differently from the annihilation position, the final cleansing and
sanctification should be looked at against the background of the original
creation. God is not likely to destroy totally what he has created as good.
The term "new creation" in itself implies this twofold dynamic: that it is
"new" bespeaks discontinuity, and "creation" refers to continuity. This is
strikingly expressed by Paul in his statement that "flesh and blood cannot
inherit the kingdom of God, nor does the perishable inherit the imperish-
able" (1 Cor 15:50), and yet it is *physical* resurrection that stands at the
forefront of that hope! Polkinghorne puts it well: "the new creation does

68. "Then I saw a great white throne and him who sat upon it; from his presence
earth and sky fled away, and no place was found for them" (Rev 20:11); "Then I saw a new
heaven and a new earth; for the first heaven and the first earth had passed away, and the
sea was no more" (Rev 21:1).

69. Moltmann, "Cosmos and Theosis," 257.

not arise from a radically novel creative act *ex nihilo*, but as a redemptive act *ex vetere*, out of old."[70]

A proper negotiation of the tension between annihilation and transformation has bearing on how we live as Christians. Just think of our daily work. If our daily work is understood to be related in some way to the coming new creation, then our work is not for nothing, not merely a way to survive. Work gains its ultimate meaning from God's future.[71]

Heaven and final consummation in Christian imagination

The hope of heaven has inspired countless artists, preachers, and faithful to imagine what the nature of eternal bliss might be.[72] Against that rich and pluriform tradition, the topic of heaven is conspicuously missing in contemporary preaching and particularly in academic theology. The omission in professional theology is so dramatic that the world's largest and most prestigious theological encyclopedia, *Theologische Realenzyklopädie*, in thirty-six volumes, has no entry on "heaven"! Nor does one find any substantive discussion among leading systematic theologians such as Pannenberg, to whom eschatology is otherwise a formative theme in theology. The only exception to this rule is Moltmann's *Coming of God*, which devotes a whole section to the topic of heaven, under the weighty heading "Cosmic Temple: The Heavenly Jerusalem."[73]

All that said, the current situation in theology (eschatology) is more complex than that. It is not that contemporary theologians were not interested in the afterlife; it is just that a robust domestication of hope for the afterlife has taken place. Unlike in the past when theologians too often erred in making the hope for the afterlife something merely spiritual and otherworldly, in contemporary scholarship the expectation is that of a pretty much this-worldly enhancement of conditions. There are even eschatological proposals, mentioned briefly in the introduction, in which the whole idea of "future" consummation has been virtually set aside.[74] Even Moltmann's discussion of cosmic eschatology under the rubric of "New

70. Polkinghorne, *God of Hope*, 116.

71. Volf, *Work in the Spirit*, 91–92.

72. Walls, *Heaven*.

73. Moltmann, *Coming of God*, 308–19.

74. Tanner, "Eschatology without a Future?" 222–37.

Heaven—New Earth"[75] is so strongly focused on the hope for the "new earth" that at times one is left wondering how much newness he hopes for. Readers are constantly warned not to be too otherworldly minded. As useful as those warnings might be to some Christians, there are also many who dare not imagine anything much in the category of the other-worldly!

An important attempt to find a radical middle between the other-worldliness of the past and the this-worldliness of the current scene comes from the British New Testament scholar N. T. Wright, a fairly traditional scholar. For biblical reasons into which I do not need to go here, he argues that although the consummation of a new heavens and a new earth is not merely a this-worldly affair, he also emphasizes that, "Heaven, in the Bible, is not a future destiny but the other, hidden, dimension of our ordinary life—God's dimension, if you like."[76] The statement in the citation "not a future destiny" is not to be taken as a total dismissal of future consummation, as N. T. Wright acknowledges the future orientation elsewhere in the New Testament, although still quite minimally.[77]

These few examples illustrate the strong and definite push in contemporary theology to intuit new creation and heaven predominantly in this-worldly terms. What should we make of this? Above, I argued that for the transition to be possible from this life to the life-to-come, a finely tuned negotiation between continuity and discontinuity has to be there. Or else, life in the resurrected body will not make sense. Enough continuity in life conditions between the old and new creation is needed. That is all good and necessary. In this regard, it is also important to critique the often too other-worldly approaches of the past. That said, I do not fully endorse this whole-scale reversal of the trend in contemporary theology which one-sidedly reduces the newness and futurity of new creation. The most important challenge to the overly this-worldly imagination is whether it is able to support a truly cosmic and comprehensive vision of God's making "all things new." If new creation merely fixes our globe's life conditions, how could that facilitate and be a part of a lasting solution to the problems of entropy and decay in the whole cosmos? Life-conditions in the renewed earth cannot be imagined apart from the widest-scale *cosmic renewal*. To put it briefly: how *cosmic* in light of our current scientific knowledge is a vision of

---

75. Moltmann, *Coming of God*, part 4.

76. Wright, *Surprised by Hope*, 19; for a similar argumentation, see Middleton, *New Heaven and New Earth*.

77. Wright, *New Testament*, 1:459–61.

a "new earth" if "cosmic" (by and large) is understood as merely referring to our globe? Nothing less than a new *heaven* and a new *earth* is the Christian vision. Consider this bold assertion of the Christian philosopher J. L. Walls: "Theism raises the ceiling on our hopes for happiness for the simple reason that God provides resources for joy that immeasurably outstrip whatever the natural order can offer."[78] With these desiderata in mind, let us piously inquire into the nature of heaven.

As is well-known and often noted, the Bible speaks only little, indeed, very little of the nature of heaven (when it is understood in its eschatological sense as opposed to a spatial reference over against the earth). In speaking of heaven, the Bible is understandably poetic: it uses metaphors, pictures, images, and similar methods, which appeal to the imagination rather than to discursive analysis.[79] These biblical symbols can be classified under three linguistic forms: *space* language, *person* language, and *time* language.[80] The first category refers to the "city" and "garden" and they harken back to the holy city, Jerusalem, and the paradise of Genesis 3. Particularly appealing to the imagination is the garden with its idea of innocence, fertility, and beauty. The main point of the city metaphor has to do with the security and the community of people. The second category (person language) relates to expressions such as "being with Christ" (Phil 1:22–23) and "seeing God face-to-face" (Matt 5:8; 1 Cor 13:12). The third category relates to expressions such as "eternal life."

Apart from the "environment" of new creation, an essential aspect of heaven is union with God. It is expressed in Thomas Aquinas's pursuit of the beatific vision; this "seeing" of God alone satisfies the endless human thirst for union.[81] Augustine put it memorably: "He shall be the end of our desires who shall be seen without end, loved without cloy, praised without weariness."[82]

Since olden times, people have speculated whether, after having "arrived" in eternity, progress and evolution will continue. It seems to me there is no reason to reject the possibility of an endless journey of new

---

78. Walls, "Heaven," 399.

79. Walls, "Heaven."; McDannell and Lang, *Heaven*; Russell, *History of Heaven*; highly accessible is McGrath, *Brief History of Heaven*.

80. Horvath, *Eternity and Eternal Life*, 124–32.

81. As explained by Walls, "Heaven," 402.

82. Augustine, *City of God* 22.30; I am indebted to Walls, "Heaven," 37.

explorations. Perhaps there are even gradations of perfection, as some biblical and traditional intuitions might indicate.[83]

What is clear is that because of bodily resurrection, life in heaven and new creation has to be embodied in nature. Here, N. T. Wright's observation is to the point, namely that Revelation's vision "is not about people leaving 'earth' and going to 'heaven,' but rather about the life of 'heaven,' more specifically the New Jerusalem, coming down from heaven to earth—exactly in line with the Lord's Prayer."[84] As to what kind of embodied life it is, we have no way of knowing for sure. The continuity-discontinuity dynamic has to be taken most seriously. What we know is that it is embodied life without death and decay.

As I have argued throughout this book, the final consummation, the "new heaven," must be imagined as cosmos-wide. The mere fixing of life conditions in one part of the cosmos, in our globe, would only be a temporary solution and fall short of "all things being made new." While human knowledge and intellectual capacities at the moment have only few resources at their disposal to imagine such a cosmic renewal, pious and humble yearning for knowing more of what is hopefully waiting us is undoubtedly appropriate.

Let us now turn once again to our younger sister faith and inquire into their imagination of the final consummation.

Paradise in Islamic imagination

What distinguishes Islam's vision of heaven among the Abrahamic traditions is that it is more transcendent and otherworldly than others. In other words, it has the least correspondence with this world, particularly when compared to Jewish eschatology. While the symbols and metaphors painting the picture of heaven are of course taken from this world, the way they are developed in the Scripture and tradition emphasize otherworldly bliss.[85] Because of the thinner relation between this world and the world to come, the youngest Abrahamic tradition's spirituality is liable to the danger of escapism, particularly in mystical traditions such as Sufism.

A typical picture of heaven is something like the following:

83. Polkinghorne, *God of Hope*, 132–33.

84. Wright, *For All the Saints*, 59; cited in Walls, "Heaven," 401.

85. For a rich account of visions and images of the afterlife, see Rustomji, *Garden and the Fire*.

Heaven is referred to as, among other things, *janna* ("garden," Q 2:35, passim), *firdaws* ("Paradise," Q 18:107, 23:11), and *'adn* ("Eden," Q 20:76, passim). Heaven is a real place with its own peculiar physical features, such as various doors (Q 21:103, 39:73). Passages in the Qur'ān describe those destined for Heaven, as well as the actions that will grant people access to its spiritual and physical pleasures. Gardens, rivers, fountains, and springs suggest an abundance of fresh water. Men will find rest in the shade of trees—with abundance of food (including fruit) and drink—lying on beds of gold and precious stones, or on sofas or carpets, and their clothes will be green and of silk and brocade. They will be wearing golden bracelets and be perfumed, while their wives will be houris with wide dark eyes (*hūr 'ayn*, Q 44:54, passim). They will be also attended by young boys serving wine.[86]

Similarly to the Christian Bible, in the Holy Qur'an heaven is often depicted with garden images:

For them [the righteous] there will be a distinct provision, fruits and they will honoured in the Gardens of Bliss, [reclining] upon couches, facing one another; they are served from all round with a cup from a spring, white, delicious to the drinkers, wherein there is neither madness, nor will they be spent by it, and with them will be maidens of restrained glances with beautiful eyes, as if they were hidden eggs. (37:41–49; see also 22:14, 23)

Obviously heaven, or as it is often called, the paradise, is a place of great enjoyment, peace, and reunion. It is to be noted that the Qur'an is not shy about offering descriptions that appeal to sensual enjoyment, including food and drink, as well as sexual pleasures with divine maidens—whether that be understood metaphorically or literally.[87] Not unlike in the Bible, there are levels of reward for the blessed ones. The details of the rewards have given Islamic exegetes a lot of food for thought over the centuries.[88]

Particularly rich and splendid accounts of heaven can be found in the Hadith, such as its having eight gates and no less than one hundred levels, the distance between each of them being as long as that between heaven and earth.[89]

---

86. Tottoli, "Afterlife."
87. Peterson, "Eschatology."
88. See Afsaruddin, "Death, Resurrection, and Human Destiny," 51–54.
89. Afsaruddin, "Death, Resurrection, and Human Destiny," 46–48.

What about the possibility of the "beatific vision," the ultimate goal of all mystical traditions, culminating in the "seeing" of God? For the Muslim tradition, the possibility of beatific vision is challenged by its uncompromising insistence on God's transcendence and the avoidance at all costs of *shirk*, the association of God with anything that is not God. Simply put: under what conditions, if any, might the sight of God be available to a resurrected person? Whereas the Asharites—while programmatically eschewing endless speculations, for which they often ridiculed the Mu'tazilites—were generally speaking open to the possibility, they also were reluctant to state a canonical opinion. A main reason why Mu'tazilites opposed the vision was simply this: because seeing is physical and God is not physical, therefore seeing God is not possible. Indeed, they insisted, God Himself had told Moses that he would not see his Lord.[90] Be that as it may, there are Muslim groups, particularly among the Shi'ites, to whom the hope and possibility of the beatific vision is an important part of their spirituality.[91]

90. Q 7:143: "And when Moses came at Our appointed time, and his Lord spoke with him, he said, 'My Lord! Show me that I may behold You!' Said He, 'You shall not see Me, but behold the mountain, and if it remains, in its place, then you shall see Me'. And when his Lord revealed Himself to the mountain He levelled it to the ground and Moses fell down senseless. And when he recovered his senses he said, 'Glory be to You! I repent to You, and I am the first of the believers.'"

91. Hermansen, "Eschatology," 320.

Epilogue
"In the End—the Beginning"

I HAVE BORROWED THE title for the epilogue from the popular version of Moltmann's eschatology, *The Coming of God* that is wittily titled, *In the End—the Beginning*. As discussed in the introduction, "end" has the dual meaning of "reaching the goal" and "coming to an end." On the one hand, the title is an apt summary of the Christian eschatological vision. It describes the core of the Christian doctrine of eschatology: the "end" is not the end as in cessation but rather an anticipation of the world's and life's consummation, the long-awaited goal.

At the same time, Moltmann's book title also reflects well my own feelings and intuitions at the end of the writing process of this eschatological reflection. Far from reaching the "end" of the theological construction of the future, I feel like much more work lies ahead of us. Surely, more questions than answers have been provided in this short book. A number of them would be worthy of another extended discussion and dialogue. This would be particularly important for a book that not only engages the wide and diverse Christian thinking about the End but also seeks to invite another major faith tradition, Islam, into the conversation.

I started the book with a musing on whether life at large, both human life and the life of this vast cosmos, can be considered meaningful, *full* of meaning. I sought to make a compelling case for a Christian establishment of meaningfulness. The same can be said of our cousin faith tradition. If so, the implication is that there is a solid basis for hoping for a fuller and a more complete consummation of life than can ever be imagined in this world, even under the best of circumstances. In this regard, even the subtitle to Moltmann's book is apt, namely *The Life of Hope!* This expectation, as argued, does not have to be—and should not be—a matter of seeking an exit, thereby forfeiting or neglecting one's duties in this single and unique life. No, not at all. Rather, the anticipation of the coming consummation gives wings to hope. Christian hope is an active and engaged waiting on the way to the final destiny.

In this short book I wanted to bring to conversation not only theological resources, Christian and Islamic, but also some resources and insights from natural sciences. If God is truly the Creator of everything—as the two cousin faiths firmly believe—it means that there is nothing in the created order void of meaning. Everything bears the mark of the Maker. Hence, what the natural sciences are discovering of the origins, workings, and the end of all things interests the theological mind. Even when there is no convergence between theology and the scientific conjectures about the coming to an end of cosmos and life, theologians do well to listen to the sciences; and to invite scientists to consider and weigh the value of religious explanations.

The last chapter, as one might expect, focused on the final consummation of everything, including human life, our planet, and the infinitely vast cosmos. Against that horizon, the words of the Seer of the last book of the Bible, Revelation, aptly summarize the breath and width and depth of the Christian vision of the desired end:

> Then I saw a new heaven and a new earth; for the first heaven and the first earth had passed away, and the sea was no more. And I saw the holy city, new Jerusalem, coming down out of heaven from God, prepared as a bride adorned for her husband; and I heard a loud voice from the throne saying, "Behold, the dwelling of God is with men. He will dwell with them, and they shall be his people, and God himself will be with them; he will wipe away every tear from their eyes, and death shall be no more, neither shall there be mourning nor crying nor pain any more, for the former things have passed away." And he who sat upon the throne said, "Behold, I make all things new." Also he said, "Write this, for these words are trustworthy and true." (21:1–5)

> "... I am the Alpha and the Omega, the first and the last, the beginning and the end." (22:13)

Bibliography

Abdalla, Mohamad. "Ibn Khaldūn on the Fate of Islamic Science after the 11th Century." In *New Perspectives on the History of Islamic Science*, edited by Muzaffar Iqbal, 29–38. Aldershot, VT: Ashgate, 2012.

Advameg, Inc. "Encyclopedia of Death and Dying." http://www.deathreference.com/Sy-Vi/Thanatology.html.

Afsaruddin, Asma. "Death, Resurrection, and Human Destiny in Islamic Tradition." In *Death, Resurrection, and Human Destiny: Christian and Muslim Perspectives*, edited by David Marshall and Lucinda Mosher, 43–60. Washington, DC: Georgetown University Press, 2014.

AI-Jayyousi, Odeh. "How Islam Can Represent a Model for Environmental Stewardship." https://www.unep.org/news-and-stories/story/how-islam-can-represent-model-environmental-stewardship.

Al-Ghazali, Abu Hamid Muhammad. *Alchemy of Happiness.* Albany, NY: Munsell, 1873.

———. *The Incoherence of the Philosophers.* Provo, UT: Brigham Young University Press, 1997. https://www.ghazali.org/works/taf–eng.pdf.

Albright, Carol Rausch, and Joel Haugen, eds. *Beginning with the End: God, Science, and Wolfhart Pannenberg.* Chicago, IL: Open Court, 1997.

Alfeyev, Hilarion. "Eschatology." In *The Cambridge Companion to Orthodox Christian Theology*, edited by Mary Cunningham and Elizabeth Theokritoff, 107–20. Cambridge: Cambridge University Press, 2008.

Amin, Adnan Z. "Preface to Islam and Ecology." In *I&E*, xxxiii–xxxv.

Aquinas, Thomas. *The Summa Theologiæ of St. Thomas Aquinas.* Taurini: Marietti, 1920. Literally translated by the Fathers of the English Dominican Province. Online Edition Copyright©2017 by Kevin Knight at https://www.newadvent.org/summa/.

Arnold, Bill T. "Old Testament Eschatology and the Rise of Apocalypticism." In *OHE*, 23–41.

Augustine. *City of God.* Washington, DC: Catholic University of America Press, 2008.

Averill, James R., et al. *Rules of Hope.* New York: Springer-Verlag, 1990.

Ayoub, Mahmoud M. "Creation or Evolution? The Reception of Darwinism in Modern Arab Thought." In *Science and Religion in a Post Colonial World: Interfaith Perspectives*, edited by Zainal Abidin Bagir, 173–90. Adelaide: ATF, 2005.

Badham, Paul, and Linda Badham. *Death and Immortality in the Religions of the World.* God, the Contemporary Discussion Series. New York: Paragon House, 1987.

Bagir, Zainal Abidin. *Science and Religion in a Post Colonial World: Interfaith Perspectives.* Science and Theology Series; 8. Adelaide: ATF, 2005.

Baker, Lznne Rudder. "Persons and the Metaphysics of Resurrection." In *Personal Identity and Resurrection: How Do We Survive Our Death?* edited by Georg Gasser, 161–76. London: Routledge, 2010.

Barker, David C., and David H. Bearce. "End-Times Theology, the Shadow of the Future, and Public Resistance to Addressing Global Climate Change." *Political Research Quarterly* 66.2 (2013) 267–79. http://prq.sagepub.com/content/66/2/267.

Barker, Gregory A., and Stephen E. Gregg. "Muslim Perceptions of Jesus: Key Issues." In *JBC*, 84–152.

Barrow, John D., and Frank J. Tipler. *The Anthropic Cosmological Principle.* Oxford: Oxford University Press, 1986.

Barth, Karl. *Church Dogmatics.* Translated by Geoffrey William Bromiley; edited by Geoffrey William Bromiley and Thomas F. Torrance. Edinburgh: T. & T. Clark, 1956–75.

———. *The Epistle to the Romans.* 6th ed. 1933. Reprint, London: Oxford University Press, 1968.

Bartholomew. "Opening Address by His All Holiness the Ecumenical Patriarch Bartholomew to the Plenary of the World Council of Churches." Commission on Faith and Order "Called to Be One Church," updated October 7, 2009. http://www.oikoumene.org/en/resources/documents/commissions/faith-and-order/x-other-documents-from-conferences-and-meetings/plenary-commission-meeting-crete-2009/opening-address-by-the-ecumenical-patriarch-bartholomew-i.

Bauckham, Richard. "Universalism: An Historical Survey." *Themelios* 4.2 (1978) 48–54.

Becker, Ernest. *The Denial of Death.* New York: Free, 1973.

Bell, Rob. *Love Wins: A Book about Heaven, Hell, and the Fate of Every Person Who Ever Lived.* New York: HarperOne, 2011.

Berry, Thomas. *The Dream of the Earth.* Sierra Club Nature and Natural Philosophy Library. San Francisco: Sierra Club, 1988.

Blichfeldt, Jan-Olaf. *Early Mahdism: Politics and Religion in the Formative Period of Islam.* Leiden: Brill, 1985.

Bloch, Ernst. *The Principle of Hope, Volume 1.* 1st American ed. Translated by Neville Plaice, et al. Cambridge: MIT Press, 1986.

Boff, Leonardo. *Cry of the Earth, Cry of the Poor.* Ecology and Justice. Maryknoll, NY: Orbis, 1997.

———. *Liberating Grace.* Maryknoll, NY: Orbis, 1981.

———. *Was Kommt Nachher? Das Leben Nach Dem Tode.* Topos-TaschenbüCher Bd. 690. Salzburg: Otto Müller Verlag, 1982.

Boisvert, Kate Grayson. *Religion and the Physical Sciences.* Westport, CT: Greenwood, 2008.

Bosch, David J. *Transforming Mission: Paradigm Shifts in Theology of Mission.* American Society of Missiology Series; No. 16. 20th anniversary ed. Maryknoll, NY: Orbis, 1991.

Boudreau, Diane, et al. "Pollution." National Geographic, 2019. https://www.nationalgeographic.org/encyclopedia/pollution/.

Braarvig, Jens. "The Buddhist Hell: An Early Instance of the Idea?" *Numen: International Review for the History of Religions* 56.2–3 (2009) 254–81.

Bracken, Joseph A., S.J. *World without End: Christian Eschatology from a Process Perspective.* Grand Rapids: Eerdmans, 2005.

Bradford, Alina. "Pollution Facts & Types of Pollution." Live Science. https://www.livescience.com/22728-pollution-facts.html.

Braswell, George W., Jr. *Islam: Its Prophet, Peoples, Politics, and Power.* Nashville, TN: Broadman & Holman, 1996.

Brown, Raymond E. *The Virginal Conception and Bodily Resurrection of Jesus.* New York: Paulist, 1992.

Brunner, Daniel L., et al. *Introducing Evangelical Ecotheology: Foundations in Scripture, Theology, History, and Praxis.* Grand Rapids: Baker Academic, 2014.

Buenting, Joel. *The Problem of Hell: A Philosophical Anthology.* Surrey, UK: Ashgate, 2009.

Bultmann, Rudolf. *New Testament and Mythology and Other Basic Writings.* Edited by Schubert M. Ogden. Philadelphia: Fortress, 1984.

Burkett, Delbert Royce. *The Blackwell Companion to Jesus.* Malden, MA: Wiley-Blackwell, 2011. https://doi.org/10.1002/9781444327946.

Calvin, Jean. "Psychopannia." In *Tracts and Treatises in Defence of the Reformed Faith,* translated by H. Beveridge, 413–90. Grand Rapids: Eerdmans, 1958.

Calvin, John. *Institutes of the Christian Religion.* Translated by Henry Beveridge, available at www.ccel.org.

Campo, Juan Eduardo. *Encyclopedia of Islam.* 2nd ed. New York, NY: Facts On File, 2016.

———. "Hell." In *Encyclopedia of Islam and the Muslim World,* edited by Richard C. Martin, 442–3. Farmington Hills, MI: Gale, 2016.

Camus, Albert. *The Myth of Sisyphus, and Other Essays.* First Vintage international ed. London: Hamish Hamilton, 1965.

Carman, John Braisted. *Majesty and Meekness: A Comparative Study of Contrast and Harmony in the Concept of God.* Grand Rapids: Eerdmans, 1994.

Cevetello, J. F. X. "Purgatory." In *New Catholic Encyclopedia,* 2nd ed., edited by Catholic University of America, 824–29. Detroit: Gale, 2003.

Chishti, Saadia Khawar Khan. "Fiṭra: An Islamic Model for Humans and the Environment." In *I&E,* 67–82.

Chittick, William C. "Muslim Eschatology." In *OHE,* 132–50.

Clark, Andy. *Natural-Born Cyborgs: Minds, Technologies, and the Future of Human Intelligence.* Oxford: Oxford University Press, 2003.

Clark, Victoria. *Allies for Armageddon: The Rise of Christian Zionism.* New Haven, CT: Yale University Press, 2007.

Clayton, Philip. "Eschatology as Metaphysics under the Guise of Hope." In *World without End: Essays in Honor of Marjorie Suchocki,* edited by Joseph A. Bracken, S.J., 128–49. Grand Rapids: Eerdmans, 2005.

———. *Mind and Emergence: From Quantum to Consciousness.* Oxford: Oxford University Press, 2004.

Clayton, Philip, and Zachary Simpson. *The Oxford Handbook of Religion and Science.* Oxford: Oxford University Press, 2008.

Cleaver, Gerald B. *Multiverse: God's Indeterminacy in Action.* West Conshohocken, PA: Templeton, 2019.

Clifford, Anne M. "Creation." In *Systematic Theology: Roman Catholic Perspectives,* 2nd ed., edited by Francis Schüssler Fiorenza and John P. Galvin, 201–53. Minneapolis, MN: Fortress, 1991.

Clooney, Francis X. *Comparative Theology: Deep Learning across Religious Borders.* Malden, MA: Wiley-Blackwell, 2010.

Clouse, Robert G. "Fundamentalist Eschatology." In *OHE,* 263–80.

Collins, John J. "Apocalyptic Eschatology in the Ancient World." In *OHE*, 40–55.

Cone, James H. *A Black Theology of Liberation*. 2nd ed. Maryknoll, NY: Orbis, 1986.

Conradie, E. M. "What Is the Place of the Earth in God's Economy? Doing Justice to Creation, Salvation and Consummation." In *Christian Faith and the Earth: Current Paths and Emerging Horizons in Ecotheology*, edited by E. M. Conradie et al., 65–96. London: Bloomsbury T. & T. Clark, 2014.

Conradie, E. M., Sigurd Bergmann, Celia Deane-Drummond, and Denis Edwards, eds. *Christian Faith and the Earth: Current Paths and Emerging Horizons in Ecotheology*. London: Bloomsbury T. & T. Clark, 2014.

Cook, David. "Early Islamic and Classical Sunni and Shi'ite Apocalyptic Movements." In *OHM*, 267–83.

———. *Studies in Muslim Apocalyptic*. New York: Syracuse University Press, 2005.

Corcoran, Kevin. "Thy Kingdom Come (on Earth): An Emerging Eschatology." In *Church in the Present Tense: A Candid Look at What's Emerging*, edited by Scot McKnight et al., 59–72. Grand Rapids: Brazos, 2011.

Costache, Doru. "Meaningful Cosmos: Logos and Nature in Clement the Alexandrian's Exhortation to the Gentiles." *Phronema* 28.2 (2013) 107–30.

Coward, Harold G. *Sacred Word and Sacred Text: Scripture in World Religions*. Maryknoll, NY: Orbis, 1988.

Cragg, Kenneth. *Jesus and the Muslim: An Exploration*. London: Allen & Unwin, 1985.

Craig, Edward. *Routledge Encyclopedia of Philosophy*. London: Routledge, 1988.

Crockett, William V., ed. *Four Views on Hell*. Grand Rapids: Zondervan, 1997.

Cunningham, Mary, and Elizabeth Theokritoff, eds. *The Cambridge Companion to Orthodox Christian Theology*. Cambridge Companions to Religion. Cambridge: Cambridge University Press, 2008.

Curry, Michael. "Presiding Bishop on the President's Action and the Paris Climate Accord." The Episcopal Church, updated June 2, 2017. https://www.episcopalchurch. org/michaelcurry/the-presidents-action-and-the-paris-climate-accord/.

Daley, Brian E. "Eschatology in the Early Church Fathers." In *OHE*, 91–110.

———. *The Hope of the Early Church: A Handbook of Patristic Eschatology*. Rev. ed. Peabody, MA: Hendrickson, 2003.

Davies, Douglas J. *The Theology of Death*. London: T. & T. Clark, 2008.

Davies, Paul C. *The Last Three Minutes: Conjectures about the Ultimate Fate of the Universe*. New York: Basic, 1994.

Davis, Stephen T., et al., eds. *The Resurrection: An Interdisciplinary Symposium on the Resurrection of Jesus*. Oxford: Oxford University Press, 1998.

Davis, W. D. *Paul and Rabbinic Judaism*. London: SPCK, 1955.

Dennett, D. C. *Darwin's Dangerous Idea: Evolution and the Meanings of Life*. New York: Simon & Schuster, 1995.

Detweiler, Nathan. "The US Plans to Withdraw from the Paris Agreement." Evangelical Lutheran Church of America, 2017. https://blogs.elca.org/advocacy/us-plans-withdraw-paris-agreement/.

Dobkowski, Michael. "'A Time for War and Time for Peace': Teaching Religion and Violence in the Jewish Tradition." In *Teaching Religion and Violence*, edited by Brian K. Pennington, 47–79. New York: Oxford University Press, 2012.

Dyson, Freeman J. *Disturbing the Universe*. New York: Harper & Row, 1979.

————. "Life in the Universe: Is Life Digital or Analogue?" In *The Far-Future Universe: Eschatology from a Cosmic Perspective*, edited by George F. R. Ellis, 140–57. Philadelphia: Templeton Foundation, 2002.

Eagleton, Terry. *The Meaning of Life: A Very Short Introduction.* Oxford: Oxford University Press, 2008.

Eaton, Heather. *Introducing Ecofeminist Theologies.* London: T. & T. Clark, 2005.

Eliott, Jaklin A. *Interdisciplinary Perspectives on Hope.* New York: Nova Science, 2005.

Ellens, J. Harold. *Heaven, Hell, and the Afterlife: Eternity in Judaism, Christianity, and Islam.* 3 vols. Santa Barbara: Praeger, 2013.

————. "Ideas of Apocalyptic Eschatology in Islam." In *End Time and Afterlife in Islamic, Buddhist, and Indigenous Cultures.* Heaven, Hell, and the Afterlife: Eternity in Judaism, Christianity, and Islam, Vol. 3, edited by J. Harold Ellens, 57–63. Santa Barbara: Praeger, 2013.

Ellis, George F. R. *The Far-Future Universe: Eschatology from a Cosmic Perspective.* Philadelphia: Foundation, 2002.

Engel, Mary Potter, and Susan Brooks Thistlethwaite. "Introduction: Making Connections among Liberation Theologies around the World." In *Lift Every Voice: Constructing Christian Theologies from the Underside*, edited by Susan Brooks Thistlethwaite and Mary Potter Engel, 1–15. San Francisco: Harper, 1998.

Erickson, Millard J. *Christian Theology.* 3 vols. in 1. Grand Rapids: Baker Academic, 1984.

Esposito, John L. *The Oxford Encyclopedia of the Islamic World.* New York: Oxford University Press, 2009. http://www.oxfordislamicstudies.com/article/opr/t236/e1107.

Exploratorium. "Global Climate Change. Research Explorer." http://www.exploratorium.edu/climate/index.html.

Fenn, Richard K. *The Persistence of Purgatory.* Cambridge: Cambridge University Press, 1995.

Filiu, Jean-Pierre, and Mehdi Khalaji. "The Rise of Apocalyptic Islam." *Policy Analysis*, November 13, 2008. https://www.washingtoninstitute.org/policy-analysis/view/the-rise-of-apocalyptic-islam-causes-and-implications.

Finger, Thomas N. *Christian Theology: An Eschatological Approach.* Scottdale, PA: Herald, 1985.

————. *A Contemporary Anabaptist Theology: Biblical, Historical, Constructive.* Downers Grove, IL: InterVarsity, 2004.

Fiorenza, Francis, and John P. Galvin. *Systematic Theology: Roman Catholic Perspectives.* Minneapolis, MN: Fortress, 1993.

Fisher, Christopher L. *Human Significance in Theology and the Natural Sciences: An Ecumenical Perspective with Reference to Pannenberg, Rahner, and Zizioulas.* Eugene, OR: Pickwick, 2010.

Francis. "Laudato Si. On Care for Our Common Home." 2019. https://www.vatican.va/content/francesco/en/encyclicals/documents/papa-francesco_20150524_enciclica-laudato-si.html.

Fromherz, Allen. "Judgment, Final." In *The Oxford Encyclopedia of the Islamic World*, edited by John L. Esposito. Oxford: Oxford University Press, 2009. http://www.oxfordislamicstudies.com/article/opr/t236/e1107.

Fudge, Edward. *The Fire That Consumes: A Biblical and Historical Study of Final Punishment.* Houston, TX: Providential, 1982.

Fukuyama, Francis. *The End of History and the Last Man.* New York: Free, 1992.

Gaborieau, Marc, et al. *The Encyclopaedia of Islam, Three.* 3rd ed. Boston: Brill, 2007.

Garrett, James Leo. *Systematic Theology: Biblical, Historical, and Evangelical,* Vol. 2. 2nd ed. Grand Rapids: Eerdmans, 1990.

Gasser, Georg. *Personal Identity and Resurrection: How Do We Survive Our Death?* London: Routledge, 2016.

Gillman, Neil. *The Death of Death: Resurrection and Immortality in Jewish Thought.* Woodstock, VT: Jewish Lights, 1997.

Goetz, Stewart, and Charles Taliaferro. *Naturalism.* Grand Rapids: Eerdmans, 2008.

Goldziher, Ignaz. *Introduction to Islamic Theology and Law.* Princeton: Princeton University Press, 1981.

Golshani, Mehdi. "Does Science Offer Evidence of a Transcendent Reality and Purpose?" In *ISHCP* 2:95–110.

———. "Islam and the Sciences of Nature: Some Fundamental Questions." In *ISHCP* 1:67–79.

Goosen, Gideon. *Spacetime and Theology in Dialogue.* Marquette Studies in Theology, 57. Milwaukee, WI: Marquette University Press, 2008.

Gorenberg, Gershom. *The End of Days: Fundamentalism and the Struggle for the Temple Mount.* Oxford: Oxford University Press, 2002.

Greene, Sidney L. "Evangelical Fundamentalists and the Science of Climate Change." In *Christian Perspectives on Science and Technology, ISCAST Online Journal* 10 (2014). http://www.iscast.org/journal/articles/Green_S_2014-10_Evangelical_fundamentalists.pdf.

Grenz, Stanley J. *Theology for the Community of God.* Grand Rapids: Eerdmans, 2000.

Griffiths, Paul J. "Purgatory." In *OHE*, 427–46.

Guessoum, Nidhal. *Islam's Quantum Question: Reconciling Muslim Tradition and Modern Science.* London: I. B. Tauris, 2011.

———. "Islamic Theological Views on Darwinian Evolution." In *Oxford Research Encyclopedia of Religion,* 2016. https://dx.doi.org/10.1093/acrefore/9780199340378.013.36.

Gutiérrez, Gustavo. *A Theology of Liberation: History, Politics, and Salvation.* Maryknoll, NY: Orbis, 1973. http://books.google.com/books?vid=isbn0883445433.

Haddad, Yvonne Y., and Jane I. Smith. "The Anti-Christ and the End of Time in Christian and Muslim Eschatological Literature." *The Muslim World* 100.4 (2010) 520–26.

Haider, Najam Iftikhar. *Shīʿī Islam: An Introduction.* New York: Cambridge University Press, 2014.

Haleem, M. A. S. Abdel. "Qur'an and Hadith." In *The Cambridge Companion to Classical Islamic Theology,* edited by Tim Winter, 19–32. Cambridge: Cambridge University Press, 2008.

Hamza, Feras, Q. "Afterlife: Islamic Concepts." In *ER* 1:159–63.

Harnack, Adolf von. *What Is Christianity? Lectures Delivered in the University of Berlin during the Winter-Term 1899–1900.* Translated by T. Bailey Saunders. 2nd rev. ed. New York: Putnam's Sons, 1908. https://www.ccel.org/ccel/harnack/christianity.html.

Hart, David Bentley. "Death, Final Judgment, and the Meaning of Life." In *OHE*, 476–89.

Haught, John F. *Is Nature Enough? Meaning and Truth in the Age of Science.* Cambridge: Cambridge University Press, 2006.

Hawking, Stephen. *A Brief History of Time: From the Big Bang to Black Holes.* 1988. Reprint, New York: Bantam, 1998.

———. *The Universe in a Nutshell*. New York: Bantam, 2001.

Hayes, Zachary. "Hell." In *The New Dictionary of Theology*, edited by Joseph A. Komonchak et al., 457–59. Wilmington, DE: Glazier, 1987.

Hayles, N. Katherine. *How We Became Posthuman: Virtual Bodies in Cybernetics, Literature, and Informatics*. Chicago: University of Chicago Press, 1999.

Hermansen, Marcia. "Eschatology." In *Cambridge Companion to Classical Islamic Theology*, edited by Tim Winter, 308–24. Cambridge: Cambridge University Press, 2008.

Hessel, Dieter T., and Rosemary Radford Ruether, eds. *Christianity and Ecology: Seeking the Well-Being of Earth and Humans*. Religions of the World and Ecology. Cambridge: Harvard University Press, 2000.

Hick, John. *Death and Eternal Life*. 1976. Reprint, Louisville, KY: Westminster John Knox, 1994.

———. *Evil and the God of Love*. 2nd reissued ed. New York: Palgrave Macmillan, 2010.

Hopkins, Dwight N., and Edward P. Antonio. *The Cambridge Companion to Black Theology*. Cambridge: Cambridge University Press, 2012.

Horvath, Tibor. *Eternity and Eternal Life: Speculative Theology and Science in Discourse*. Waterloo, ON: Wilfrid Laurier University Press, 2006.

Iqbal, Muzaffar. "In the Beginning: Islamic Perspectives on Cosmological Origins—II." In *ISHCP*, edited by Muzaffar Iqbal, 2:397–418. Burlington, VT: Ashgate, 2002.

———. *Studies in the Making of Islamic Science: Knowledge in Motion*. Islam and Science: Historic and Contemporary Perspectives, Vol. 4. Aldershot, UK: Ashgate, 2012.

Jacobsen, Knut A. "Three Functions of Hell in the Hindu Traditions." *Numen: International Review for the History of Religions* 56.2–3 (2009) 385–400.

Jeffery, Arthur. *The Foreign Vocabulary of the Qurʾān*. Leiden: Brill, 2007.

Johnson, Elizabeth A. *Friends of God and Prophets: A Feminist Theological Reading of the Communion of Saints*. New York: Continuum, 1998.

———. "Losing and Finding Creation in the Christian Tradition." In *Christianity and Ecology: Seeking the Well-Being of Earth and Humans*, edited by Dieter T. Hessel and Rosemary Radford Ruether, 3–21. Cambridge: Harvard University Press, 2000.

Jones, Lindsay, ed. *Encyclopedia of Religion*. 2nd ed. 15 vols. Detroit: Macmillan Reference USA, 2005.

Juergensmeyer, Mark, et al. *The Oxford Handbook of Religion and Violence*. New York: Oxford University Press, 2013.

Kamali, Mohammad Hashim. *The Dignity of Man: An Islamic Perspective*. Cambridge: Islamic Texts Society, 2002.

———. *Freedom, Equality and Justice in Islam*. Cambridge: Cambridge Islamic Texts Society, 2002.

Kant, Immanuel. *Kant's Critique of Judgement*. Translated with an introduction and notes by J. H. Bernard, 2nd rev. ed. London: Macmillan, 1914. https://oll.libertyfund.org/title/bernard-the-critique-of-judgement.

Kärkkäinen, Veli-Matti. *Christ and Reconciliation*. A Constructive Christian Theology for the Pluralistic World, Vol. 1. Grand Rapids: Eerdmans, 2013.

———. *Christian Theology in the Pluralistic World: A Global Introduction*. Grand Rapids: Eerdmans, 2019.

———. *Creation and Humanity*. A Constructive Christian Theology for the Pluralistic World, Vol. 3. Grand Rapids: Eerdmans, 2015.

———. *Doing the Work of Comparative Theology*. Grand Rapids: Eerdmans, 2020.

———. *Hope and Community. A Constructive Christian Theology for the Pluralistic World*, Vol. 5. Grand Rapids: Eerdmans, 2017.

———. "Hope, Theology of." In *Global Dictionary of Theology: A Resource for the Worldwide Church*, edited by William A. Dyrness and Veli-Matti Kärkkäinen, 404–5. Downers Grove, IL: InterVarsity, 2008.

———. *An Introduction to the Theology of Religions: Biblical, Historical, and Contemporary Perspectives*. Downers Grove, IL: InterVarsity, 2003.

———. "Meaningful Life in a Meaningless Cosmos? A Short Reflection for Good Times— and Bad." *Dialog: A Journal of Theology* 59.2020–5–14 (2020) 1–4.

———. *Spirit and Salvation. A Constructive Christian Theology for the Pluralistic World*, Vol. 4. Grand Rapids: Eerdmans, 2016.

Karras, Valerie A. "Eschatology." In *The Cambridge Companion to Feminist Theology*, edited by Susan Frank Parsons, 243–60. Cambridge: Cambridge University Press, 2002.

Kateregga, Badru D., and David W. Shenk. *Islam and Christianity: A Muslim and a Christian in Dialogue*. Scottdale, PA: Herald, 1997.

Keller, Catherine. *Apocalypse Now and Then: A Feminist Guide to the End of the World*. Boston: Beacon, 1996.

Kenney, Jeffrey T. "Millennialism and Radical Islamist Movements." In *OHM*, 688–714.

Khalidi, Tarif. *The Muslim Jesus: Sayings and Stories in Islamic Literature*. Convergences. Cambridge: Harvard University Press, 2001.

Khan, Nazir, Amal Qutub and Mahdi Qasqas. "Divine Duty: Islam and Social Justice." Collection: Justice in Islam, 2020. https://yaqeeninstitute.org/nazir-khan/divine-duty-islam-and-social-justice#ftnt5.

Klein, F. A. *The Religion of Islám*. London: Paul, Trench, Trübner, 1906.

Komonchak, Joseph A., et al. *The New Dictionary of Theology*. Wilmington, DE: Glazier, 1987.

Kurzweil, Ray. *The Singularity Is Near: When Humans Transcend Biology*. New York: Viking, 2005.

LaHaye, Tim, and Jerry B. Jenkins, "Left Behind." http://www.leftbehind.com/.

Langmead, Ross. "Transformed Relationships: Reconciliation as the Central Model for Mission." *Mission Studies* 25.1 (2008) 5–20.

Largen, Kristin Johnston. *Baby Krishna, Infant Christ: A Comparative Theology of Salvation*. Maryknoll, NY: Orbis, 2011.

Leirvik, Oddbjørn. *Images of Jesus Christ in Islam*. 2nd ed. New York: Continuum, 2010.

Libreria Editrice Vaticana. "Catechism of the Catholic Church." https://www.vatican.va/archive/ENG0015/__P2I.HTM.

Lieberman, Philip. *Uniquely Human: The Evolution of Speech, Thought, and Selfless Behavior*. Reprint, Cambridge: Harvard University Press, 1993.

Louw, Daniel J. "Cura Animarum as Hope Care: Towards a Theology of the Resurrection within the Human Quest for Meaning and Hope." *Hervormde Teologiese Studies* 70.1 (2014) 1–10.

Löwith, Karl. *Meaning in History*. Phoenix Books. Chicago: University of Chicago Press, 1957.

———. *Meaning in History: The Theological Implications of the Philosophy of History*. Chicago: University of Chicago Press, 1949.

Luther, Martin. *Lectures on Genesis: Chapters 26–30*, in *Luther's Works*, Vol. 5, 76.

———. *Luther's Works*. Edited by Libronix Digitl Library, Jaroslav Pelikan and Helmut T. Lehman. American ed. 55 vols. Minneapolis, MN: Fortress, 2002.

Mabrouk, Layla. "The Soul's Journey after Death: An Abridgment of Theologian Ibn Al-Qayyim's Kitabar-Ruh." https://ia600205.us.archive.org/34/items/KitabAlRuhSummary-IbnAlQayyim/23713846-The-Souls-Journey-After-Death.pdf.

Maguire, Daniel C. *The Moral Core of Judaism and Christianity: Reclaiming the Revolution*. Minneapolis, MN: Fortress, 1993.

Mahmutćehajić, Rusmir. *The Mosque: The Heart of Submission*. New York: Fordham University Press, 2006.

Marshall, David, and Lucinda Mosher. *Death, Resurrection, and Human Destiny: Christian and Muslim Perspectives*. Washington, DC: Georgetown University Press, 2014.

Martin, Richard C. *Encyclopedia of Islam and the Muslim World*. 2nd ed. Farmington Hills, MI: Gale, 2016.

Martindale, Paul. "A Muslim-Christian Dialogue on Salvation: The Role of Works." *Evangelical Missions Quarterly* 1 (2010) 69–71.

Mattson, Stephen. "5 (Stupid) Reasons Christians Reject Environmentalism." Sojourners, updated April 22, 2013. https://sojo.net/articles/5-stupid-reasons-christians-reject-environmentalism.

McCall, Theodore David. *The Greenie's Guide to the End of the World: Ecology and Eschatology*. Hindmarsh, Australia: ATF, 2011.

McDannell, Colleen, and Bernhard Lang. *Heaven: A History*. New Haven, CT: Yale University Press, 1988.

McDermott, Gerald R. "Will All Be Saved?" *Themelios* 38.2 (2013) 232–43.

McDonald, Gregory. *The Evangelical Universalist*. 2nd ed. Eugene, OR: Cascade, 2012.

McFague, Sallie. *A New Climate for Theology: God, the World, and Global Warming*. Minneapolis, MN: Fortress, 2008.

McGinn, Bernard. *Antichrist: Two Thousand Years of the Human Fascination with Evil*. 1st ed. San Francisco: HarperSanFrancisco, 1994.

McGrath, Alister E. *A Brief History of Heaven*. Blackwell Brief Histories of Religion. Malden, MA: Blackwell, 2003.

———. *A Fine-Tuned Universe: The Quest for God in Science and Theology*. Gifford Lectures, 2009. Louisville, KY: Westminster John Knox, 2009.

———. *A Theory of Everything (That Matters): A Brief Guide to Einstein, Relativity, and His Surprising Thoughts on God*. Carol Stream, IL: Tyndale Momentum, 2019.

McKnight, Scot, et al., eds. *Church in the Present Tense: A Candid Look at What's Emerging*. Grand Rapids: Brazos, 2011.

McNamara, Patrick, and Wesley Wildman. *Science and the World's Religions*. 3 vols. Santa Barbara, CA: Praeger, 2012.

Meagher, David K., and David E. Balk. *Handbook of Thanatology: The Essential Body of Knowledge for the Study of Death, Dying, and Bereavement*. 2nd ed. London: Routledge, 2017.

Merritt, Jonathan. "Is God Going to Incinerate the Earth? And Does It Matter?" *Religious News Service*, March 26, 2019. https://religionnews.com/2013/05/21/is-god-going-to-incinerate-the-earth-and-does-it-matter/.

Meshal, Reem A., and M. Reza Pirbhai. "Islamic Perspectives on Jesus." In *The Blackwell Companion to Jesus*, edited by Delbert Royce Burkett, 232–49. Malden, MA: Wiley-Blackwell, 2011.

Middleton, J. Richard. *A New Heaven and a New Earth: Reclaiming Biblical Eschatology.* Grand Rapids: Baker, 2014.

Migliore, Daniel L. *Faith Seeking Understanding: An Introduction to Christian Theology.* 2nd ed. Grand Rapids: Eerdmans, 2004.

Míguez Bonino, José. *Doing Theology in a Revolutionary Situation.* Confrontation Books. Philadelphia: Fortress, 1975.

Miller, William D. "Da'wah." In *ER* 4:2225–26.

Misner, Charles W., et al. *Gravitation.* New York: Freeman, 1973

Mohler, Albert. "Modern Theology: The Disappearance of Hell." In *Hell Under Fire: Modern Scholarship Reinvents Eternal Punishment,* edited by Christopher W. Morgan and Robert A. Peterson, 15–41. Grand Rapids: Zondervan, 2009.

Moltmann, Jürgen. *The Coming of God: Christian Eschatology.* Minneapolis, MN: Fortress, 1996.

———. "Cosmos and Theosis: Eschatological Perspectives on the Future of the Universe." In *The Far-Future Universe: Eschatology from a Cosmic Perspective,* edited by George F. R. Ellis, 249–65. Philadelphia: Templeton Foundation, 2002.

———. *God in Creation: A New Theology of Creation and the Spirit of God.* The Gifford Lectures, 1984–85. 1st Fortress ed. Minneapolis, MN: Fortress, 1993.

———. *In the End, the Beginning: The Life of Hope.* Translated by Margaret Kohl. Minneapolis, MN: Fortress, 2004.

———. "Is There Life after Death?" In *EWEG,* 238–55.

———. *The Spirit of Life: A Universal Affirmation.* Minneapolis, MN: Fortress, 2001.

———. *Theology of Hope: On the Ground and the Implications of a Christian Eschatology.* London: SCM, 1967.

———. *The Way of Jesus Christ: Christology in Messianic Dimensions.* 1989. Reprint, Minneapolis, MN: Fortress, 1993.

Morgan, Christopher W., and Robert A. Peterson, eds. *Hell Under Fire: Modern Scholarship Reinvents Eternal Punishment.* Grand Rapids: Zondervan, 2009.

Morris, Henry M. *The Beginning of the World: A Scientific Study of Genesis 1–11.* Denver: Accent, 1977.

Mosher, Lucinda, and David Marshall. *The Community of Believers: Christian and Muslim Perspectives.* Washington, DC: Georgetown University Press, 2015.

Moule, C. F. D. *The Meaning of Hope: A Biblical Exposition with Concordance.* Philadelphia: Fortress, 1963.

Murphy, Nancey C. *Bodies and Souls, or Spirited Bodies?* Cambridge: Cambridge University Press, 2006.

———. "The Resurrection Body and Personal Identity: Possibilities and Limits of Eschatological Knowledge." In *RTSA,* 202–18.

Murray, Michael. "Three Versions of Universalism." *Faith and Philosophy* 16.1 (1999) 55–68.

Nagel, Thomas. *Mind and Cosmos: Why the Materialist Neo-Darwinian Conception of Nature Is Almost Certainly False.* New York: Oxford University Press, 2012.

———. *The View from Nowhere.* New York: Oxford, 1986.

NASA. "Hubble Space Telescope." https://www.nasa.gov/content/goddard/2017/highlights-of-hubble-s-exploration-of-the-universe.

———. "Origins of Life: Free Online Course." https://astrobiology.nasa.gov/news/origins-of-life-free-online-course/.

———. "Universe 101. Big Bang Concepts." https://wmap.gsfc.nasa.gov/universe/bb_concepts.html.

Nasr, Seyyed Hossein. "Islam, the Contemporary Islamic World, and the Environmental Crisis." In *I&E*, 85–105.

———. "Islam and Science." In *The Oxford Handbook of Religion and Science*, edited by Philip Clayton and Zachary Simpson, 71–85. Oxford: Oxford University Press, 2008.

———. *Man and Nature: The Spiritual Crisis in Modern Man*. Rev. ed. Chicago: Kazi, 1997.

———. *The Need for a Sacred Science*. Albany, NY: State University of New York Press, 1993.

The National Conference of Commissioners on Uniform State Laws. "*Uniform Determination of Death Act*." 1981. http://www.lchc.ucsd.edu/cogn_150/Readings/death_act.pdf.

Neely, Brent J., and Peter G. Riddell, eds. *Islam and the Last Day: Christian Perspectives on Islamic Eschatology*. Occasional Papers in the Study of Islam and Other Faiths, 4 (2013–14). Wantirna, Australia: Melbourne School of Theology Press, 2014.

Neiman, Susan. *Evil in Modern Thought: An Alternative History of Philosophy*. Princeton, NJ: Princeton University Press, 2004.

Novello, Henry L. *Death as Transformation: A Contemporary Theology of Death*. London: Routledge, 2016.

Nusselder, André. *Interface Fantasy: A Lacanian Cyborg Ontology*. Cambridge: MIT Press, 2009.

O'Donnell, Patrick S. "Mutazili School." In *Encyclopedia of Islam*, edited by Juan Eduardo Campo, 511–14. New York: Facts on File, 2016.

Ohlander, Erik. "Ash'Ari, Abu Al-Hasan Al- (260/873–324/935 OR 936)." In *Encyclopedia of Islam and the Muslim World*, 2nd ed., edited by Richard C. Martin, 111–12. Farmington Hills, MI: Gale, 2016.

Oktar, Adnan. "Harun Yahya." http://harun-yahya.net.

Onof, Christian J. "Jean Paul Sartre: Existentialism." In *Internet Encyclopedia of Philosophy: A Peer-reviewed Academic Resource*. https://www.iep.utm.edu/sartre-ex/.

Ortner, Sherry B. "Is Female to Male as Nature Is to Culture?" In *Women, Culture, and Society*, edited by Michelle Zimbalist Rosaldo and Louise Lamphere, 67–87. Stanford, CA: Stanford University Press, 1974.

Ostřanský, Bronislav. *The Jihadist Preachers of the End Times: ISIS Apocalyptic Propaganda*. Edinburgh: Edinburgh University Press, 2019.

Oxford Islamic Studies Online. http://www.oxfordislamicstudies.com/article/opr/t236/e0223.

Özdemir, İbrahim. "Towards an Understanding of Environmental Ethics from a Qu'ranic Perspective." In *I&E*, 3–37.

Pascal, Blaise. *Pascal's Pensées*. New York: Dutton, 1958. https://www.gutenberg.org/files/18269/18269-h/18269-h.htm.

Pannenberg, Wolfhart. "Contributions from Systematic Theology." In *The Oxford Handbook of Religion and Science*, edited by Philip Clayton, 359–71. Oxford: Oxford University Press, 2006.

———. *Systematic Theology*. Translated by Geoffrey William Bromiley. 3 vols. Grand Rapids: Eerdmans, 1991, 1994, 1998.

————. "Theological Questions to Scientists." In *Beginning with the End: God, Science, and Wolfhart Pannenberg*, edited by Carol Rausch Albright and Joel Haugen, 37–50. Chicago: Open Court, 1997.

————. *Theology and the Kingdom of God*. Edited by Richard John Neuhaus. Philadelphia: Westminster, 1969.

Parfit, Derek. *Reasons and Persons*. Oxford: Oxford University Press, 1986.

Parker, Amanda. "Torment in the Grave and a Christian Response." In *Islam and the Last Day: Christian Perspectives on Islamic Eschatology*, edited by Brent J. Neely and Peter G. Riddell, 11–17. Wantirna, Australia: Melbourne School of Theology Press, 2014.

Parry, Robin A., and Christopher H. Partridge, eds. *Universal Salvation? The Current Debate*. Grand Rapids: Eerdmans, 2003.

Paul VI. *Gaudium et Spes: Pastoral Constitution on the Church in the Modern World* (Vatican II), #36. Available at www.vatican.va.

Peacocke, Arthur. "Chance and Law in Irreversible Thermodynamics, Theoretical Biology, and Theology." In *Chaos and Complexity: Scientific Perspectives on Divine Action*, edited by Robert John Russell et al., 139–42. Berkeley, CA: Center for Theological and the Natural Sciences, 1995.

Peters, Ted. "Introduction: What Is to Come." In *RTSA*, viii–xvii.

————. "Theologians Testing Transhumanism." *Theology and Science* 13.2 (2015) 130–49.

————. "The Trinity in and beyond Time." In *Quantum Cosmology and the Laws of Nature: Scientific Perspectives on Divine Action*, edited by Robert John Russell et al., 263–91. Berkeley, CA: The Center for Theology and the Natural Sciences, 1993.

Peterson, Daniel C. "Eschatology." In *The Oxford Encyclopedia of the Islamic World*, edited by John L. Esposito. Oxford: Oxford University Press, 2009; Oxford Islamic Studies Online. http://www.oxfordislamicstudies.com/article/opr/t236/e0223.

Pigliucci, Massimo. "Science and Fundamentalism: A Strategy on How to Deal with Anti-science Fundamentalism." In *EMBO reports* 6.12, 1106–9.

Pihlström, Sami. "A Meaningful Life in a Meaningless Cosmos? Two Rival Approaches." *Cosmos and History: The Journal of Natural and Social Philosophy* 3.1 (2007) 4–17.

Pinnock, Clark H. "Annihilationism." In *OHE*, 462–73.

————. "The Conditional View." In *Four Views on Hell*, edited by William Crockett, 135–66. Grand Rapids: Zondervan, 1997.

————. *A Wideness in God's Mercy: The Finality of Jesus Christ in a World of Religions*. Grand Rapids: Zondervan, 1992.

Plantinga, Harry. "Institutes of the Christian Religion." http://www.ccel.org.

Polkinghorne, John. "Anthropology in an Evolutionary Context." In *God and Human Dignity*, edited by R. Kendall Soulen and Linda Woodhead, 89–103. Grand Rapids: Eerdmans, 2006.

————. "Eschatology: Some Questions and Some Insights from Science." In *EWEG*, 29–41. Harrisburg, PA: Trinity, 2000.

————. *The God of Hope and the End of the World*. New Haven, CT: Yale University Press, 2002.

————. *The Quantum World*. Princeton, NJ: Princeton University Press, 1985.

Rahemtulla, Shadaab. *Qur'an of the Oppressed: Liberation Theology and Gender Justice in Islam*. Oxford: Oxford University Press, 2017.

Rahner, Karl. *Foundations of Christian Faith: An Introduction to the Idea of Christianity*. Translated by William V. Dych. New York: Crossroad, 1982.

————. *On the Theology of Death.* Translated by Charles H. Henkey. New York: Herder & Herder, 1961.

Ratzinger, Joseph. *Eschatology: Death and Eternal Life.* Translated by Michael Waldstein. Washington, DC: Catholic University of America, 1988.

————. "Instruction on Christian Freedom and Liberation." 1986. http://www.vatican. va/roman_curia/congregations/cfaith/documents/rc_con_cfaith_doc_19860322_ freedom-liberation_en.html.

Ravi, N. S. R. K. "A Comprehensive Listing of References to Jesus ('Isa) in the Qur'an." 2016. https://www.namb.net/apologetics-blog/a-comprehensive-listing-of-references-to- jesus-isa-in-the-qur-an/.

Roberts, Deotis J. "Dignity and Destiny: Black Reflections on Eschatology." In *Cambridge Companion to Black Theology,* edited by Dwight N. Hopkins and Edward P. Antonio, 211–20. Cambridge: Cambridge University Press, 2012.

Robinson, Neal. "Ash'ariyya and Mu'tazila." In *The Routledge Encyclopedia of Philosophy,* edited by Edward Craig, 1:519–23. London: Routledge, 1988. http://www. muslimphilosophy.com/ip/rep/H052.

————. *Christ in Islam and Christianity.* New York: State University of New York Press, 1991.

Rosaldo, Michelle Zimbalist, and Louise Lamphere, eds. Stanford, CA: Stanford University Press, 1974.

Ross, Kenneth R. "Christian Mission and the End of Poverty: Time for Eschatology." *Mission Studies* 24.1 (2007) 79–97.

Ruether, Rosemary Radford. "Ecofeminism—The Challenge to Theology." In *DEP. Deportate, Esuli, Profughe* 20 (July 2012) 22–33. https://www.unive.it/pag/fileadmin/ user_upload/dipartimenti/DSLCC/documenti/DEP/numeri/n20/06_20_-Ruether_ Ecofeminism.pdf.

————. "Eschatology in Christian Feminist Theologies." In *OHE,* 328–42.

Russell, Jeffrey Burton. *A History of Heaven.* Princeton, NJ: Princeton University Press, 1997.

Russell, Robert J. *Cosmology: From Alpha to Omega: The Creative Mutual Interaction of Theology and Science.* Minneapolis, MN: Fortress, 2008.

————. "Cosmology and Eschatology: The Implications of Tipler's 'Omega-Point' Theory for Pannenberg's Theological Program." In *Beginning with the End: God, Science and Wolfhart Pannenberg,* edited by Carol Rausch Albright and Joel Haugen, 195–216. Chicago: Open Court, 1997.

————. *Time in Eternity: Pannenberg, Physics, and Eschatology in Creative Mutual Interaction.* Notre Dame, IN: University of Notre Dame Press, 2012.

Rustomji, Nerina. *The Garden and the Fire: Heaven and Hell in Islamic Culture.* New York: Columbia University Press, 2009.

Sachedina, Abdulaziz Abdulhussein. *The Islamic Roots of Democratic Pluralism.* New York: Oxford University Press, 2001.

Saeed, Abdullah. "The Nature and Purpose of the Community (Ummah) in the Qur'ān." In *The Community of Believers: Christian and Muslim Perspectives,* edited by Lucinda Mosher and David Marshall, 15–28. Washington, DC: Georgetown University Press, 2015.

Salah, Ali Mohammed. "Signs of the Last Hour | Dr. Ali Mohammed Salah." 2014. https:// www.youtube.com/watch?reload=9&v=E02rab4-HoA.

Saritoprak, Zeki. *Islam's Jesus.* Gainesville, FL: University Press of Florida, 2014.

Scherer, Glenn. "Christian-Right Views are Swaying Politicians and Threatening the Environment." In *Grist: Environmental News and Commentary*, October 27, 2004 (online edition), n.p. http://www.grist.org/article/scherer-christian.

Schleiermacher, Friedrich. *The Christian Faith.* Edited by H. R. Mackintosh and J. S. Stewart. Edinburgh: T. & T. Clark, 1999.

Schwarz, Hans. *Eschatology.* Grand Rapids: Eerdmans, 2000.

Sells, Michael A. "Armageddon in Christian, Sunni, and Shia Traditions." In *The Oxford Handbook of Religion and Violence,* edited by Michael Jerryson et al., 467–95. Oxford: Oxford University Press, 2013.

Siddiqui, Mona. "Death, Resurrection, and Human Destiny: Qur'ānic and Islamic Perspectives." In *Death, Resurrection, and Human Destiny: Christian and Muslim Perspectives,* edited by David Marshall and Lucinda Mosher, 25–42. Washington, DC: Georgetown University Press, 2014.

Smart, Alan, and Josephine Smart. *Posthumanism: Anthropological Insights.* Toronto: Toronto University Press, 2017.

Smith, Jane Idleman, and Yvonne Yazbeck Haddad. *The Islamic Understanding of Death and Resurrection.* Oxford: Oxford University Press, 2002.

Smith, Jane I. "Reflections on Aspects of Immortality in Islam." *Harvard Theological Review* 70.1–2 (1977) 85–98.

Snyder, C. R. "Hypothesis: There is Hope." In *Handbook of Hope. Theory, Measures, and Applications,* edited by C. R. Snyder, 3–21. San Diego: Academic, 2000.

Soskice, Janet M. "Resurrection and the New Jerusalem." In *The Resurrection: An Interdisciplinary Symposium on the Resurrection of Jesus,* edited by Stephen T. Davis et al., 41–58. Oxford: Oxford University Press, 1997.

Soulen, R. Kendall, and Linda Woodhead, eds. *God and Human Dignity.* Grand Rapids: Eerdmans, 2006.

Spencer, Andrew. "Three Reasons Why Evangelicals Stopped Advocating for the Environment/It's Not Theology, It's Politics." *Christianity Today,* June 14, 2017 (online edition). https://www.christianitytoday.com/ct/2017/june-web-only/three-reasons-evangelicals-dont-advocate-for-environment.html.

Spitzer, Robert J. *New Proofs for the Existence of God: Contributions of Contemporary Physics and Philosophy.* Grand Rapids: Eerdmans, 2010.

Stevenson, Tyler Wigg. "Revelation's Warning to Evangelicals: *Left Behind* May Be Hazardous to Our Health." *Reflections* 92 (Spring 2005) 35–39.

Stieglecker, Hermann. *Die Glaubenslehren des Islam.* Paderborn, Germany: Schöningh, 1962.

Sumegi, Angela. *Understanding Death: An Introduction to Ideas of Self and the Afterlife in World Religions.* Malden, MA: Wiley Blackwell, 2014.

Tabor, James D. "Ancient Jewish and Early Christian Millennialism." In *OHM*, 252–66.

Talbott, Thomas. *The Inescapable Love of God.* 2nd ed. Eugene, OR: Cascade, 2014.

———. "Universalism." In *OHE*, 446–58.

Tanner, Kathryn E. "Eschatology without a Future?" In *EWEG*, 222–37.

Thagard, Paul. *The Brain and the Meaning of Life.* Princeton, NJ: Princeton University Press, 2010.

Thomassen, Einar. "Islamic Hell." *Numen: International Review for the History of Religions* 56.2–3 (2009) 401–16.

Tillich, Paul. "The Right to Hope." *The University of Chicago Magazine* 58 (1965) 16–21.

———. *Systematic Theology.* Chicago: University of Chicago Press, 1963.

Tipler, Frank J. *The Physics of Immortality*. London: Weidenfeld & Nicolson, 1994.

Tottoli, Roberto. "Afterlife." In *Encyclopaedia of Islam, Three*, edited by Kate Fleet et al. Boston: Brill, 2007. http://dx.doi.org/10.1163/1573-3912_ei3_COM_22930.

Troeltsch, Ernst. "On the Historical and Dogmatic Methods in Theology [1898]." Translated by Jack Forstman (orig. German text in *Gesammelte Schriften*, 2:728–53 [Tübingen: Mohr, 1913]). http://faculty.tcu.edu/grant/hhit/Troeltsch,%20On%20the%20Historical%20and%20Dogmatic%20Methods.pdf.

Troll, Christian W., et al., eds. *We Have Justice in Common: Christian and Muslim Voices from Asia and Africa*. Berlin: Konrad-Adenauer-Stiftung, 2010.

Trumbower, Jeffrey A. *Rescue for the Dead: The Posthumous Salvation of Non-Christians in Early Christianity*. Oxford: Oxford University Press, 2001.

Tsirpanlis, Constantine N. "The Concept of Universal Salvation in Saint Gregory of Nyssa." *Studia Patristica* 17.3 (1982) 1131–44.

Tug, Salih. "Death and Immortality in Islamic Thought." In *Death and Immortality in the Religions of the World*, edited by Paul Badham and Linda Badham, 86–92. New York: Paragon House, 1987.

Tuveson, Ernest L. *Redeemer Nation: The Idea of America's Millennial Role*. Chicago: University of Chicago Press, 1968.

Ukaogo, Prince O., et al. "Environmental Pollution: Causes, Effects, and the Remedies." In *Microorganisms for Sustainable Environment and Health*, edited by Pankaj Raj Chowdhary et al., 419–30. Amsterdam: Elsevier, 2020.

United Nations Climate Change. "Islamic Declaration on Climate Change." Updated August 18, 2015. https://unfccc.int/news/islamic-declaration-on-climate-change.

Volf, Miroslav. *Work in the Spirit: Toward a Theology of Work*. Eugene, OR: Wipf & Stock, 2001.

Vroom, Hendrik. *No Other Gods: Christian Belief in Dialogue with Buddhism, Hinduism, and Islam*. Grand Rapids: Eerdmans, 1996.

Walls, Jerry L. *Heaven: The Logic of Eternal Joy*. Oxford: Oxford University Press, 2002.

———. *Hell: The Logic of Damnation*. Notre Dame, IN: University of Notre Dame Press, 1992.

Ware, Kallistos. "Dare We Hope for the Salvation of All? Origen, St. Gregory of Nyssa and St. Isaac the Syrian." In *The Inner Kingdom*, 193–216. Crestwood, NY: St. Vladimir's Seminary Press, 2001.

———. *The Orthodox Way*. Rev. ed. Crestwood, NY: St. Vladimir's Seminary Press, 1995.

Watt, William Montgomery. *Muslim-Christian Encounters: Perceptions and Misperceptions*. London: Routledge, 1991.

Welker, Michael. "Resurrection and Eternal Life: The Canonic Memory of the Resurrected Christ, His Reality, and His Glory." In *EWEG*, 279–90. Harrisburg, PA: Trinity, 2000.

Westhelle, Vitor. "Liberation Theology: A Latitudinal Perspective." In *OHE*, 311–27.

Wiker, Benjamin, and Jonathan Witt. *A Meaningful World: How the Arts and Sciences Reveal the Genius of Nature*. Downers Grove, IL: InterVarsity, 2006.

Wikipedia contributors. "Dabiq (Magazine)." Wikipedia, The Free Encyclopedia. https://en.wikipedia.org/w/index.php?title=Dabiq_(magazine)&oldid=1027602761.

———. "Rumiyah (magazine)." Wikipedia. https://en.wikipedia.org/w/index.php?title=Rumiyah_(magazine)&oldid=1019533677.

WikiShia contributors. "Grave Sins." *WikiShia*. https://en.wikishia.net/view/Grave_Sins.

———. "An Online Encyclopedia of the School of Ahl Al-Bayt." WikiShia. https://en.wikishia.net/view/Main_Page.

Wilkinson, David. *Christian Eschatology and the Physical Universe*. London: T. & T. Clark, 2010.

Wilkinson Microwave Anisotropy Probe. "Cosmology: The Study of the Universe." Updated June 3, 2011. http://map.gsfc.nasa.gov/universe/WMAP_Universe.pdf.

———. "What Is the Inflation Theory?" April 16, 2010. http://map.gsfc.nasa.gov/universe/WMAP_Universe.pdf.

Winter Tim, ed. *The Cambridge Companion to Classical Islamic Theology*. Cambridge: Cambridge University Press, 2008.

Wittgenstein, Ludwig. *Tractatus Logico-Philosophicus*. Translated by C. K. Ogden. New York: Harcourt, Brace & Company, Inckegan, 1922. Project Gutenberg eBook: https://www.gutenberg.org/files/5740/5740-pdf.pdf.

World Council of Churches. "Together Towards Life: Mission and Evangelism in Changing Landscapes." Commission on World Mission and Evangelism/WCC, updated September 6, 2012. https://www.oikoumene.org/resources/documents/together-towards-life-mission-and-evangelism-in-changing-landscapes.

Wright, N. T. *For All the Saints: Remembering the Christian Departed*. Harrisburg, PA: Morehouse, 2003.

———. *The New Testament and the People of God*. Christian Origins and the Question of God, Vol. 1. Minneapolis, MN: Fortress, 1992.

———. *The Resurrection of the Son of God*. Christian Origins and the Question of God, Vol. 3. Minneapolis: Fortress, 2003.

———. *Surprised by Hope: Rethinking Heaven, the Resurrection, and the Mission of the Church*. New York: HarperOne, 2008.

Zauzmer, Julie. "Vatican Leaders Dismayed by Reports that United States Will Leave Paris Climate Accord." *The Washington Post*, June 1, 2017 (online edition). https://www.washingtonpost.com/news/acts-of-faith/wp/2017/06/01/vatican-leaders-dismayed-by-reports-that-united-states-will-leave-paris-climate-accord/?utm_term=.94ba3ecb1887.

Zizioulas, John D. "Preserving God's Creation: Three Lectures on Theology and Ecology: Lecture One." *King's Theological Review* 12.1 (1989) 1–5.